CW01645254

Charles Chaplin
1907–1987

Artist, Engraver, Printmaker

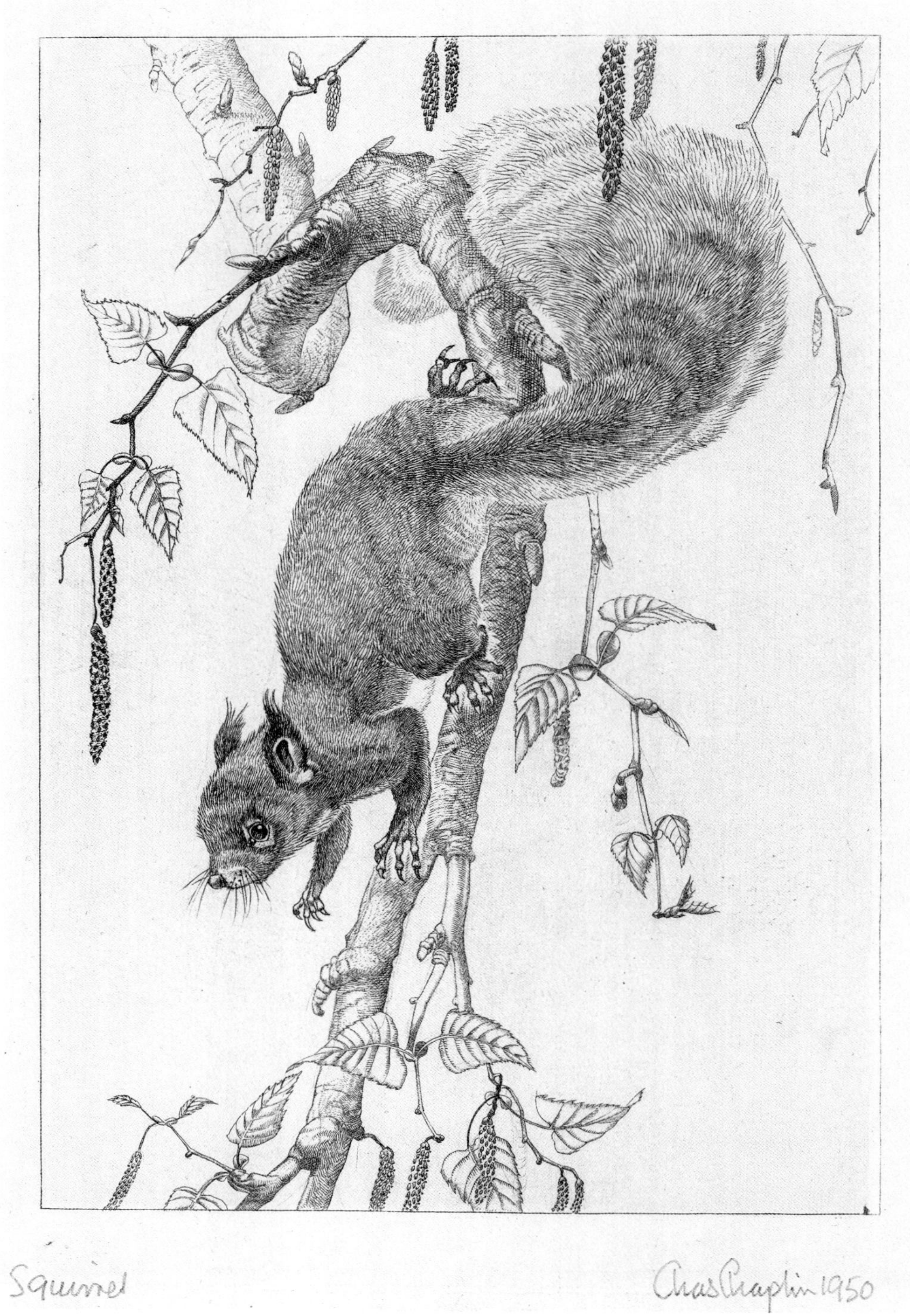

Squirrel, line engraving, 190 x 133 mm, 1950

Charles Chaplin 1907–1987

Artist, Engraver, Printmaker

with a catalogue of prints

JON CHAPLIN

'You teach me a little about engraving and I'll teach you a little about art'

ROBERT AUSTIN TO CHARLES CHAPLIN

OBLONG

Published in Great Britain by Oblong Creative Ltd, 2005

Text © Jon Chaplin 2005

No part of this book may be reproduced in any form or by any means without prior permission in writing from the publisher and the copyright holders.

ISBN 0 9536574 7 7

MAIN JACKET ILLUSTRATION
Brambles and Plough, line engraving,
165 x 265 mm, 1978

BACK JACKET ILLUSTRATION
Reed Warbler, line engraving,
223 x 150 mm, 1951

FLAP ILLUSTRATION
Photographic portrait of Charles Chaplin
by Bassano, *c.* 1950

DESIGNED AND PRODUCED BY OBLONG CREATIVE LTD, WETHERBY LS23 7BJ, UK

Contents

To our children Elizabeth, Sara and Jon,
grandchildren so loved by
Grandpa Charlie

Introduction

Jon Chaplin has written a personal, affectionate and detailed account of the life and work of his father, Charles Herbert Arthur Chaplin. The artist is revealed as he saw himself, a gifted amateur who modestly resisted any promotion or commercialisation of his art. Charles Chaplin's preferred medium was intaglio printmaking,[1] and in this area he was to prove that he was no dabbler with the engraving burin or etching needle. His skill and artistic ability, particularly in the exacting and difficult medium of line engraving, brought recognition and admiration from his peers and resulted in a body of work remarkable for its distinctive style.

Chaplins's first prints were etchings, which were executed in the early 1920s, a period when the popularity of this art form was at its peak. The hegemony of etching as the true printmaking technique for artistic expression had been promoted since the middle of the nineteenth century, and the founding of The Royal Society of Painter-Etchers (RE) in 1880 established the dominant position of the medium. This was upheld and reinforced by the academic establishments and many of the print publishers. Chaplin had been apprenticed at a commercial printing works (where he was employed for the rest of his working life) and was adept at line engraving on copper. For centuries line engraving had been considered a purely reproductive and commercial medium and, in spite if its acceptance as a fine art by the RE,[2] many graphic artists considered its inherent requirement for precision left little room for artistic expression. From a young age Chaplin would have been aware that very few artists used line engraving when producing their original prints. His tutors at the evening classes he attended at the Watford School of Art would also have instilled in him the desirability of etching or drypoint, rather than engraving, for original printmaking. No doubt Chaplin would initially have been quite happy to conform to the exclusive use of etching or drypoint. Both these techniques would have appealed to his desire for spontaneity in his art, allowing him to work directly onto the copper plate even out in the open where he could observe and experience the local landscape that he enjoyed so much. Chaplin's

1 For an explanation of the intaglio printmaking techniques of etching, engraving, drypoint and aquatint, see the section Notes to the Catalogue on page 97.

2 The RE was founded in 1880 as the Royal Society of Painter-Etchers. In 1888 it became The Royal Society of Painter-Etchers and Engravers in order to accommodate a growing number of members who were important and accomplished reproductive engravers. For a full account of the history of the RE see Martin Hopkinson, 'No Day Without a Line', Ashmolean Museum, 1999.

earliest works demonstrate his graphic ability with these techniques and the ease with which he adopted the freedom they afforded him.

However, by the early 1930s Chaplin began to work on the plate with aquatint and also to exploit his skill with the engraved, rather than the etched, line. Indeed the use of line engraving had been gaining slowly in popularity amongst artists for the last few years. As early as 1930 Malcolm Salaman, editor of the annual publication, Fine Prints of the Year, noted that there was now, '... a growing school of graphic artists ... attracted by the orderly precision and beauty of the graven line.'[3] Salaman mentioned in particular the work of Robert Austin, Stanley Anderson and Harry Morley, all graphic artists who had studied at the School of Engraving at the British School in Rome and who had been influenced by the brilliance of the engravings of the early Italian Renaissance masters. These artists conveyed their enthusiasm for the medium to their students at the Royal College of Art, and to fellow artists at the RE. The concurrent exhibitions and publications on the earlier masters of engraving by the influential curators at the British Museum, Campbell Dodgson and Arthur Hind, also engendered a growth in interest in this printmaking technique. As described later in this book, Charles Chaplin's fortuitous meeting with Malcolm Osborne at the 1947 annual exhibition of the RE led to his period of part time study at the Royal College of Art under the tutelage of Robert Austin. Austin encouraged his use of engraving and was much impressed by his skill. He was minded to receive some instruction from Chaplin on the use of the burin! In return he helped him to discover more fully the artistic potential of the medium.[4] It was no doubt Austin's own engravings of exquisite simplicity that fired Chaplin's enthusiasm to develop his engraving skills with the same degree of artistry. From this time on Chaplin was to use engraving exclusively for his prints.

Although he gained immensely from his period of study at the Royal College of Art, Chaplin was not comfortable with the artistic establishment and never actively sought the company of other artists. He was also aware of the new post-war movements in art, but felt no need to widen his approach to his subject matter along avant-garde lines, seeing his art purely as a personal and accurate record of the world around him. Post-war printmaking was for the most part focussed on large, colourful images, produced by lithography or linocut. The more traditional black and white prints were produced less and less by artists who realised that the market and the collectors of such prints had virtually disappeared. However, the annual exhibitions at the Royal Academy and the RE still provided a small band of

[3] Malcolm C. Salaman, editor, *Fine Prints of the Year. Annual Review of Contemporary Etchers and Engravers*, 1930, p. 1.

[4] The occasion is described later in the book when Robert Austin said to Chaplin, 'You teach me a little about engraving, and I'll teach you a little about art'. (Page 33)

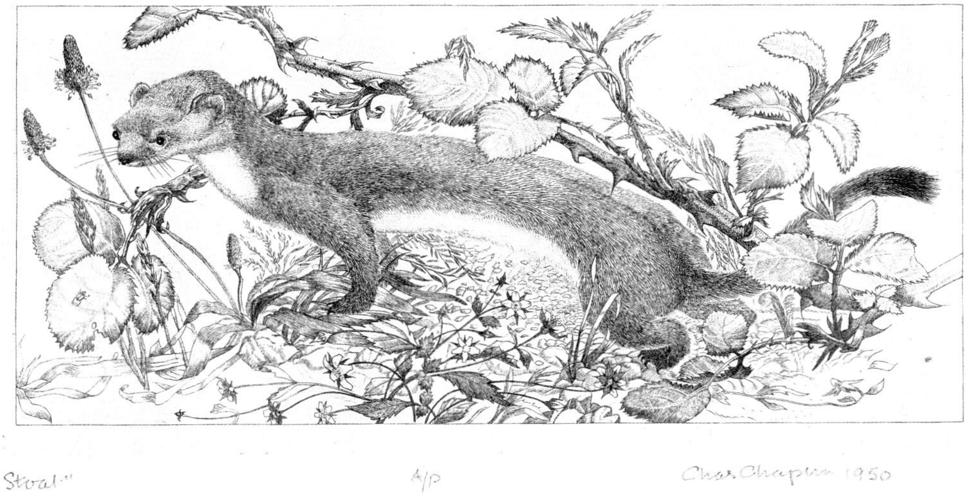

Stoat, line engraving, 92 x 200 mm, 1950, selected as a presentation print for members of the Print Collectors Club

enthusiasts with a showcase for etchings and engravings and Chaplin continued to exhibit regularly with both establishments. His fellow artists always admired his work, and he was elected an Associate of the RE in 1950 and a Fellow in 1962. His diploma work, for his election as an Associate member, was a delightful engraving of a stoat — alert, tense and sleek, the creature is a fine example of Chaplin's observational skills and his technical mastery. It was selected as a presentation print for the members of the Print Collectors Club of the RE that year.[5] Chaplin continued to produce a remarkable number of engravings over the next few decades. His subject matter continued to be the familiar landscape, but his ability to use the burin to produce engraved lines of finesse and sculptural energy imbued many of his later prints with an almost surreal quality; a characteristic rarely seen within this genre.

The quality and range of Chaplin's prints are illustrated in the catalogue in this book and provide an invaluable record of the work of this little known but exceptional artist. His legacy of over one hundred brilliant etchings and engravings secures him a place amongst the finest printmakers of the twentieth century.

Hilary Chapman, 2005

[5] The Print Collectors Club was affiliated to the RE. Members paid an annual subscription which included the choice of a Presentation Print by an RE each year.

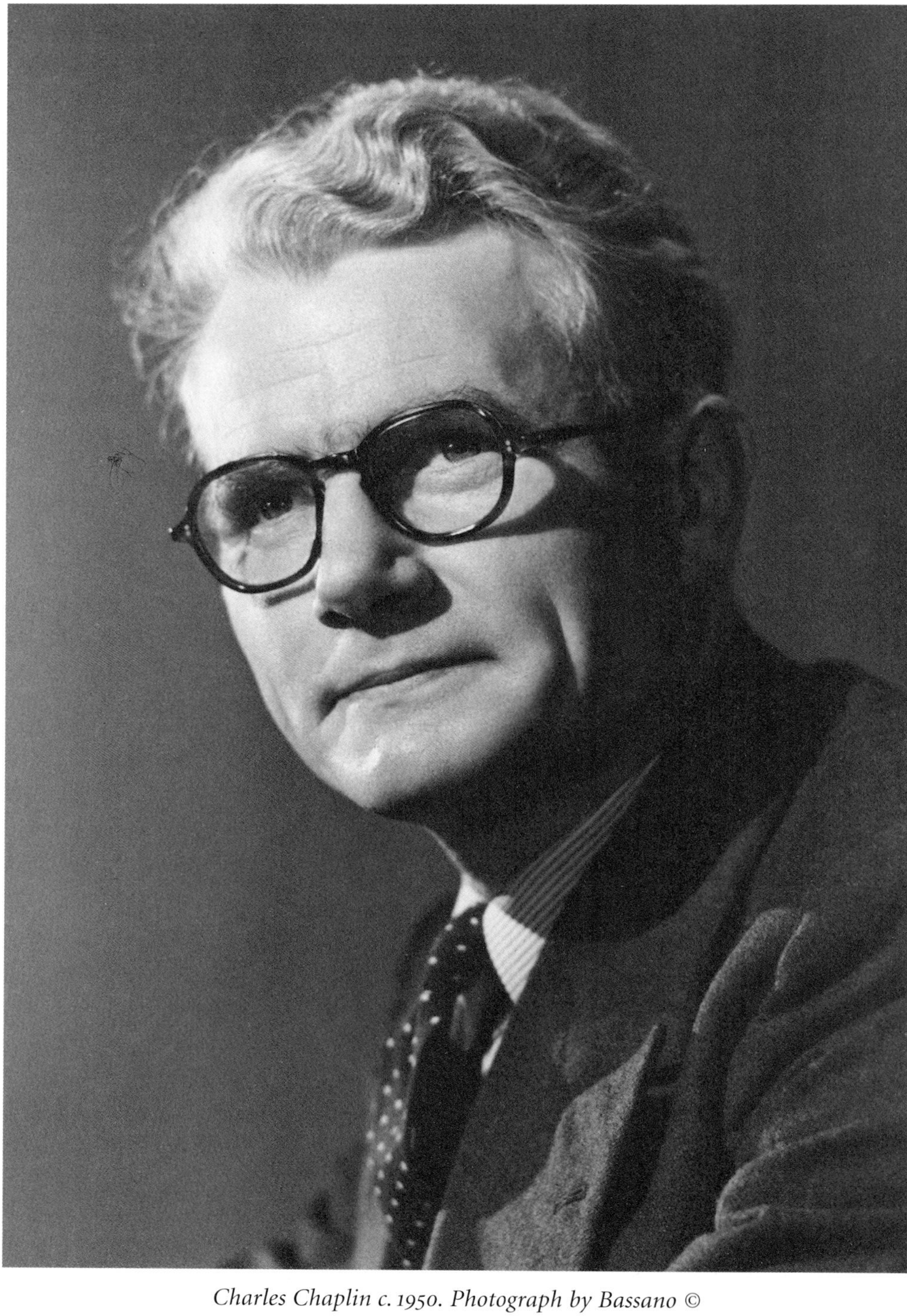

Charles Chaplin c. 1950. Photograph by Bassano ©

Author's Preface and Acknowledgements

MORE TIMES that I care to remember during my own life, in answer to the question 'Have you inherited any of your father's talent?', I have had to reply 'No, not at all'. However, after much consideration, I have concluded that my own lack of artistic talent need not disqualify me from writing this book! I have always been intensely interested in engraving as an artistic technique and, as far as printing is concerned, most of our immediate family and many of our friends have been in the printing industry all their lives.

I spent many hours as a child and as a young man sitting on a high stool alongside my father in his studio as he engraved — in the darkness apart from the strong light projected through a screen above, and reflecting brightly from the surface of the polished copper. The air would be thick with fumes from the printing inks and chemical materials, and from the pungent smoke issuing from his pipe. He rarely spoke, except perhaps to answer my occasional question, or to tell me to stop disturbing him. Although my mother thought my time could be more usefully spent concentrating on my homework, I always felt that watching him was important. I would be mesmerised watching the graver, slowly and deliberately pressed into the plate, raising thin coils of glinting copper from the point as he twisted the plate from side to side on its worn leather sandbag. He would take an evening to engrave one square inch of a plate, constantly and with infinite patience referring to his sketches propped alongside, or to a model; he might take six months to complete a plate to his own high standards, which could include removing or changing different parts of the image already apparently completed. Our sessions would usually conclude at 9.30 pm with mother calling him for his grilled sausage supper, which I would share, after which he would return alone to his studio for further work into the late hours.

In writing this book I have tried to account for the details of my father's life that are relevant to his work, and to describe his work in a factual and objective, rather than in an analytic and critical way for which I would in any case not be qualified. Nevertheless, his work is intimately linked with his own life, in the surroundings of countryside and wildlife, in the rural and agricultural activities which fascinated him, and in his extended family which he loved so dearly. So, in spite of my intentions, the text may occasionally disclose a personal reflection!

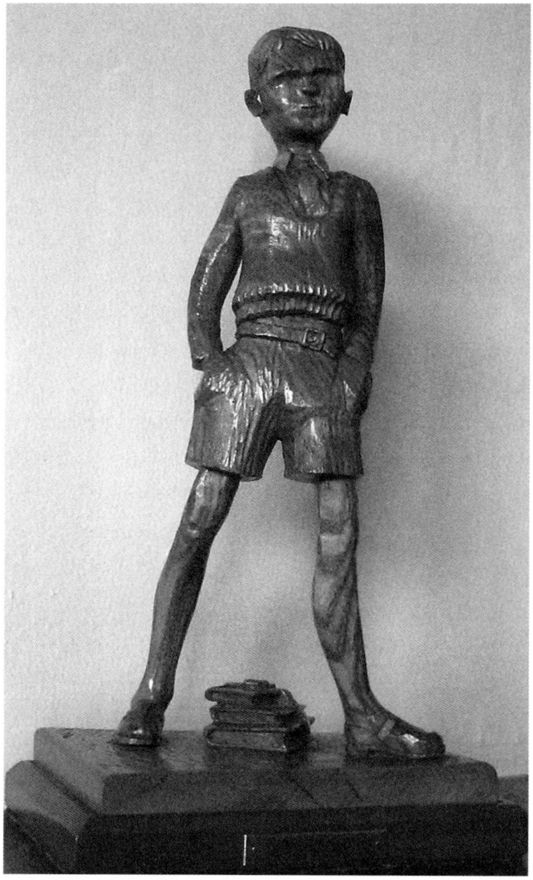

'Ex Libris'. Carving of the artist's son aged eight

I have been able in all but two cases to use an original print (preferably one from a limited edition or an artist's proof) for reproduction as an illustration of the plate in the catalogue or in the book generally. In his last years, with unusual foresight, the artist put together a collection of all his prints for his grandson, Jon; many of the illustrations are taken from prints in this collection, the remainder from my own, or as acknowledged in the text.

The reproductions of the artist's work appearing in this book are, of course, 'illustrations' of his work, and as such cannot approach the quality, refinement and clarity of the original proofs printed by the artist himself directly from the engraved plate. My father was a perfectionist in all matters relating to printed reproductions, and I have no doubt that he would not have been satisfied with these illustrations had he been able to see them himself. They are, however, the best that can be achieved by modern printing technology, and, in the catalogue section, will at least serve to identify the artist's work. I would like to take this opportunity also to thank Derek Brown of Oblong for his attention to the quality of the reproduction, as well as for his skill and assistance in the design and production of the book.

The idea for the book first occurred some twenty-five years ago, as my secretary, Ruth Griffiths, typed up my father's notes on many of his prints, in many cases directly from his own manuscripts. These notes have been invaluable to me, having formed the basis for the Catalogue, and I have to thank Ruth for her hard work and patience all those years ago. I am also profoundly grateful to my daughter-in-law, Nicola Chaplin, and my son-in-law Philip Brett, for their work in word processing, revising and correcting my own manuscripts of the book. Without their enthusiastic and skilful endeavours the book would not have happened.

In addition I owe much to friends with whom I have discussed various aspects of the artist's life and work, and whose stories and words I have sometimes quoted, as well as to others who have kindly assisted in my research: G. A. D. Bourne, MBE (Group Commandant Royal Observer Corps), David Cave, Catherine Casely (Ashmolean Museum, Oxford), John Francis Chaplin, Rev. Gavin Collins, Simon Fenwick (RWS/RSPP, Bankside Gallery), Muriel Good, Corrie Graddon, Dennis Hallbery and A.W. Potter (Royal Academy of Arts) have all contributed and I thank them warmly. My son, Jon, has provided encouraging advice and practical help in connection with many aspects of the publication of this book. I acknowledge the authorship of the poems by Chaplin's friend, Paul Wigmore, reproduced in connection with 'Floating Oakleaf' (133) and 'New Forest Ghost' (135). Although I have had much help from others, I take responsibility for statements made in the book; my research has been as thorough and accurate as I could make, and if any errors or omissions come to light I apologise for these.

I met Hilary Chapman at the beginning of 2003 in connection with her exhibition in April of that year of some of my father's early work at the 20th Century Gallery in the Fulham Road, London. This exhibition, and Hilary's encouragement, was the impetus I needed to get the book started. If some thirty-seven of my father's early works could cause such interest in a hitherto comparatively unknown artist, it seemed that there could be much more potential interest in his lifetime's achievement of 136 prints. Since our first meeting, Hilary has provided me with continuous encouragement and inspiration, as well as good advice in writing and producing this book. In thanking her for writing an Introduction, I acknowledge her valuable contribution to the book as a whole.

Finally my wife, Betty, and I have had huge enjoyment recalling together the events of my father's life. Betty has known him since I first took her home to Highfield Way when she was just sixteen! I have benefited so much from her patience and wisdom, and I am so grateful for her constant support. It has been a wonderful opportunity for us both to look back and appreciate our own lives, as reflected in the artist's work.

Charles Chaplin: A Memoir

The Early Years
1907–1939

CHARLES CHAPLIN was born on 12 January 1907 into a large family living in Jubilee Road, Watford. In the years leading up to the First World War his elder and younger brother and five elder and one younger sister, together with his father, a railway worker, and his mother would have found living conditions cramped in the small, two-up two-down Victorian terrace — its cooking and heating range in the living room adjacent to a tiny scullery, and the WC outside. Yet the sitting room at the front of the house, with its tidy lace curtains, elaborate cast iron fireplace, and elegant Edwardian porcelain vases, remained in pristine condition always ready to welcome visitors.

His elder brother, Frank John Chaplin, a gifted artist, was to become a role model for the young Charles, who later recorded that by the age of seven he had become aware of the art of drawing and painting by watching his brother, Frank, and that even as a boy he wanted to be an artist. He regarded Frank's untimely death in the First World War not only as a personal tragedy in his life, but also as a setback in his own art career; throughout his life Chaplin referred to the inspiration he received from his elder brother.

Chaplin attended school in Alexandra Road, Watford, and by his own account was not a promising scholar. Allowing for his short and disrupted education, his notes and correspondence subsequently demonstrate a clear articulate and creative mode of expression, even if the spelling and punctuation was variable. At the age of twelve he lost his right eye in an accident during a street game — knocking flints together to make sparks, and he was told then that his artistic ambitions were over. In fact, the surgeons at Moorfields even advised him not to continue making his small pencil sketches, as the strain of this would be likely to damage his remaining left eye. The lack of a right eye clearly affected the whole of his life, and his achievements in his chosen art of engraving are particularly remarkable when considered in the light of this major disability. So much of his work is engaged with design, distance, light, perspective, contrast and detail, and yet there is no clue as to this severe limitation of his physical resources. Throughout his life his first task on rising was to insert his prosthetic eye, and the last to remove it before retiring, a little ceremony seen only by his family, which he used to conduct in a quaintly theatrical manner and invariably with wry good humour. The prosthetic was an excellent match to the good eye, and few people were ever aware of it even when, as he examined his work closely, he would characteristically incline his head a little to the left. Throughout his life as an artist there would be no further reference by him to the missing eye, except perhaps to his young son, and later to his grandchildren, when he would refer to his 'spare eye' kept in a small box in his personal drawer with the admonition '*Be good — I'll keep my eye on you!*'.

Chaplin left school early, and in due course began to attend the Watford School of Art under the principal, Mr Arthur Scott. For many years he remained a student at evening classes. At the same time he and his parents signed indentures as an apprentice engraver with the Sun Engraving Company Ltd, subsequently Sun Printers Ltd.

Sun Printers was one of two major printing works in Watford, as well as being one of the largest gravure printing plants in the world. In 1945 it was acquired by Hazell, Watson and Viney Ltd, and in 1964 Hazell, Sun and Purnells merged to form the British Printing Corporation Ltd, though Sun Printers remained the largest

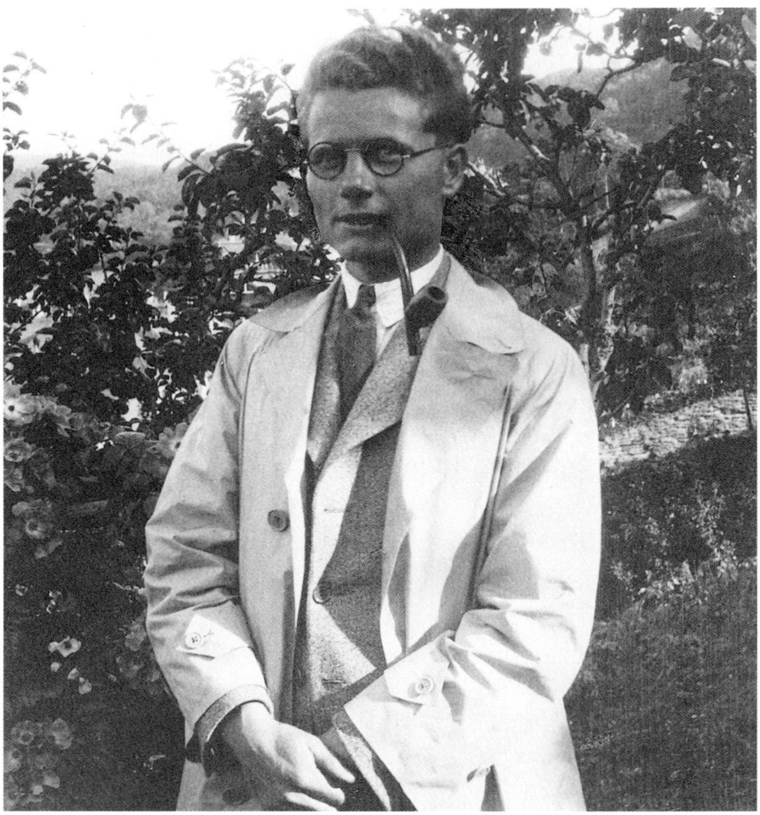

Charles Chaplin as a young man, c. 1928

single unit in the new group. The site of Sun Printers' works at Whippendell Road, Watford, extended to twenty-one acres, and employed some 2,500 people.* At some time Sun Printers was using some 1,250 tons of paper each week to produce six million copies of weekly and monthly magazines. Besides the main gravure process and gravure rotary machine departments, the plant included composing, foundry, letterpress, warehouse and bindery, and a gravure ink factory.

Chaplin remained an employee at Sun Printers, first as a journeyman later as a manager, for nearly fifty years. He harboured a love-hate relationship with the printing industry, once expressing it thus: 'If I had not lost an eye I would possibly have been allowed to study art full-time; however, through print [i.e. the printing industry], I have been able to meet many famous artists, Munnings and Annigoni among them.' He was also grateful to the Sun Engraving Company for the supply of copper plate — see note to 'It is Finished!' (6). Throughout his working life he remained a member of the Society of Lithographic Artists Designers and Engravers, the trade union usually known as 'SLADE'!

As a youth, Chaplin attended St John's Church in North Watford. He was baptised 'Charles Herbert Arthur Chaplin', and confirmed there by the Bishop of St Albans, Dr Furze. Rev. Reggie James was the vicar at St John's, and the young men were members of the Guild of Sammary. The event is recorded in Chaplin's first print, the small drypoint 'Gerald and I' (1). This reference in a plate to himself, or a member of his family, or a friend, in the pictorial context of some event during his life, is characteristic of much of his work, to such an extent even that his art becomes — whilst not as overtly autobiographical as in this case — a close reflection of his own life.

Referring to his first efforts at plate making Chaplin wrote: 'My copper plate career started by using a dart as a point on a small piece of copper, standing outside in the open air (one could work in the rain like this).' The prints of the early years up to the beginning of the Second World War were virtually all drypoints or etchings, executed simply, many of them needled directly on to the copper whilst standing in the open at the site of his subject. Although a fully qualified journeyman engraver, he had not yet begun to apply his engraving skills to his art. The subjects of his prints at this time are invariably rural locations around Watford, particularly in Cassiobury Park. His lifelong fascination with trees can be seen in much of his early work; he seeks to capture their transient character and moods according to many varying conditions of light, season, climate and perspective.

His mode of transport to these widespread locations around Watford and indeed, after his marriage, around Rickmansworth as well, was his bicycle. This he

* The buildings are now demolished and the site has been completely redeveloped.

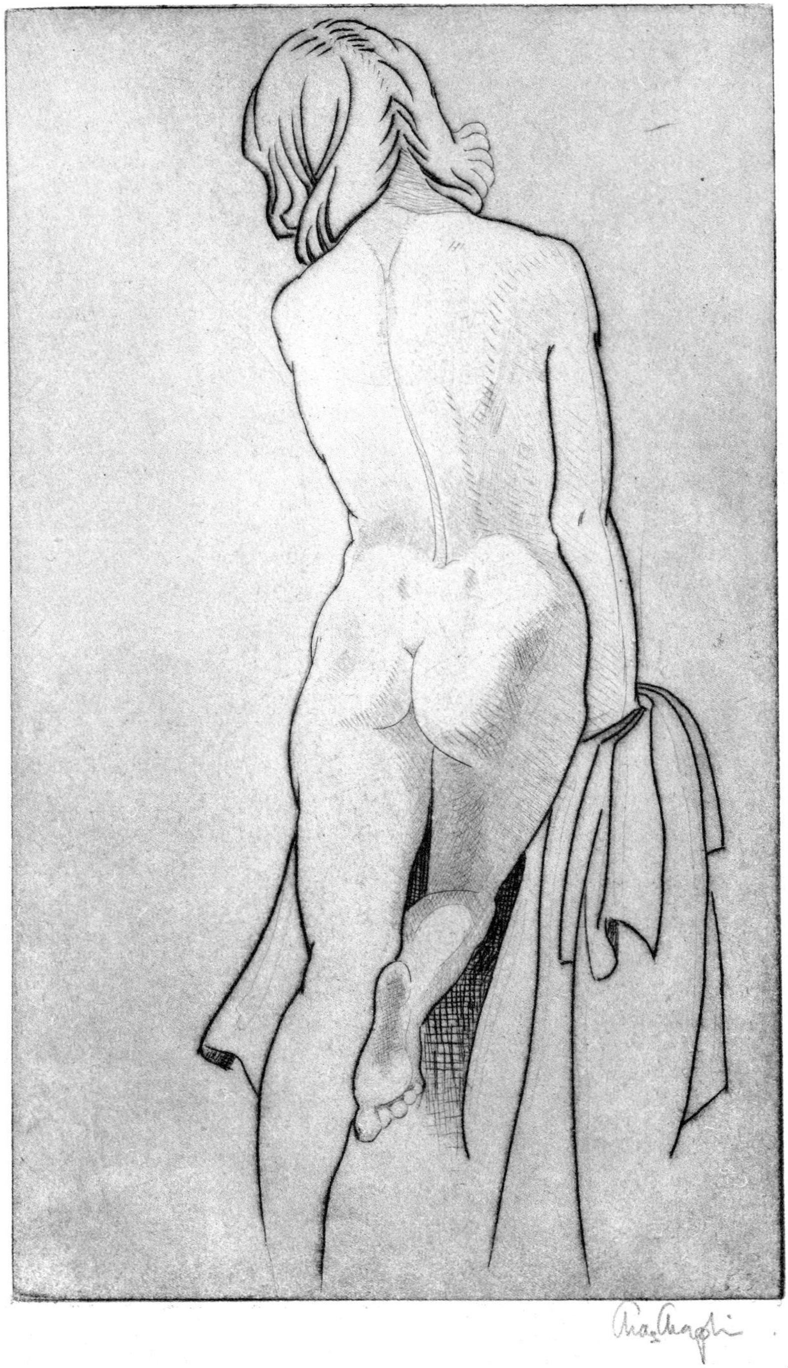

Life study needled direct on to copper (drypoint), 248 x 145 mm, c. 1930

had elaborately adapted and constructed to carry his sketching box and stand, stool, lunchbox and the other essential equipment for a peripatetic artistic. Not until 1952 did he acquire a motor car, and, with some courage passed his driving test at the second attempt at the age of forty-five. Thereafter his range and the location of his subjects extended considerably!

In the early 1930s, his attendance at life classes at the Watford School of Art reflects his desire to master the human form. Whilst he never attempted portraiture, other than in simple pencil sketches or pastels, figures do appear in a number of the early images, for example 'Farm Worker' (4), 'The Clearing' (5), 'Hilltop' (8), 'Hillside' (10), 'The Bathers' (18) and 'Binding Reeds' (32). A large number of pencil and chalk sketches of the human figure exist from this time, but he translated only a few of these studies to the copper plate: see (12), (13), (14), and (19).

In 1934 Chaplin married Elsie May Howick, a clerk working at Hoover Limited in Perivale, Middlesex, and the couple moved into a newly built house in Highfield Way, Rickmansworth. This was to be their home, and the artist's studio, until 1985. The house was built on a pleasant, leafy, and, by today's standards, spacious estate developed by Metropolitan Railway Estates (sympathetically portrayed in Betjamin's 'Metroland'). At first, one of the bedrooms served as a studio, but later the garage was converted to a purpose-built studio, with the advantage, among others, that the powerful fumes from the printing inks, acids and other chemicals no longer wafted through the house.

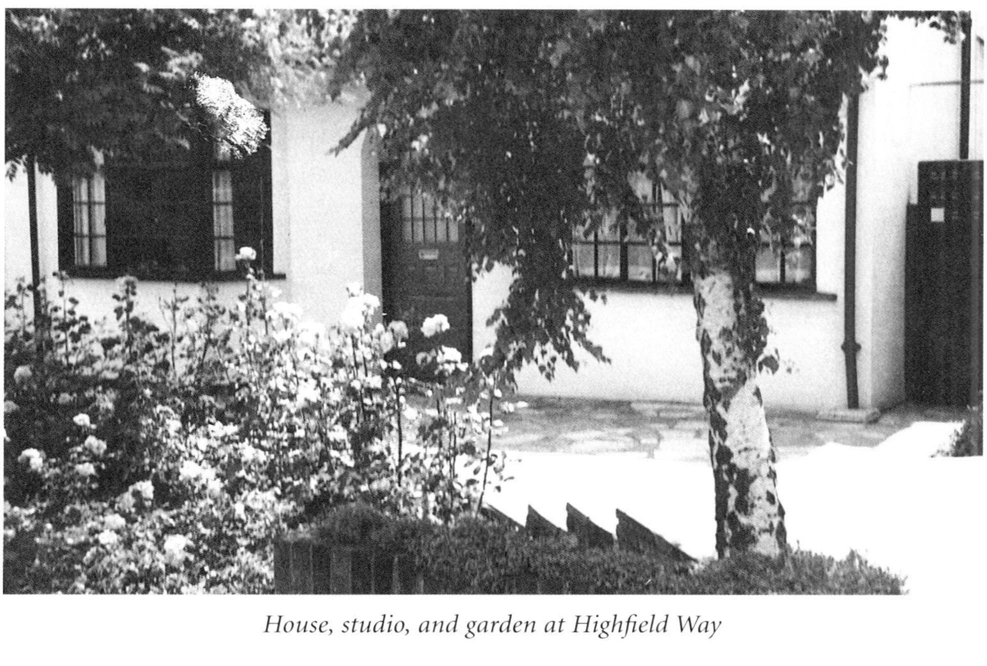

House, studio, and garden at Highfield Way

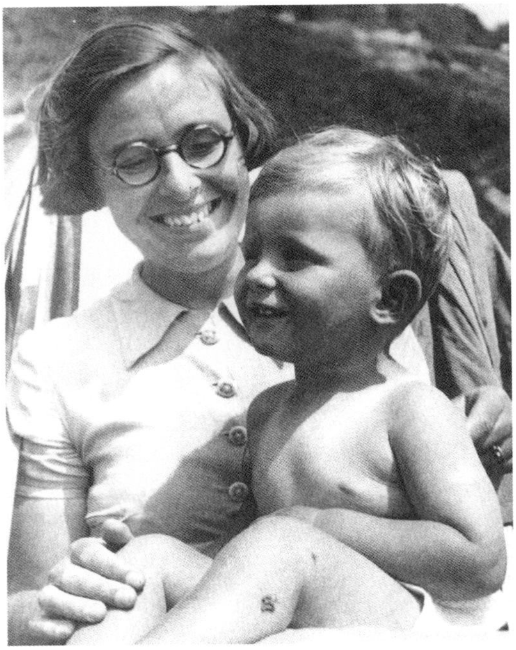

May with the author, 1937

At the end of 1935, their child was born in a neighbour's house — a son, Jon, with May's maiden name 'Howick' as an additional given name. In the future May was to suffer miscarriages, and no further children were born. Perhaps not surprisingly, no plates were made between 1933 and 1936, a lean period which, like other subsequent short periods of the absence of plate production, reflected personal and domestic distractions in the life of an essentially amateur, though dedicated, artist. Chaplin always lived two lives — his 'working' life, and his life as an artist. His work life as an employee of a large printing company secured the economics for his other life, his life as an artist, which embraced and was interwoven with his family, friends, and the society of other artists. The former life extended from 9 o'clock to 5 o'clock on weekdays, and the latter was compressed into the remainder of his time, effectively evenings and weekends. Given the amount of time available for his art, the production and printing of some 110 plates before he retired from full time employment in 1970 is impressive.

The first objective recognition of Chaplin as an artist had occurred as a young man of 18 when, as he noted proudly on a proof, his etching 'After Rain' (3) was highly commended by the Hertfordshire Art Society. His style and skill both as an artist and a printer developed strongly during the 1930s. A further approbation came in 1938 when *The Artist* magazine commended a small line engraving 'Winter Sun' (30). He was eventually persuaded by friends to submit 'Melting Snow' (31) to the Royal Academy; this was accepted and hung in the 1939 Summer Exhibition. Although Chaplin's style as an artist had still far to develop he had tasted a recognition, which for him was a major encouragement, and he had begun a relationship with the Royal Academy which remained important to him to the end of his career as an artist. In the subsequent years to 1984, a further thirty-two of the artist's prints were hung in RA Summer Exhibitions. Later in his life, with many years of the highest quality and most successful art behind him, he took a more critical view of the work of his early years. Writing in 1975 he said:

It was not until 1939 when I first exhibited at the Royal Academy and was made a member of the Royal Society of Painter-Etchers and Engravers, that my work seemed to be worthwhile. It is only my work after 1939 that I feel is worth selling, the ones previous to this can only be of interest, and show how I myself progressed — very slowly indeed — to my present plates, such as they are.

Perhaps an over-harsh judgement, particularly in the light of the undoubted interest and charm of the early years' work.

The war had now started, and with it came significant changes to Chaplin's domestic and artistic life. In October 1939 he qualified as a member of the Royal Observer Corps, No. 16385, and his personal war service began.

Wartime 1940–1949

DESPITE TURBULENCE on the world stage, this decade witnessed a prolific artistic output from Chaplin, with over forty prints, representing over a quarter of his total production. In this decade his initial success at the Royal Academy was repeated with prints hung at the Summer Exhibitions in 1940, 1943, 1947, 1948 (two) and 1949. His skills developed greatly as he moved from the simpler etchings and drypoints of the earlier years to the more demanding and larger line engravings, which became his predominant medium. In the latter years of the decade, the influence of his studies at the Royal College of Art becomes evident in an increasing artistry in the design of his images. The subject matter of his prints throughout the decade is, again, predominantly trees, with outstandingly personal characteristics attributed to his favourite chestnuts, silver birches, beeches and willows, observed in all four seasons, in all weathers, and especially lit by or reflected in water, lakes, rivers and winter floodwater. The second half of the decade sees a collection of animal and bird studies, totally different to any of his previous (or subsequent) work, though many of these still retain the favoured trees and rural scenes, now retained as a background or subsidiary feature.

Chaplin's work in the Sun Engraving Company was judged to be of a key national importance, and exempted him from conventional military service. However, service in public defences was required, and for this a service medical was necessary. Chaplin duly presented himself for examination at a military establishment in Uxbridge, and, as a physically fit and healthy man, passed through the routine tests with ease. When it came to the sight test, he took the test for the left eye normally; he then engaged his typically mischievous tendency when covering his left eye with his hand for the test on the right eye, by surreptitiously spreading his fingers apart so that he could read the test letters with his left eye. At the end of the proceedings he came before the Chairman of the Medical Board, and affected surprise on hearing that he had passed the medical A1; he was asked whether his preference was for the Army or the RAF. Chaplin drew attention to his artificial eye, which had not been spotted by the examiners, and in a farcical gesture, removed it from its socket as evidence. He was asked why he had not informed the examiners of this disability, and is said to have replied: 'You are the doctors!'.

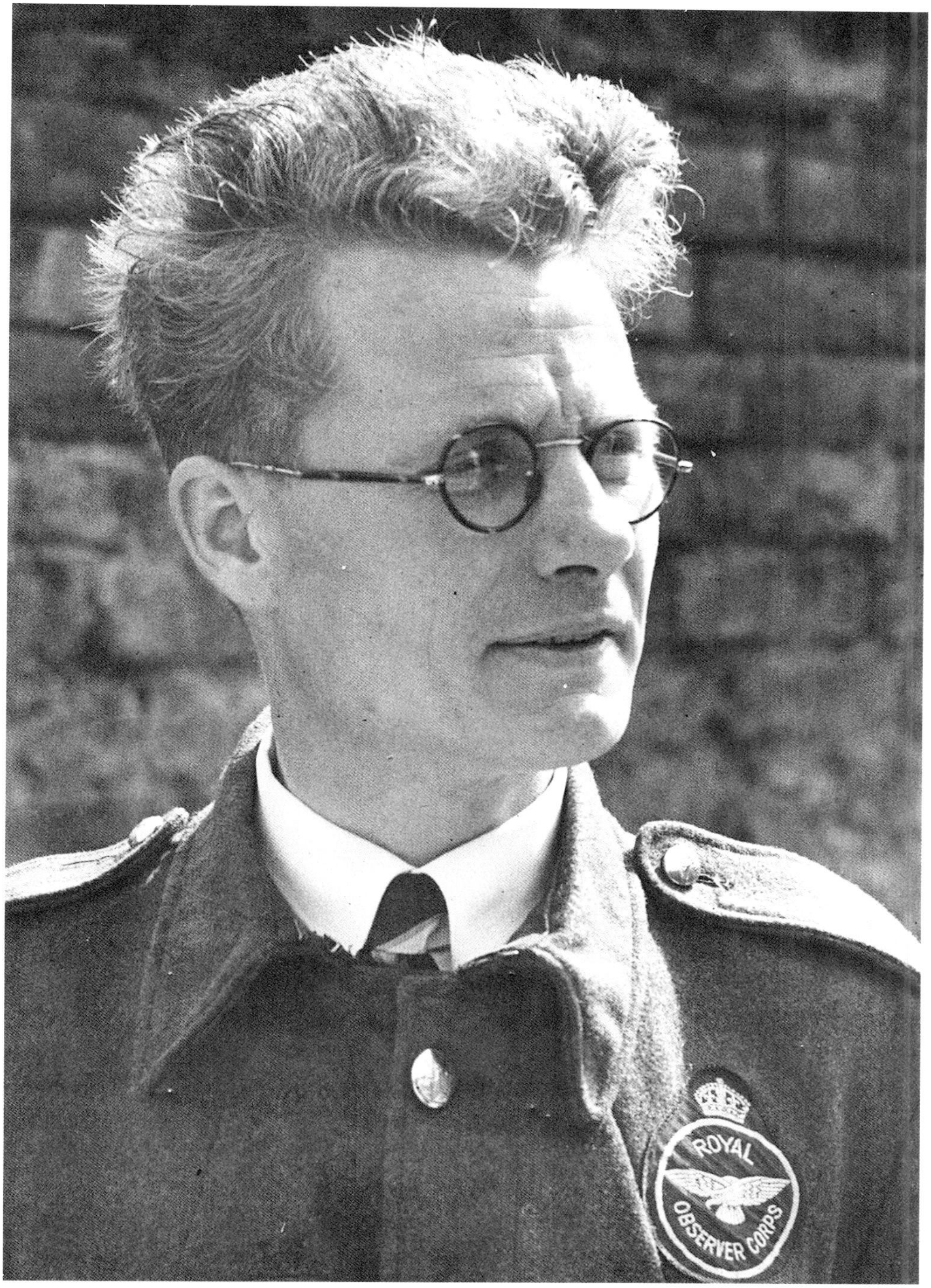

Chaplin in Royal Observer Corps uniform, c. 1940

Curiously, the revelation of this disability did not prevent his selection and training for his preferred service, the Royal Observer Corps, where accurate vision in both daylight and darkness was prerequisite. The ROC had been described as 'one of the most important and least known of our defence services — watchers of the skies, the eyries of the ROC.' It had been formed in 1925 as a civilian organisation under the direct command of Fighter Command with its Commandant an active service Air Commodore. Its observation posts were at first mainly in the South East, manned for 24 hours a day, with the purpose of watching the skies over England, observing both friendly and enemy aircraft, plotting their course, and giving early warning of their attack destinations. Air raid warnings were sounded from the basic ROC information. The ROC also guided home lame or lost bombers, and called up the Air-Sea Rescue Service for fighter pilots shot down in the sea. By 1943 there were some 1400 posts throughout the British Isles. The Rickmansworth post had been founded in 1933, and was codenamed 'Fox 1'. Of Chaplin's role in the team of some twenty observers* at F1 a colleague subsequently wrote:

> The shy chap with the cheery grin and mop of golden hair soon became a favourite at the Post, although in the early days we did not realise that he was an artist until the cartoons started going up on the guard-room noticeboard. Then we sat up and took notice. None of us knew that he had lost an eye until he came on for night duties minus the artificial optic, and then we marvelled more than ever at his uncanny knack of spotting high flying aircraft when for most of us they were just a sound in the sky. One of the amazing things about Charlie was his memory. Something would happen on the Post, and next day on the noticeboard there would be a faithful art record of amazing details which made us gasp. We got to recognise various members better through Charlie's all-seeing recordings of the passing scene.
>
> (Berwydd Davies, *West Herts Post*, 25 January 1951)

The simplicity, hilarity and brashness of cartoons must be at the opposite pole to the seriousness, complexity and beauty of engravings, and yet Chaplin's prodigious creativity inspired both during the war years. Perhaps the cartoons, and their manic, almost black, humour, relieved the otherwise unbearable tensions and fears of wartime both for himself, and for his colleagues. A large number of these cartoons exist — a truly sideways look at the war. They are executed in bold pencil and ink, and many are colourworked in watercolour. Pungent, saucy and irreverent comments erupt from the mouths of the completely recognisable observers, as well as from the pet rabbit, the horse in the field next to F1, even from worms emerging

* Besides the artist, members of the ROC Post at F1 *c.* 1942 were: W. G. Adams, H. S. Batsford, E. K. Bloom, A. M. Brown, F. V. Burgess, L. B. Davies, I. Courtney, R. C. Dean, W. Gammon, F. Giddins, H. G. Green, L. H. Griffiths, L. R. Lindsay, J. MacKensie, A. Moffat, Page, A. R. Pitkin, Potter, Rattle, B. A. Smith, D. H. M. Symon, F. Welles-Kay, S. E. Worley and E. Wright

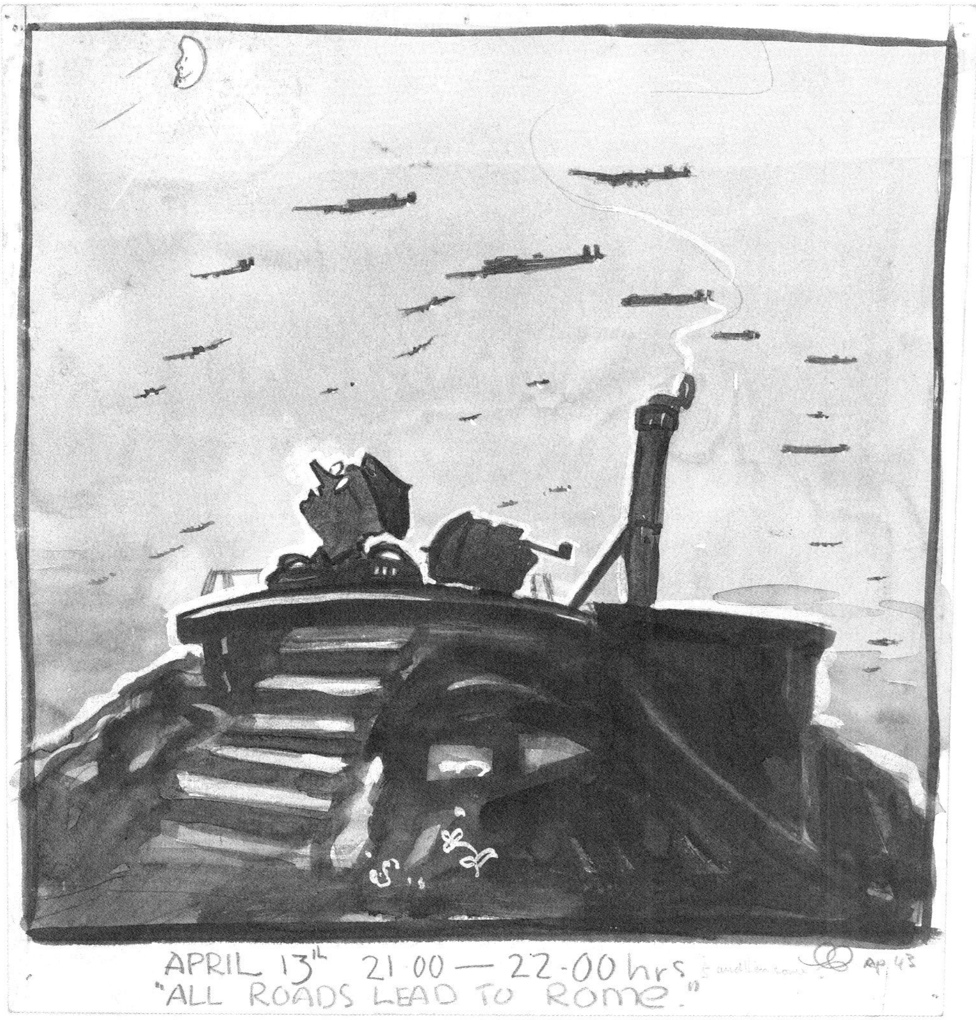

from their holes, and flowers and inanimate objects — all of them had a wry comment on life in F1. Many years later, after Chaplin's death, G. A. D. Bourne, MBE, who eventually became Group Commandant, ROC Watford, wrote to the author as follows:

The Post was a happy one, with many 'characters', mostly good. All were enthusiasts. Some had special talents, and I call to mind Giddings, the gardener; Peggy Green the radio wizard; Edgar Wright a brilliant aero technician with Handley Page who would have gone far had it not been for a fatal air crash; Ian Courtney who died the same way, and your father whose professional skill as an engraver coupled with a vivid imagination enabled him to see humour in the most mundane incidents of the daily routine. Charlie, the artist, captured

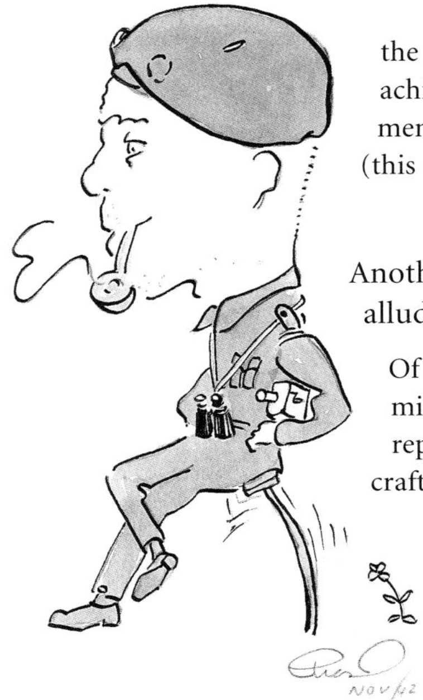

> the sprit of 'Ricky' Post in a way which could not have been achieved by any historian. For over 40 years I carried a perfect mental picture of a carthorse chewing through F1's phone cable (this actually happened) with the caption 'Why F1 went dead.'
>
> (Bourne to Jon Chaplin 10 September 1989)

Another incident recalled by Bourne in his letter perhaps alluded to Chaplin's defective sight:

> Of course I knew of your father very well at the time, but he missed one golden opportunity when Fox 1 and a brother Post reported a 'corrected height' to Watford (HQ), then saw the aircraft flapping its wings, and realised that it was an outsize rook.

For Chaplin there was much humour in wartime as well as the opportunity to exercise the sketchpad and pencil, but war was not a game. In 1943 he held the ROC First Class Certificate, and was appointed an official instructor in aircraft recognition. Chaplin's artistic power of observation was indeed applied to the war effort. A colleague, a local press reporter, said of him:

> The amazing thing about Charlie was his passion for perfection. Long before the big brass of the Observer Corps had recognised the need for detailed recognition, he was telling us how to recognise an aircraft at a glance by its 'sit' in the sky. I think he was the first to say 'I don't know you chaps by your clothes alone' — that was before the days of uniform — 'but by the way you walk and by the set of your heads on your shoulders.' But he became our instructor in many more things than aircraft recognition. I learned a great deal from him — nature love that made me feel humble. We watched many sunsets, and Charlie explained the ever changing colours, telling me what to expect in the next few minutes. He made it a living experience, rather than a fleeting night. 'You don't just see beauty, you feel it' he would say.
>
> (Berwydd Davies)

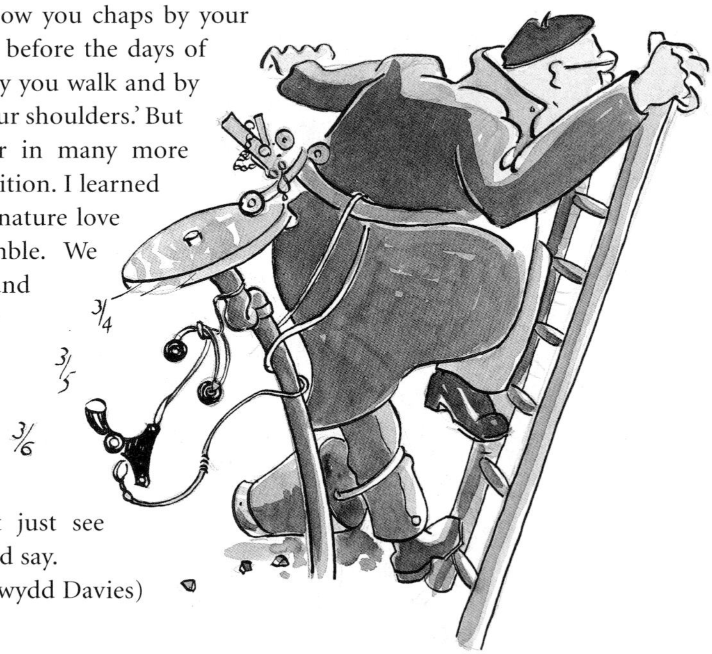

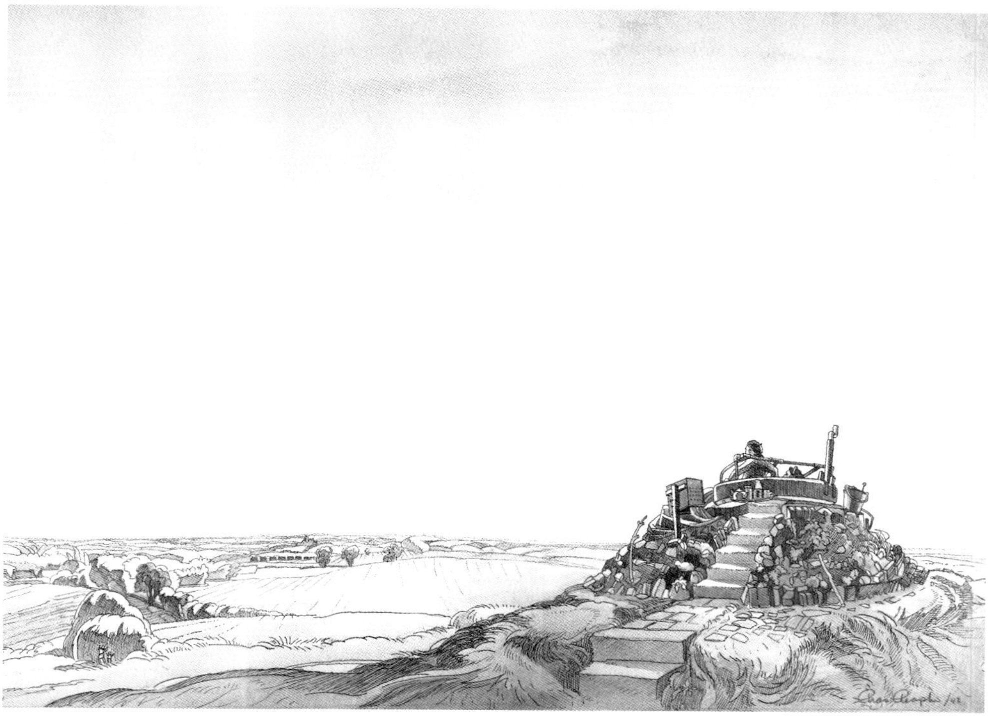

Fox 1 ROC Post, pen and ink, 380 x 510 mm, as published in the Illustrated London News, 1943

Chaplin served many night duties, both at Rickmansworth's F1 and at 'Centre' in Kings Langley. He was also sent to other observation posts throughout the South East, accompanied always by his sketchbook. In an article describing the work of the ROC, the *Illustrated London News** published four of the artist's pen-and-ink drawings of ROC posts at work. The first (see this page), a view of F1 itself described coyly as 'typical of the many country posts manned by the ROC,' was captioned: 'With telescope and glasses a wide expanse of sky can be kept under constant survey. This Post was made by its members and consists of a large section of concrete conduit.' The second, a view of the Kings Langley Post (though not mentioned as such!) was captioned: 'Plotting a sneak raider: long before this German aircraft comes into view, various ROC posts have been waiting for him. He is here seen skimming through a valley, with the observer providing second-by-second plots of his movements.' The third illustrates a Post by the sea: '"In the drink": a pilot has baled out over the sea: his position is plotted from the observation post, and the air-sea rescue authorities are advised. In this picture a shaft of sunlight has caught the tiny speck on the horizon.' Finally, the fourth drawing

* *Illustrated London News*, 1 May 1943, pages 492–493

illustrated a night raid on the outskirts of London: 'Accurate sound readings on every aircraft, with cross-bearings from other posts, are relayed to the ROC centres; there they are correlated and passed to Fighter Command, Ack-ack and the Ministry of Home Security.'

However, the only copper plate Chaplin made of overtly wartime activity, the soft ground etching and engraving 'View from Brunswick Tower' (48) was produced from drawings made whilst on duty for the ROC at Windsor Castle. The pace and superficiality of cartoons did not mix well with the labour and intensity of line engraving.

The nights, and some days, of ROC duty, together with his full time employment, did not leave the artist much time for sketching expeditions into Watford, now some five miles from his new home in Rickmansworth. While he continued throughout this decade to produce a number of images from Cassiobury Park in Watford, his attention began to turn nearer home, to the beautiful and largely unspoilt area of former disused gravel pits, now a series of tranquil lakes lying between the River Colne and the Grand Union Canal to the south of Rickmansworth — Batchworth Lake, Bury Lake, Stockers Lake and Springwell Lake. These expansive waterways were bordered by huge willows and poplars, and the wild water and land based undergrowth gave sanctuary to a large variety of wild animals, birds and waterfowl. The many waterways and open spaces were intersected by quiet paths of privacy which, to an artist working quietly and without moving for hours on end, afforded an exciting intimacy with nature. Weather changes had a radical effect on this scenery, rendering a warm placid and reassuring view on a summer's day into an uncompromisingly wild and menacing scene during a winter storm. The mystery of mist and fog would melt backgrounds into nothingness, and light from moving clouds, driven by gentle breezes or fierce gales across the sun, or moon, would constantly change before the artist's gaze. Chaplin never represented a clear blue sky. He was fascinated by the light, the trees, and the constantly changing atmosphere in these places. Examples of his work on these subjects during this period can be seen in 'Silver Birches and Snow' (39), 'Willows' (41), 'Spring' (42), 'Evening Glow' (43), 'Hoar Frost' (47), 'Stockers Farm' (49), 'Tree Tops and Snow' (51), and 'Split Willow' (55). He also began to explore another area nearer home in Rickmansworth with a more conventional rural beauty, the Chess valley. This is a Chiltern beauty spot, to the north of the town, where Chaplin's bicycle would often be spotted wending its way home at dusk. Examples of images from this area in this period are 'Sunshine Wind and Rain' (46), 'Early Spring' (68), 'Evening Light — Chess Valley' (69) and 'Chess Valley' (71).

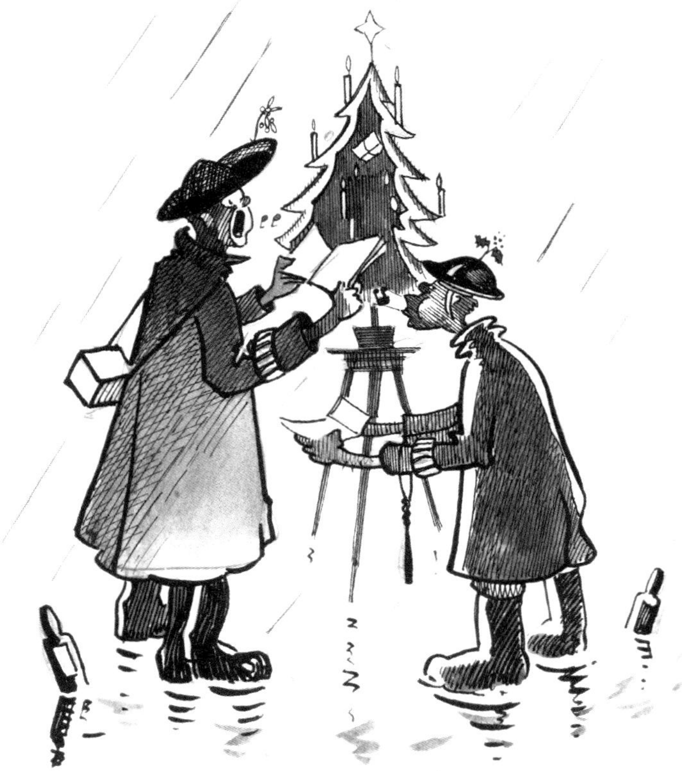

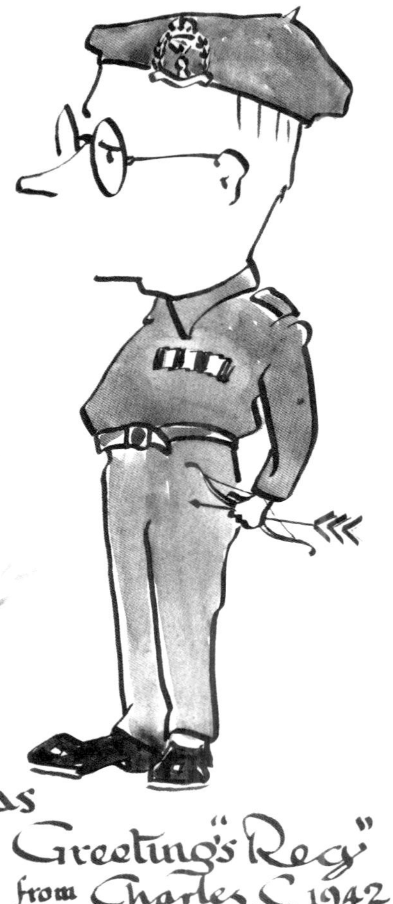

Some Christmas cartoons by the artist, including a self-caricature (above)

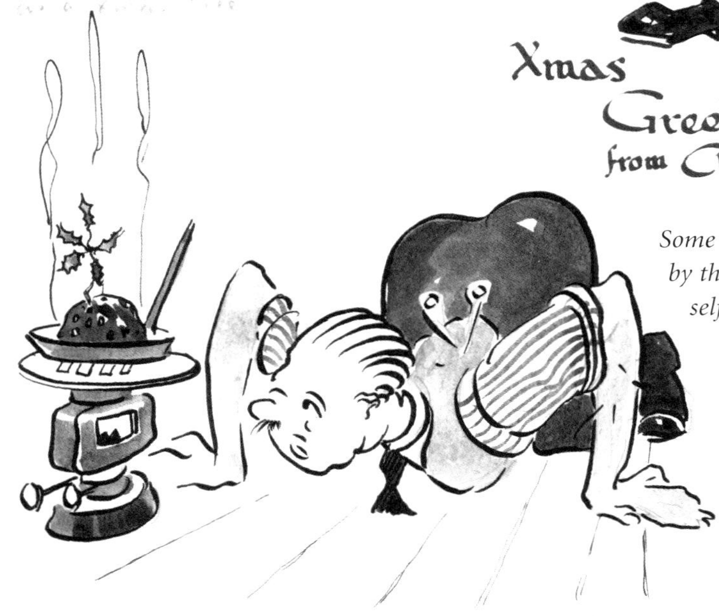

The ending of the war came as a profound relief to Chaplin and his family, and on VE Day the residents of Highfield Way organised a huge bonfire and street party in the centre of the road, still not made-up; neighbours recall Chaplin as the master of ceremonies and generally acting as the life and soul of the party.

Following the war an event occurred of profound significance to the quality and maturity of Chaplin's work. In the course of his duties at the Sun Engraving Company, Chaplin had to meet many editors of art and other popular magazines which were printed at the Sun works, and for which he had quality control responsibilities. One of these was Edgar Ainsworth of *Picture Post*, who encouraged him in many ways. Chaplin wrote later:

> It was Mr Ainsworth who introduced me one very wet Saturday afternoon, at an exhibition of the Royal Society of Painter-Etchers and Engravers, to Mr Malcolm Osborne. By this time I had already exhibited 5 or 6 works at the Royal Academy Summer Exhibitions, much to my surprise. Mr Osborne was very charming and made my small efforts seem worthwhile. The outcome of our introduction was that the customary educational requirements were waived, and I was allowed to become an external student at the Royal College of Art on Saturdays.*

A new world of skill and quality opened up for the artist. Hitherto he had been largely self-taught, apart from his commercial apprenticeship and evenings at the Watford School of Art, although he had always been strongly motivated and was increasingly creative. At the RCA he was an etching and engraving student for the whole of the academic terms 1947–1948 (student no 9), and 1948–1949 (student no 72) and for 9 months of each of these years his every Saturday was absorbed in practicing his art, and learning more from others. Works completed whilst a student at RCA included 'Pelican' (52), 'Coleshill Pond' (59), 'Garden Snail' (60), 'Cassiobury Park, View from Golf Course' (61), 'Close Friends' (62), 'Willows Cassiobury' (63), 'Fieldmouse' (64), 'Frog and Toad' (65), 'Wren' (66), and 'Evening Light, Chess Valley' (69). These show progressive developments in subject matter and style, and culminate in two of Chaplin's more important and recognised works, 'Farm Corner' (67) and 'Early Spring' (68). Of the series of animals and birds started here at the RCA, more later.

Chaplin's tutor was Robert Austin, later to become President of the Royal Society of Painter-Etchers and Engravers. In the collection of the artist's son, there is a proof of 'Farm Corner' (67) annotated as having been printed by Austin at the college. At the Department of Engraving there were tensions between Chaplin, a

* 'C. H. A. Chaplin RE Discusses his Engravings', *RE Journal*, No. 7, 1985

mature student and a highly skilled commercial engraver, and the other younger students bursting with artistic creativity, but finding the techniques of engraving hard to acquire. On one occasion Austin drew attention to the straightness of Chaplin's lines, comparing them unfavourably with the softer more flexible lines of a fellow student. Later, when the two students were together, the fellow student overlooked Chaplin's work and said: 'I wish I could do straight lines like you — I can't keep my hand steady enough!' The effect of joining the RCA was at the same time to boost and to wobble Chaplin's confidence. Chaplin wrote:

> This [joining the RCA] was a great boost to my art career, until I saw the wonderful work being done by students half my age. Robert Austin, however, paid me the greatest compliment of my life when he saw my first engraved plate on Saturday morning. He descended from his pedestal and said: 'Chaplin, you teach me a little about engraving, and I will teach you a little about art'. After this I felt less embarrassed at being a part-time student at the RCA.' When Chaplin eventually left his Saturday studies at the college, he was delighted when Austin called him into his office to present him with two of his engravings.*

Chaplin's medium hitherto had been predominantly etching, although in the later half of the 1940's he began to turn more to engraving; whilst attending the RCA and thereafter, his medium becomes predominantly line engravings, perhaps another influence of the RCA?

The strange, and unfinished, study of a pelican, 'Pelican' (52), had been made following Chaplin's enrolment at the RCA, and there followed a remarkable series of animal and bird studies, originally no doubt influenced by other contemporary students doing similar subjects at the College. The series was made between 1947 and 1951 and consists of 'Pelican' (52), 'Garden Snail' (60), 'Fieldmouse' (64), 'Frog and Toad' (65), 'Wren' (66), 'Dragonfly and Passion Flower' (70), 'Frog' (72), 'Stoat' (73), 'Robin' (75), 'Butterflies and Buddleia' (76), 'Mole' (77), 'Squirrel' (79), 'Bullfinch' (81) and 'Reed Warbler' (82); perhaps 'Two's Company' (136) — a magpie — can be added for completeness, though not made until 1980. These representations of little creatures are all of immense charm, although different collectors have different favourites. They all reflect the artist's deep love of nature and his personal sensitivity to flora and fauna.

In artistry and skill the series develops strongly in the later stages, with 'Stoat' (73), 'Squirrel' (79), 'Bullfinch' (81), and 'Reedwarbler' (82) featuring among Chaplin's best work. 'Stoat' (73) was Chaplin's diploma plate for his Associateship of the Royal Society of Painter-Etchers and Engravers, and a presentation print for

* Ibid

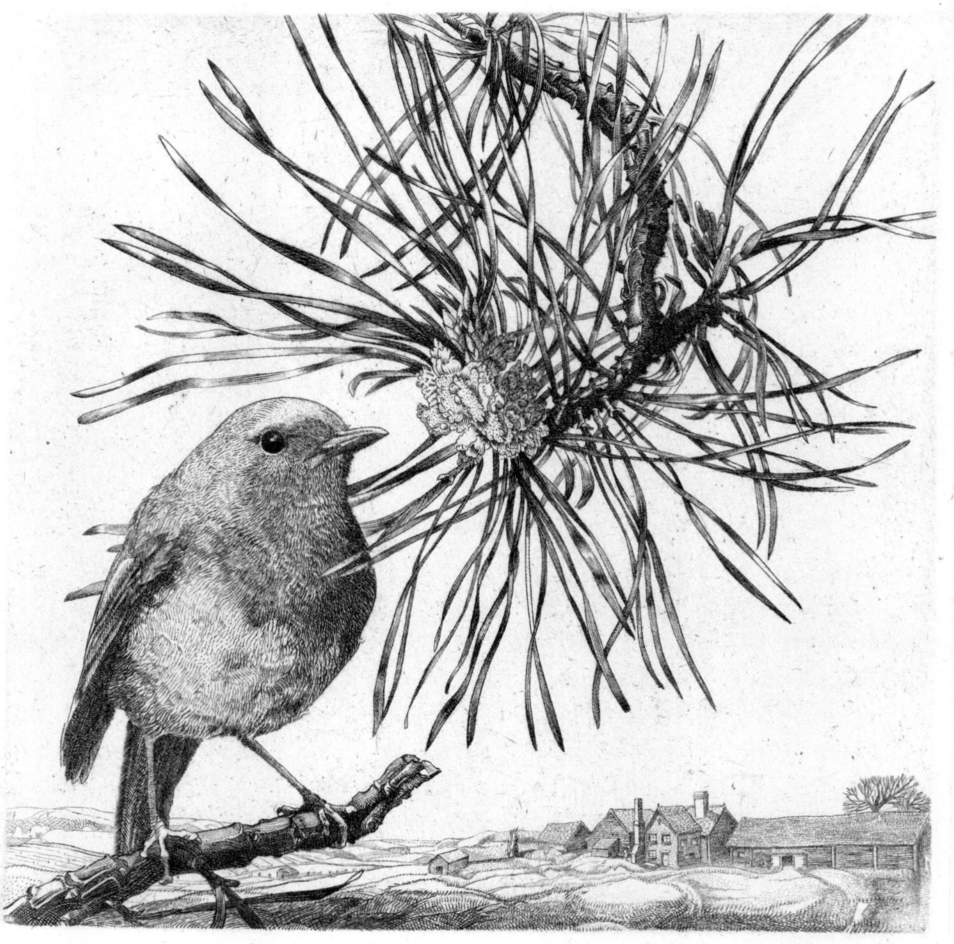

Robin, line engraving, 125 x 125 mm, 1950

the Print Collectors Club. The arts reporter in the *West Herts Post* of 8 June 1950 recorded:

> Mr Chaplin is a remarkable artist who works from memory. He tells me he caught a fleeting glance of the stoat while out on a country walk. He went home and transferred the picture onto copper whilst the memory was still fresh. The plate has captured the strength and ferocity of the hunter of the hedgerows.

Chaplin's observation of nature was acute, up close and personal. He wrote to a correspondent:

> I am interested in all animals, especially small ones: their artistic beauty fascinates me, and whilst studying them of course like to find out their habits and ways of life. The frog I

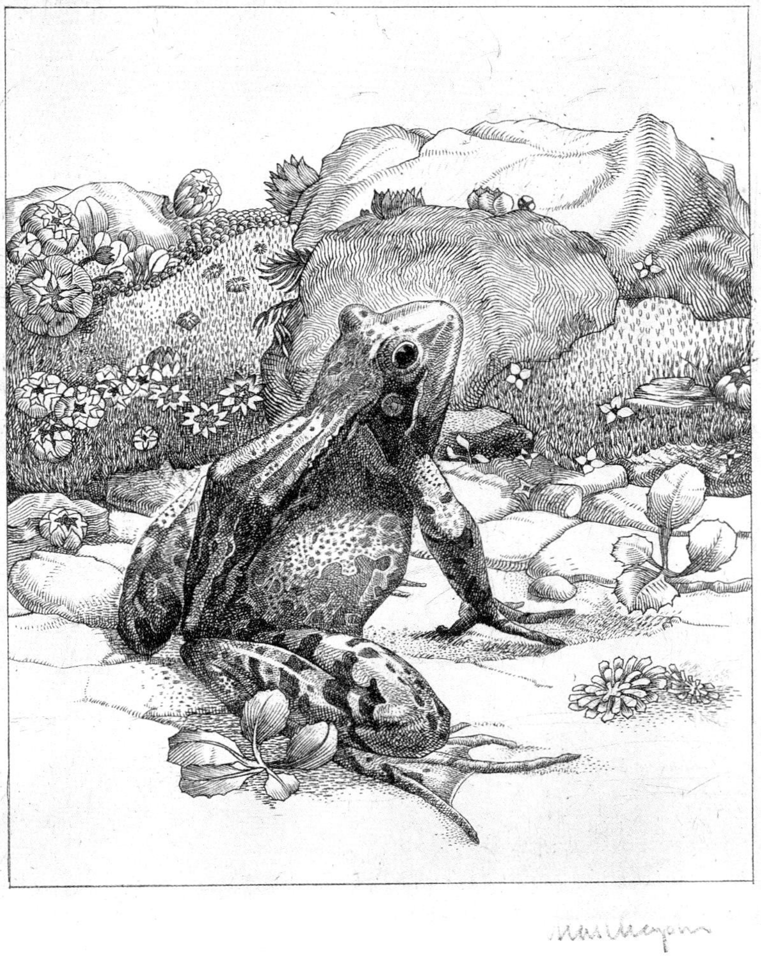

Frog, line engraving, 123 x 100 mm, 1949

collected quite small, and when grown up was friendly and a remarkable model. The toad, which I kept for months, was never friendly, but surly, keeping still and not seeming to be interested in the proceedings at all. Snails I have kept too — they are most exacting to draw, requiring a great deal of concentration.

His relationship with the model frog and toad was further explained to another correspondent as follows:

The frog was an extremely patient model for many weeks. He became a member of the Chaplin family, and was fed on the fattest and juiciest worms available as a reward for his friendly co-operation. He retired to the garden where we still meet him now and again. The toad was not quite so interesting as a model, rather surly and not too friendly. He too roams the garden now. His texture of lumps and bumps was delightful to engrave, and his eye was a jewel.

The *Daily Telegraph* art correspondent, commenting on the RA Summer Exhibition of 1949, picked out Chaplin's 'minute and meticulous frog'.

Of 'Mole' (77) he wrote to a collector:

It gave me great pleasure recently to open a small box sent to me by a friend — I found a mole inside. I am not a naturalist, but the lives and habits of these creatures intrigue me, so that I immediately made pencil sketches and notes of the mole. My notes would keep, even if the mole, being dead, did not. To me the beauty of the mole, apart from being one of God's small creatures, was in its smooth grey fur growing in all directions; and, in direct contrast, the wonderment of its powerful and workmanlike hands most suitably designed for tunnelling in the earth. Its long pink and clean snout protruding from such a furry body was also noted, as were the small weak eyes.

The deep personal involvement of Chaplin with the subject matter of his art is well illustrated here in these ephemeral subjects, and is typical of all his work.

In 1948 Chaplin met Muriel Took, an old school friend home in Great Britain for a visit. She had married a Canadian, Mr Brodie, from Ontario, Canada. They chatted over happy days at Alexandra Road School and the neighbours in Jubilee Road in Watford where they had both lived. Conversation turned to art and Chaplin's emerging success as an engraver. Chaplin gave her six prints, and in 1949, following her return to Canada she showed these to Nicolas Hornyansky of the Society of Canadian Painter-Etchers and Engravers. They were submitted to the Ontario Royal Museum where five prints were exhibited and 'Fieldmouse' (64) was illustrated in the catalogue.

Thus begun an association with Canada, and the Society of Canadian Painter-Etchers and Engravers ('CPE'), in particular, which Chaplin greatly valued in the coming years. It was invigorating for him to receive recognition outside Great Britain, particularly in a progressive country such as Canada where artists' printwork was excitingly modern and different, and where traditional engraving seemed almost extinct!

'Farm Corner' (67) was the artist's presentation print to the CPE, and this print, together with others was subsequently included in the Society's Archives Collection; it was exhibited again in the Archives Exhibition in Hamilton in 1978, and was reproduced in *Artviews* (Ontario, Canada) the same year. In 1950, an earlier print made in 1948 'Early Spring' (68) became the diploma plate for the artist's Associateship of CPE and the Honorary Members Print for the year. A couple of years later

'Summer, Underhill Farm' (89) received the George A. Reid Silver Memorial Award of CPE, 1952. In the following years up to 1971 a number of the artist's proofs are recorded as having been exhibited at CPE exhibitions in Hamilton (including the Centennial Print Exhibition, Montreal Museum of Fine Arts, 1967), many subsequently going on tour in Toronto, Vancouver, Quebec, Montreal and other cities in Canada. Chaplin was intrigued with the interest and almost quizzical acclaim that greeted his work in Canada, possibly because of its apparently old-fashioned style. For him the attitudes there contrasted with the atmosphere prevailing at the Royal Society of Painter-Etchers and Engravers in London. Of the annual CPE exhibition in the Royal Ontario Museum a reporter wrote:

> Most daring of their innovations is the habit of using a jury consisting of any members who want to turn up. In the very antithesis of secret voting, they argue lustily and vote by show of hands. If something is turned down then, there is no mystery about the reasons. Our preview of this boldly chosen selection indicated that, more than in the past the exhibition will run the full way from the almost extinct practice of detailed engraving, represented here by Chaplin of England, to forceful contemporary compositions such as the distinguished wood engraving 'The Nets' by Valius.*

Another critic, Hugh Thomson, said:

> Possibly the most outstanding contribution is by Britain's C. H. A. Chaplin who is exhibiting etching, mezzotint, drypoint and engraving, with finest attention to details without stiffness. In fact his style is extremely varied.

Following these exhibitions and the resulting sales, the artist enjoyed a healthy correspondence with collectors in Canada. Prints sent out to CPE exhibitions and not sold were exchanged with Canadian printmakers and he acquired a collection of many fine modern prints, very different from his own.

Despite the turmoil of war and the domestic hardship and deprivation of the post war years, the 1940s had been a period of significant development for Chaplin in the maturity of his art, and in his recognition in the wider world of art.

* Pearl McCarthy, *Globe and Mail*, Toronto, 4 March 1959

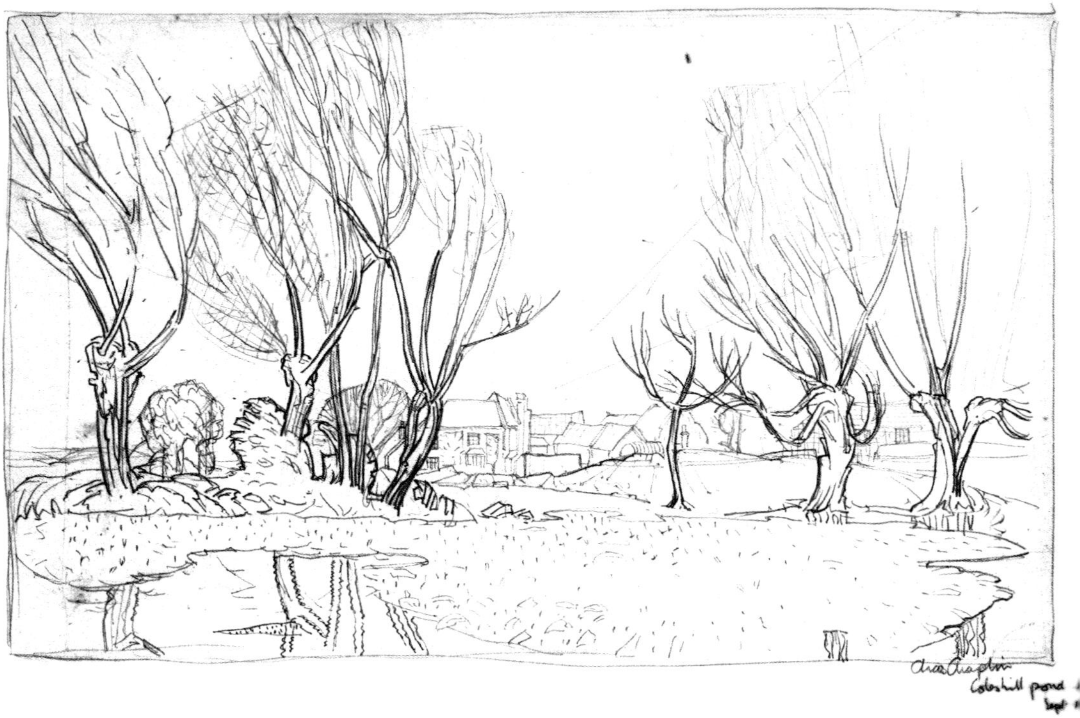

ABOVE: *Coleshill Pond, Amersham, pencil sketch, c. 190 x 300 mm, 1946. Preparatory sketch for catalogue no. 59, a line engraving of which no example could be located for inclusion in this book*

Work and Art 1950–1969

BY 1950 THE WAR and immediate post-war years and their restrictions were receding, and during the next two decades Chaplin consolidated his skills as an artist, whilst still bound by the restraint of full-time employment in order to earn his living. His responsibilities as an employee increased as he moved in various capacities from skilled journeyman to a middle manager in the large printing factory. He was involved first directly in production, then quality control, later customer liaison. This last function, perhaps the most stressful, involved frequent travelling to customers' premises in London, Manchester and elsewhere, and thrust him into the middle of the often conflicting interests of production and the customer. His family expanded during this period, providing him with absorbing new personal interests. He exhibited his work widely, having twenty prints exhibited at the RA Summer Exhibitions, missing only the years 1957, 1958 and 1968. He became a member of the Royal Society of Painter-Etchers and Engravers (now the Royal Society of Painter-Printmakers — 'RE') and showed much work at their annual exhibitions. The subject matter of his work during the 1950s continued to concentrate on trees and the area of water at Rickmansworth, but is greatly extended by inspiration he received on travels to a number of different places in Spain, and, nearer to home, in Sussex, Hampshire and Dorset.

In 1950 he began a relationship with the RE which was to last thirty-five years, and during which he exhibited sixty-seven works at the Society's annual exhibitions at the Conduit Street Gallery until 1979, and at Bankside Gallery from 1981. He exhibited nearly every year, missing the years 1957, 1972, 1973, 1980 and 1984, all of these due to ill health at the time. In the earlier years he would submit between three and six prints at each exhibition, some of these representing earlier work before he became a Member of the Society; later he settled down to exhibiting one or two a year, usually of new contemporary work.

It is not known how Chaplin first became involved with the RE, but it may be assumed that it was through the introductions and encouragement of Malcolm Osborne and Robert Austin, with both of whom he had worked closely during his studies at the Royal College of Art, 1947–1949. In any event, the diploma print for his Associateship of the Society, the line engraving 'Stoat' (73), engraved in 1949,

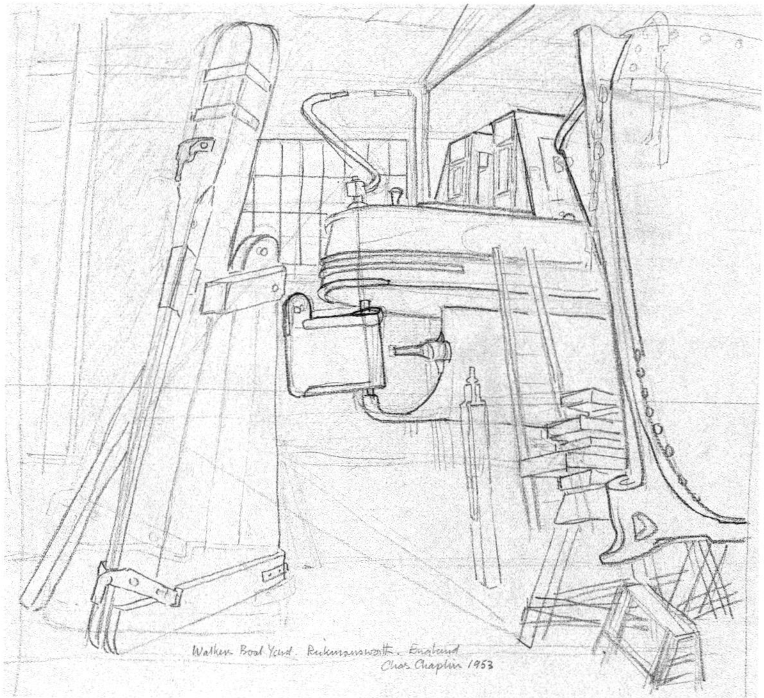

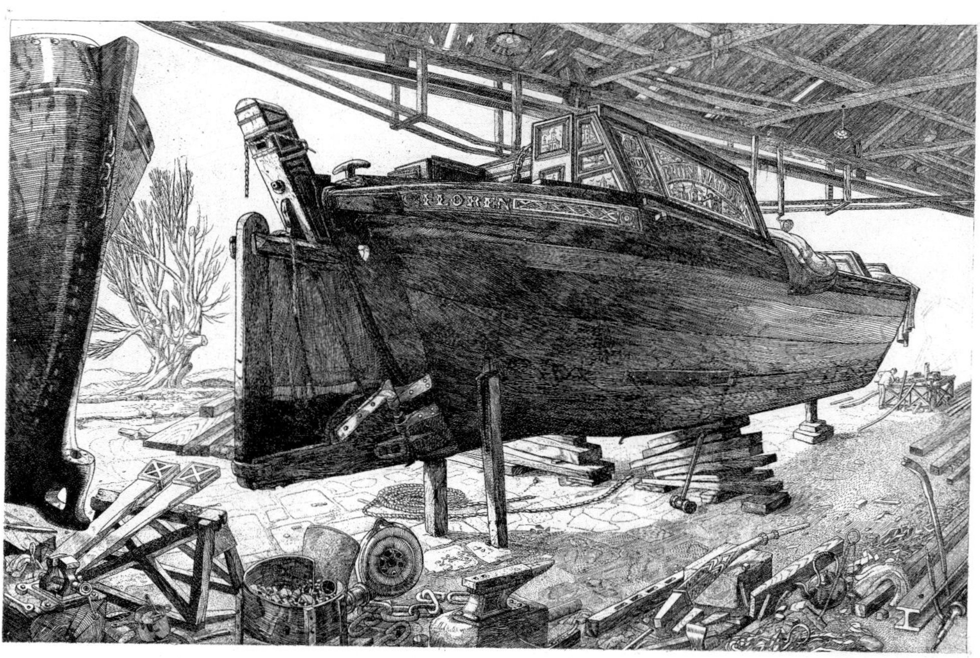

Pencil sketch (top) made in 1953 and referred to by Chaplin when engraving 'Under Repair' (below), line engraving, 204 x 305 mm, 1968

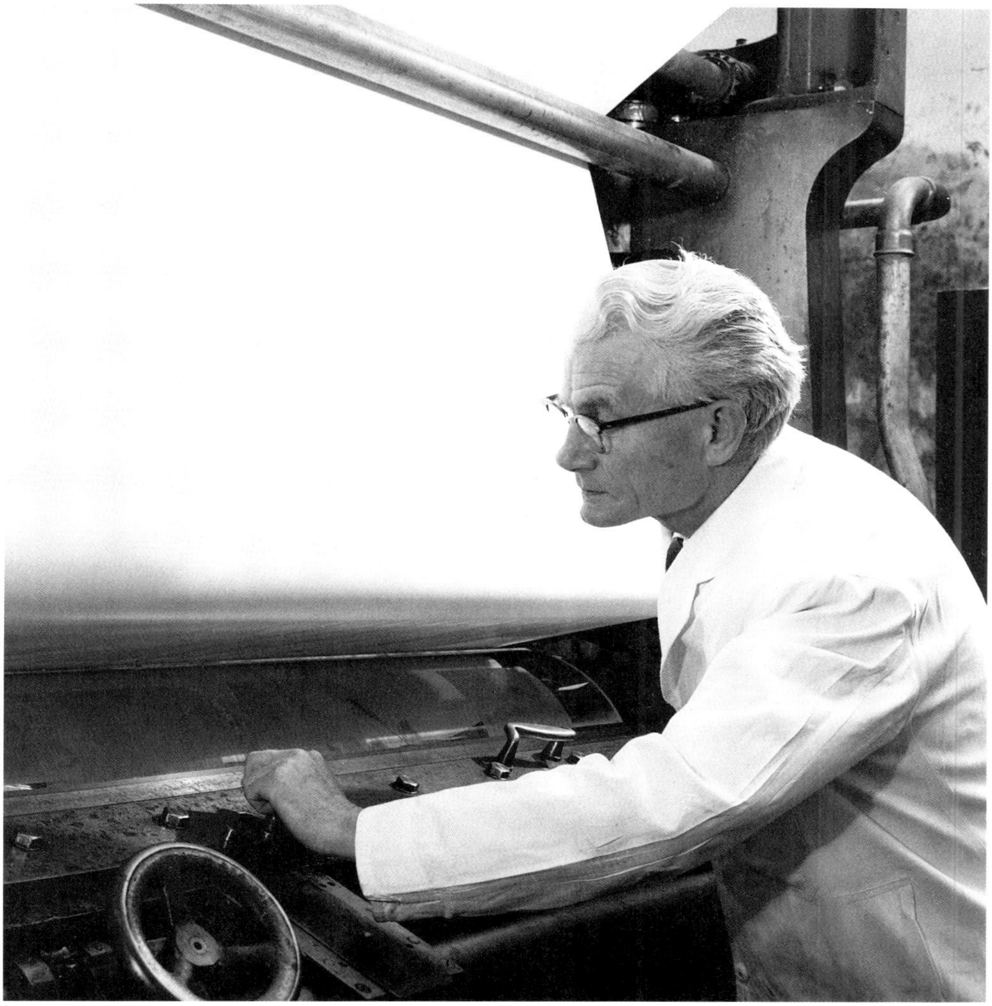

Chaplin at work at Sun Engraving, c. 1960

was perhaps one of the best prints he made. He was elected an Associate Member, and this print with five others was hung at his first RE Exhibition in 1950. He became a Fellow of the Society in 1962, his diploma print being the line engraving 'Forest Glade' (103). However, the Society never became one of the artist's principal interests, partly due to the time travelling to London that this would have involved, and partly, no doubt, due to Chaplin's shyness and general unsociability. Looking back in 1981 on his relationship with the RE, he wrote:

I find I cannot travel up to London these days, so I have lost contact with the members, and many of them about my age have passed on. Not one of the RE members live within striking distance of me, so I do not see any other artist, etchers or engravers. There are no etchers or engravers in Rickmansworth or Watford. We are surely a rare breed.

A couple of years later, complaining that the proceeds of his sales barely covered the expenses of an RE exhibition, he wrote:

So really the RE is a dead loss. I feel that the move of their premises [to Bankside} has not worked out, and I am sure that, because I do not attend meetings and exhibitions of the Society, interest in my work suffers.

In spite of his rather ambivalent attitude to the Society, he appreciated the influence it had on his work. At the end of his artistic life in 1985 he referred to leaving his Saturday studies at the RCA, and his subsequent relationship with the RE:

Some time later I was elected a member of the RE where I met many fine copper-plate artists. The mere fact that I was among them and their exhibitions improved my art knowledge. Mr Norman Janes purchased a print of one of my works for his wife's birthday, which greatly encouraged me. The younger members of the Society were very friendly, bearing in mind that I did not consider myself then to be one of them as I was not an RCA student. But I always felt that the RE was a little standoffish. I fully agreed with Charles Bartlett in his article in the *Journal* No. 5 that the Society was changing, and needed changing. The whole atmosphere has changed, but for me it has been a little too late, for I am sure that very few members of the Society will know me personally as I have not visited London for some years. Although I did not speak much at the Society's meetings, I did listen and I acknowledge the great help the Society generally gave me.*

In April 1987, Chaplin received a letter from Michael Spender, the Secretary of the Society, informing him that he had been unanimously elected an 'Honorary Retired Member of the Society'.

The Council wish me to express its admiration of your contribution to the exhibitions and affairs of the Society over the years and to send you every best wish in your retirement from active participation.

Three days later, Chaplin had died.

Chaplin's visit to Spain in 1951 was very different from anything he had done before, since he had rarely moved far from home, even in the United Kingdom. As on most of his sketching expeditions, May remained at home. He travelled by car with two old friends, Bob and Peter North, who both spoke Spanish fluently and undertook all the driving and the administrative chores of the tour. Their destination was

* C. H. A. Chaplin RE discusses his engravings: *RE Journal* No. 7, 1985, p. 20.

Marbella on the South Coast. In an old Ford V8 car the three week journey over some 3,500 miles was for him physically quite demanding. However, as a non-driver, he was able to occupy the back seat and contemplate and absorb the passing scenery. Occasionally he would make a plea to stop in order to sketch a briefly glimpsed subject. His companions were not artists, although they were sympathetic to art; they afforded him every opportunity to sketch on the brief stops within their hectic schedule, although the peace and quietude of his customary method of observation was lacking.

In these circumstances the artist was not able to use one of his usual techniques for rapid plate-making, namely needling direct onto waxed copper, but he was at least able to make copious pencil sketches, many of them consisting of tiny details only. He refined, reworked and developed these in the months following his return. In terms of print however, the outcome of the experience in Spain was only six works: a mezzotint 'Mystery of Spain' (84), a softground etching and drypoint 'Bullfight' (85), a drypoint 'Spain' (86), a linocut 'Spain' (87) and the only line engravings 'Segovia, Spain' (90), and 'Siesta' (101). Chaplin certainly shared the love of his companions for Spain, its excitement, colour and mystery, but it seems that, for the purposes of his artistic expression, the pressures of travel did not suit his detailed and contemplative style of observation. Years later he would frequently speak of the colour and drama of Spain and the deep impression it had made on him, yet neither the quantity nor the quality of his subsequent output seem to reflect this. For example, he wrote:

> My simple sketches of trees in Spain will always refresh and remind me that the trees I saw were not products of my imagination, but that the grotesque and fantastic shapes really did exist.

Moreover, the effect of 'Bullfight' (85) does not quite seem to achieve his own description of the incident:

> [in the bullring] techniques of pencil drawing were forgotten; to capture the speed and grace of movement in the drama was now the objective. The young matador is shown [in the pencil sketch] making his last pass, for within five seconds of this move he was fatally gored — it was while the matador was being carried from the ring that the sketch was made. From this sketch I made the soft ground etching 'The Bullfight'. In this type of sketch the thinking comes after and not before. The carefully studied sketches I have made, and the training and observation in the past, enabled me to make this quick sketch under conditions of great mental excitement with a crowd, either roaring or deathly silent, surrounding me.

In summary, Chaplin's Spanish experience was probably of less importance to him artistically, than in the broadening of his personal horizons and in the further development of his acute perception of nature and people.

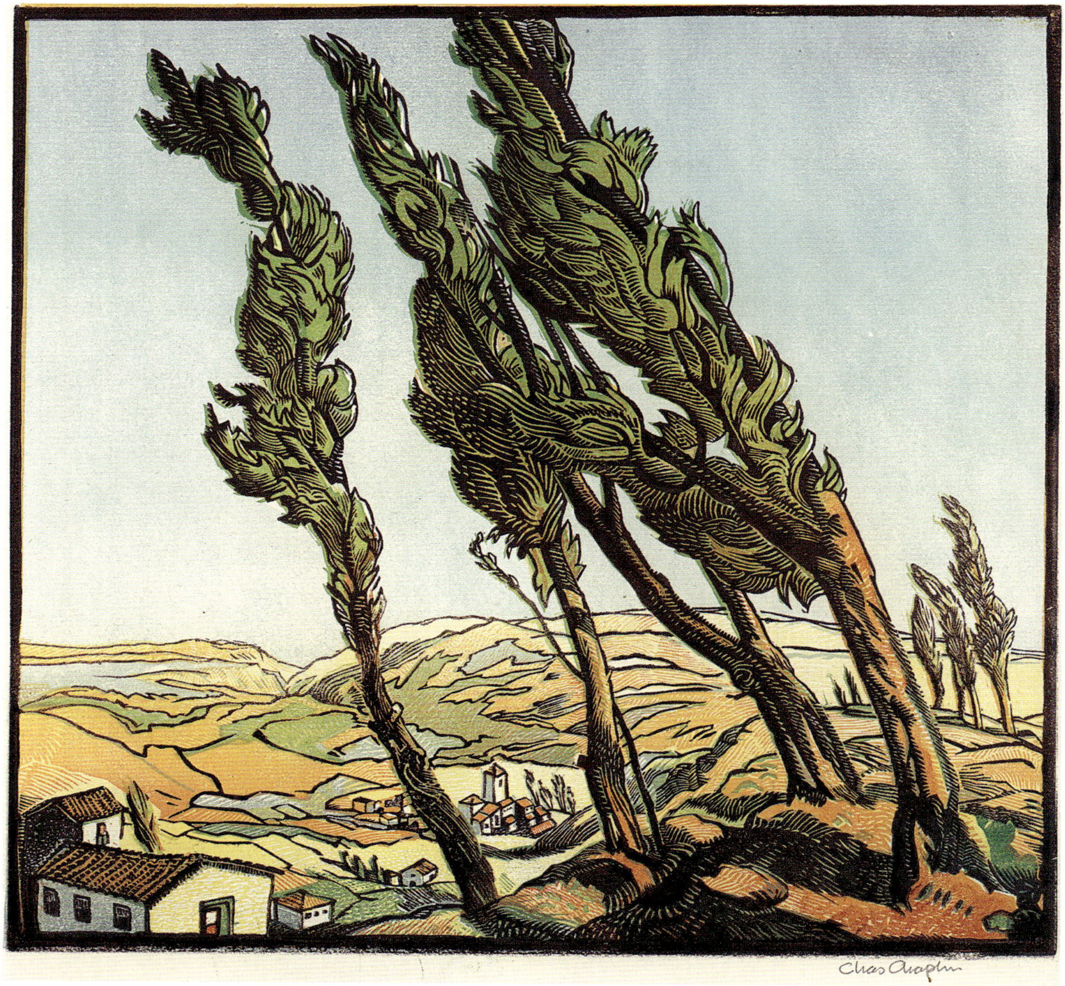

Spain, five-colour linocut, 265 x 285 mm, 1952

By the early 1950's the artist had also spent several summer holidays with his family in Lyme Regis in Dorset. They stayed in a simple farm on the coast to the west of the town where the land had slipped into the sea. The farm itself consisted of an ancient stone farmhouse and several random and irregular barns, all of which seemed to cling perilously to rocky outcrops in the hills which tumbled unevenly down to the sea. The area was very remote, the farm being approached along a rough narrow lane leading to the main road a mile away. The terrain, the thick woodland and the hedgerows in the area were wild and unkempt. A visit to the town entailed a walk of several miles across undulating fields, where rabbits would scatter ahead of the walker. The rocky beach, reached after a scramble down the steep loose cliffs was noted for ammonites and other large fossils. The peace and quiet of the area and the old-fashioned, almost primitive, nature of the farming there appealed to the artist, and in undisturbed isolation he was able to do much pencil sketching, as well as much colour work, mainly in pastels and oils. Two line engravings resulted from these visits: 'Underhill Farm (with cats)' (88), and 'Summer, Underhill Farm (with Mr Bowditch)' (89). In both the artist begins to observe and explore decrepit rural buildings and rural clutter, a fascination which was to continue and develop more strongly later in his career. Both images were exhibited at the RA, in 1952 and 1953 respectively, and were successful and popular with collectors.

Another sketching expedition at about this time took the artist to Sussex. For him the joy in these excursions which were devoted solely to finding material for his artistic expression, can be sensed in his notes on 'Ancient Crafts' (102):

> The sketches and notes for this plate were made on a Monday in September, 1953 during a sketching tour of ten days in Sussex with my friends, Reg Allen and Peter Neighbour, who drove the car. Both are artists. We toured the lanes and byways, lunching at pubs, staying at country hotels at night, having immense fun and games, and also enjoying the sketching — Reg and Peter in watercolours and I in pencil. My only colour medium was a sixpenny packet of school blackboard chalk in six colours, bought at a small village. This was my first use of chalks.

However, in some ways, the change in the character of Chaplin's work between the 1940s and the 1950s in best exemplified in 'Scarecrow' (83), a line engraving completed in 1951. The attitude of the scarecrow, perched incongruously on the top of a hill overlooking a park and watercress beds, appears to be one of declamation, or possibly questioning. This led many artists, collectors and observers to enquire of the artist as to the 'meaning' of the image. He found such enquiries amusing, and whilst never expressly *denying* that the image had any particular meaning, he would invariably turn the question around, asking the enquirer as to what meaning he might have found. There were many suggestions: philosophical, political, social — even sexual — motives were at one time or another attributed to the artist. As far as I know, Chaplin himself never accepted any of these attributions, and he continued to be entertained by them. In his notes to the engraving, his own explanation was somewhat more prosaic:

> The sketches for 'The Scarecrow' were made during a lunch-hour break in the watercress beds of Cassiobury Park, Watford. The watercress growers had made it to keep the birds off the young newly-planted watercress. Like all my plates, this is a composite study, the

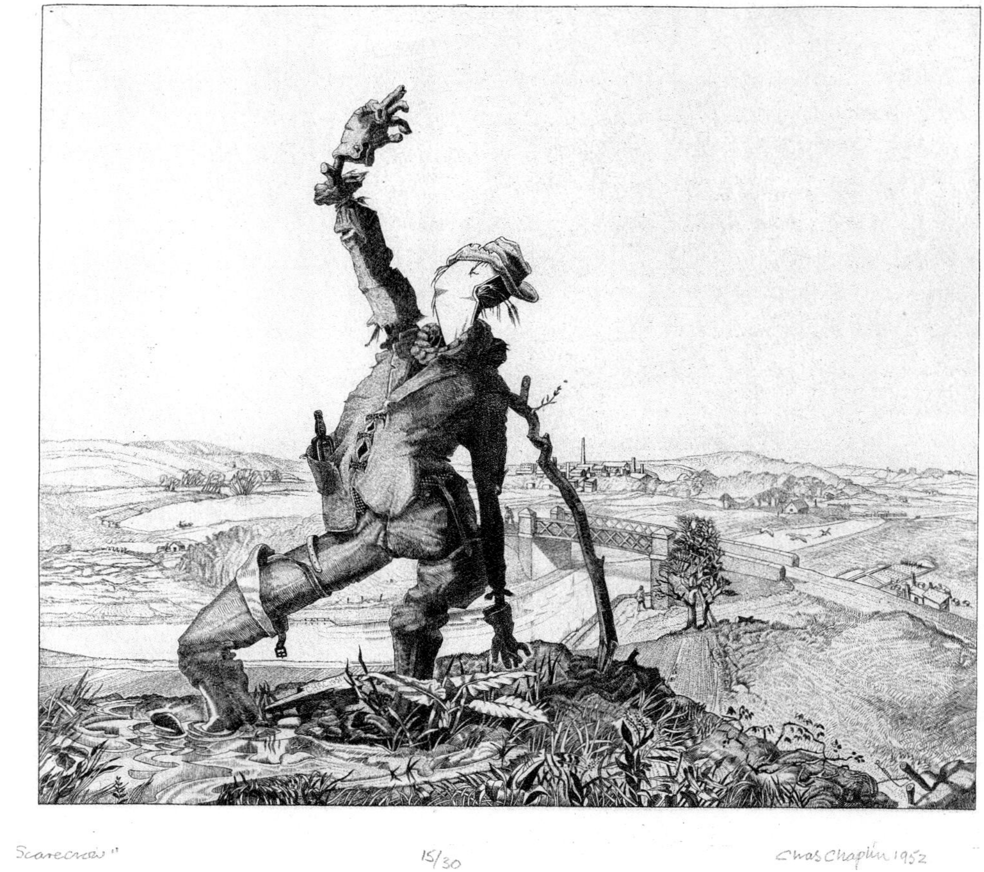

Scarecrow, line engraving, 220 x 252 mm, 1951

scarecrow being placed in a nearby setting, and as nearly always, the other objects are not always in exact proportion. The scarecrow, which is an exact study, was soon destroyed by children. Whilst making the drawings for this plate I saw many kingfishers, a rare bird in 1951, but now completely disappeared from this area. I used to talk to the old lady with a feather in her hat, each day — she is shown crossing the bridge. The small figure passing under the bridge was a friend with whom I went out sketching every lunch our, and is a well known pastel artist now — James Fry. The small figure at the watercress beds shed is a Mr Sansom, a well known local character and grower of watercress. His sons still carry on the business.

For many years 'Scarecrow' did, however, hold a personal secret. This became something of a mystery when the artist himself wrote of the plate: 'A young lady's name is engraved on this plate (at her request) which my wife has failed to find after all these years.' The mysterious identity of the young woman was not revealed until 2003 when, following her death, the lady's daughter sold* a number of prints (including 'Scarecrow') which formed a collection of the artist's work which the artist had given her over a period of several years. The actual print of 'Scarecrow' given to the young lady fifty years earlier was bought at the sale and is now owned by Mr Oliver Cave, a nephew of the artist's son.

The artist continued to explore creatively the locality near his home in Rickmansworth, especially the area of lakes, canal, and rivers to the south of the town which were all accessible by a walk or a cycle ride of a mile or two. He produced a series of prints of waterside and winter subjects, 'Melting Snow and Floodwater' (91), 'Old Willows' (92), 'Winter's Reflections' (93), 'Evening Patterns' (94)'Tree Patterns' (95), 'Winter Snow' (96), 'Silver Birches in Winter' (97), and 'Old Willow and Moorhens' (98) which were exhibited at the RA and widely elsewhere. These effectively developed his themes of the intensity and the enigma of light and reflection, through trees, skies and water, and in the changing moods of sun, moon, cloud, rain, snow and ice.

Chaplin was always highly focussed on his art, but not to the exclusion of social and family activities. By 1954 his son, Jon, had begun to study law at Magdalen College, Oxford and subsequently at Gray's Inn, London. A few years later, in 1959, Jon married a local teacher, Elizabeth Ann Cave, whose father and three brothers were also involved in the printing industry in Watford. By now Chaplin had replaced his trusty bicycle with a car, and was able to make termly visits to Oxford with May. He enjoyed the magnificence of the ancient buildings, and the peace and tranquillity of the colleges, but was never tempted to capture these on paper or copper. Later he threw himself with energy and enthusiasm into helping with his son's new house and garden, contributing many long week-ends labouring in the garden, constructing drives and terraces, erecting a shed and planting trees. His interest in the design and infrastructure of gardens continued throughout his life. Soon his grandchildren began to arrive — Elizabeth Louise in 1960, Sara Ann in 1962 and Jon Edward in 1966 — and he, with May, applied himself diligently to babysitting, nursing and eventually storytelling and games with the young children. Frequent personal references to events in the lives of his extended family begin to appear in his work from this time.

* See catalogue: Hilary Chapman Fine Prints, 20th Century Gallery, London, April 2003

The artist had begun to take annual holidays with May in the New Forest, Hampshire in the late 1950s, on some occasions together with their son's family. Invariably they stayed at the Watersplash Hotel in Brockenhurst, then a simple, quiet and friendly family hotel where they could spend lazy afternoons chatting with the proprietor, Brian Foster, about the surrounding forest and the location of different roads and paths in the forest that could provide the deepest isolation. In their different ways they were both completely charmed by the forest. They liked nothing better than to drive the car off the road and follow the tracks (possible still in those days) for a mile or more, deep through the thick dark trees until a clearing was reached. Here they would set up camp for the day, May laying out the packed lunch and arranging the deck chairs in the sun, whilst Charlie operated the primus stove to brew frequent pots of fresh tea. Charlie would wander off with his complex sketching stool and materials to find an unusual tree or setting, and May would settle down with her knitting, tapestry or a book. It was a rare, tranquil and idyllic setting which they could enjoy together, far from the pressures of commercial print or the domestic grind.

A huge volume of pencil sketches and pastels was amassed by the artist during these holidays. In the decade following 1960, these led to a series of five line engravings: 'In the New Forest (with pheasant)' (99), 'Sunlight and Shade, New Forest (with deer)' (100), 'Forest Glade (with teddy bear)' (103), 'Edge of Forest (with tree stump)' (104) and 'Tree Patterns, New Forest (with large stag)' (113); to these can be added the last complete plate engraved by the artist much later in 1984, 'New Forest Ghost' (144). All but 'Tree Patterns' were exhibited at Summer Exhibitions, with many resulting sales; 'Forest Glade (with teddy bear)' was the diploma plate for the artist's Fellowship of the RE, and a presentation print for the Print Collectors Club.

For Chaplin, part of his fascination for the New Forest lay in its history, which seemed to imbue the ancient trees with additional character and mystery. His notes disclose:

> I visit the New Forest in Hampshire almost every year for a short holiday and make many pastel and pencil studies. So far I have engraved several plates of the older wooded areas. The Forest has been a Crown possession since the days of the Normans and is now in the care of the Forestry Commission. Some areas are fenced off from the cattle, semi-wild horses, cows, deer and other wild life. The area covered by the Forest is some 100 square miles.

And in another note:

> I have made many studies in the New Forest in pastel and some engraved plates, mostly of the old and veteran trees, which are now fast declining. There are glades, moors and marshes which have scarcely changed since William the Conqueror in A.D. 1079. It is the

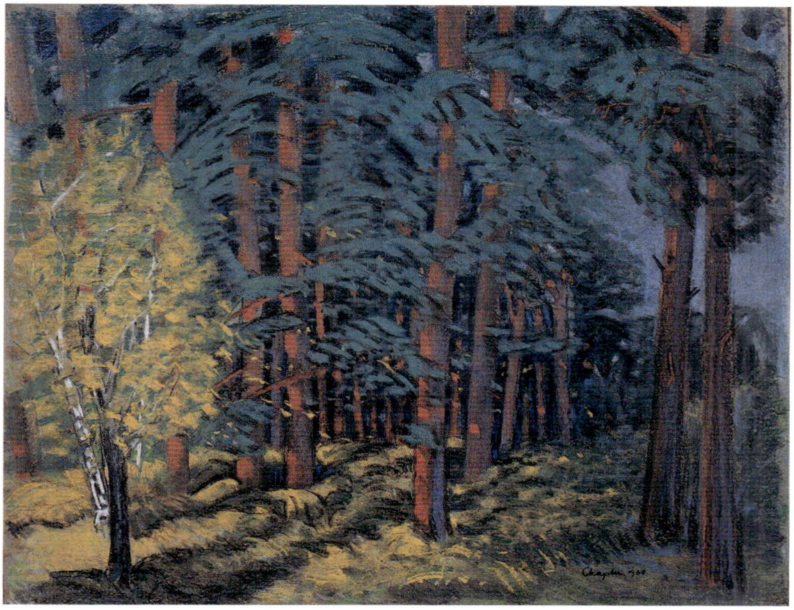

Scots Pine, Rhinefield Walk, New Forest, pastel, c. 410 x 610 mm, 1967, reproduced in Tree News by Felix Publishing, 2004 (by kind permission of John Francis Chaplin: phtograph by Tom Reeves, Lewes, Sussex)

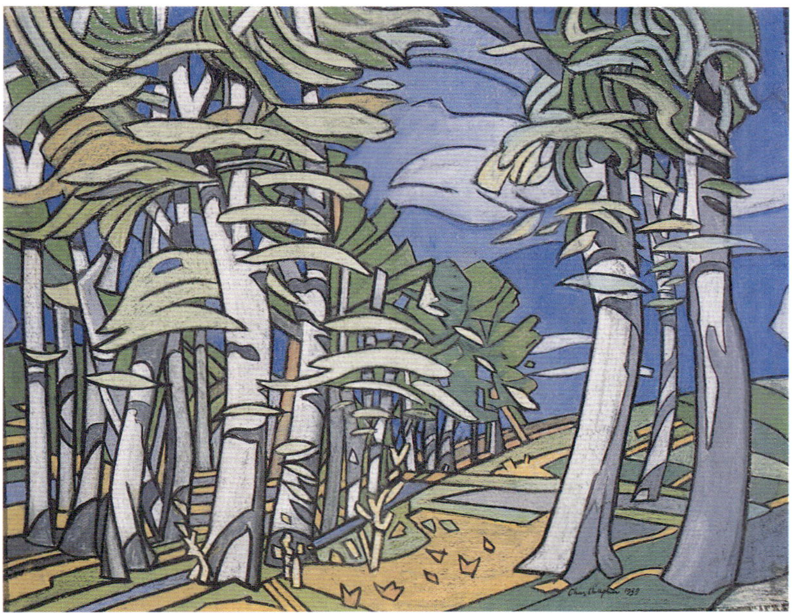

The New Forest, pastel, c. 410 x 610 mm, 1970 (by kind permission of John Francis Chaplin: phtograph by Tom Reeves, Lewes, Sussex)

finest forest in England. My pastels and engravings cannot do justice to such a wonderful area, which has given me such pleasure. I have always made my stays in the New Forest at Brockenhurst which is full of ancient history, as the Romans were here in about the year A.D. 70.'

In the latter years of the 1960s, as Chaplin approached retirement, he began to develop an interest, already represented in a number of his earlier works, in rural scenes and artefacts; these are not countryside scenes of classical beauty with sweeping hills, fields and woodland, nor busy and well-ordered objects serving contemporary rural industries. They are, rather, scenes of rural chaos and dereliction, objects of mechanical obsolescence left where abandoned to rust and rot, and minutely and accurately observed and recorded. They disclose an almost obsessional curiosity and fondness for history and the life of the rural community in an age which had then gone. Examples are the line engravings 'Allotment Hut' (105), 'Hedgerow Study' (108), 'Farm Corner' (107), 'Going for a Song' (110), and 'Put out to Grass' (111). The last three of these are significant in that they are based on subjects found at Knightscote Farm, Harefield, Middlesex, where the artist was to derive most of his inspiration during the years following his retirement — more of this later.

The final print of this group, 'Put out to Grass' (111) is personally significant in the artist's life. He had worked nearly fifty years for his employer. The increased responsibilities of the later years had proved stressful, and his former robust health had begun to deteriorate. In May, 1970 he was hospitalised for a major operation. He convalesced for two months and on returning to work in a still weakened state was shocked to discover that, without being informed, he had been moved from the large office he previously occupied in the Watford factory, to a small corner in a production area. His title and responsibilities had been downgraded without consultation with him. He was sixty-three years of age, and the combination of these circumstances led to his sudden and unplanned early retirement that summer. By today's standards 'early retirement at sixty-three' is almost a contradiction in terms, but he had worked nearly fifty years believing that he would be entitled to retire at age sixty-five, but not before. At the time he wrote in correspondence with his Swedish friends: 'I am 63. Proper retirement age is 65, so I am now unemployed until I reach 65.' For a loyal, proud, shy and sensitive man to be forced to leave work in these circumstances was a severe psychological blow. As far as the printing industry was concerned he had certainly seen the straws blowing in the wind; the advent of automation, the beginnings of computer control, the new printing technologies, Union demarcation and intransigence, and the gradual loss

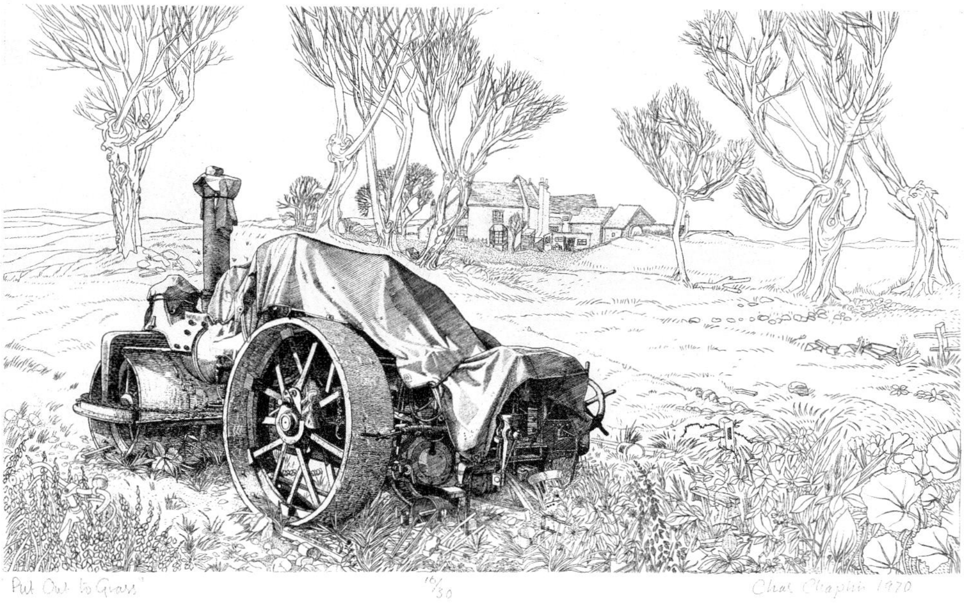

Put out to Grass, line engraving, 183 x 302 mm, 1970

of British printing business to overseas competition with its greater productivity. These factors eventually led to the complete closure of the large printing plants in Watford and the virtual disappearance of the British printing industry as Chaplin had known it. He had been caught in the wrong place at the wrong time. His pension was small, although just adequate, and a lifetime of May's careful housekeeping had ensured that the mortgage on Highfield Way was paid off; however his pension would not be paid to May if she should be widowed. Unlike previously, the proceeds of the sales of his prints were to become more material to their way of life, the continuation of the costs of his art, and the need to provide for May in the event of his prior death. He and May managed to take a holiday in Brockenhurst in the late Summer, but depression and further ill-health set in. Further operations followed in May and June 1971. It was not until he reached the age of sixty-five in 1972 that physical and mental recovery seemed attainable, and not until 1974 that his artistic output began to recover. In these circumstances, both the subject matter, and the title of, 'Put out to Grass' can be felt as a sad and ironic commentary on a self-perceived failure in the artist's life.

Retirement 1970–1987

For Chaplin, retirement signified the cessation of full-time employment and the gaining of total freedom to follow his artistic activities. It did not become a period of reduced activity, but produced a flowering of his energy and talents in which he developed new approaches to his art, new styles of engraving and new interests. Retirement, however, did not start easily, and 1970 was a very unsettled year. After his major operation in the Spring, and the trauma of being forced out of work in his view two years early, after returning from Brockenhurst he wrote to a correspondent in the Autumn: 'We have not settled down this year; we do not know if we will stay in Rickmansworth.'

Although he had been able to do much work during his recent holiday in the New Forest — having completed some twenty large pastels and much other pencil sketching — he seemed to have lost some of his confidence. In September 1970 he wrote to Ann Hook, Honorary Secretary of the CPE:

> I am afraid that our RA exhibitions are continuing to change, and to change very considerably in style, and my plates will not be acceptable. Of course I can be hung at the RE without having to pass the selection committee which is required at the RA. The general public, however, seem to want my work more than ever, and I hope now that I am retired I can get down to doing more plates. I do not intend to alter my style or outlook.

Chaplin's plate output was greatly reduced in the early years following retirement, the only line engraving hung in the Summer Exhibitions between 1969 and 1974 being 'Cactus and Shells' (112) in 1971, a print that he did not care for much himself and which he was disappointed to see hung in preference to 'Tree Patterns, New Forest' (113) which he had submitted at the same time. He had been diagnosed as suffering from Meuniere's disease, a disease of the inner ear which caused giddiness. By Christmas 1970 he was forbidden by his doctor to drive his car. In spite of this, and with much difficulty he continued with sketching and pastel work, but his sketching expeditions now had to be conducted on foot, carrying all his relatively heavy equipment with him. In the Spring of 1971 he had two operations on his ear which, although leaving him completely deaf in the affected ear, did improve the symptoms of giddiness, and enable him gradually to resume his work.

A few years earlier Chaplin's younger brother, Edward, had taken the tenancy of a farm in Harefield, Middlesex, only a few miles from Rickmansworth. Prior to this

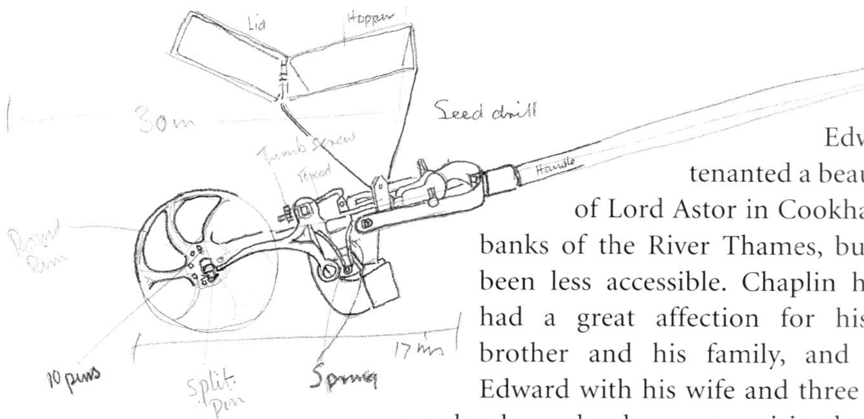

Edward had tenanted a beautiful farm of Lord Astor in Cookham, on the banks of the River Thames, but this had been less accessible. Chaplin had always had a great affection for his younger brother and his family, and now that Edward with his wife and three boys were much closer he began to visit the farm — Knightscote Farm — increasingly frequently. This was to become an absorbing interest in Chaplin's life, and a significant influence in the development of his art. The first image of Knightscote Farm appeared in 'Farm Corner' (107), engraved in 1967, and about which Chaplin notes:

> At this time, my brother was the farming tenant, but since then, the Greater London Council [which owned the farm] have taken a great interest in the farm, which is in the London green belt area, and with the co-operation of the farming tenants, have made the farm into an education farm. They have established only recently a farm walk, and for the last few years, Open Days, when the farm is open to the public. Over 2,000 visitors during the day have been recorded. A great number of farm machines and tools and animals are on show, with many old and ancient crafts being performed. All this was organised by the tenant farmer, Frank Townshend, a dairy farmer who had a Fresian herd of over 250 cattle. School visits are a daily feature.

The 'show' of machines and tools started in this way. Chaplin met Dennis Hallbery who was bird-watching on the farm, and together they began to accompany Townsend, the new tenant farmer, on his visits to surrounding farms in pursuit of his hobby of collecting old tractors, mostly lying abandoned in fields or barns. In the course of these visits Townsend would be given or would purchase many other smaller machines and old rural tools and implements also abandoned on the farms. To start with these were thrown randomly into a disused chicken shed at Knightscote. Chaplin and Hallbery shared an interest in these objects, and began to clean and arrange them, and then to repair, organise and display them. This was the beginning of a substantial collection which was eventually purchased by the GLC

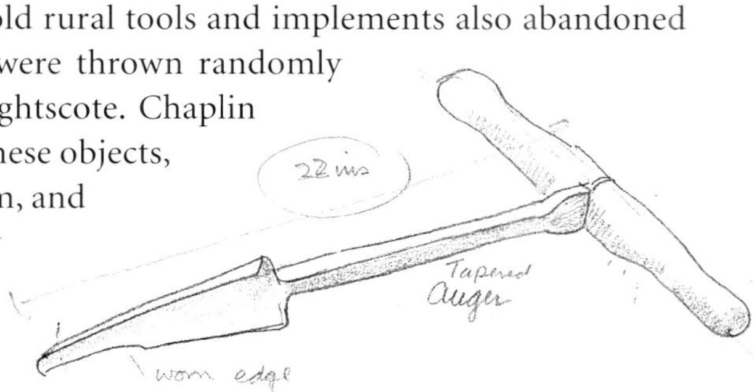

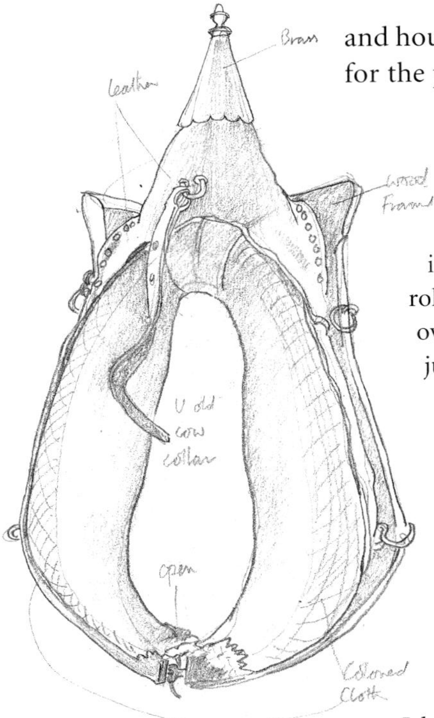

and housed properly in a large barn built by them specially for the purpose of becoming a country museum.

The first open day at the farm was in August 1973 and was a washout, although the second, in September, proved very successful. Chaplin wrote:

> It is a very mixed crowd that visits the farm, mostly all interested in the animals, old tractors, farm carts, steam rollers and demonstrations. I repair, renovate and show over 200 small antique farm tools of all sorts, and show just those prints that are connected with the farm.'

Through his association with Knightscote, Chaplin had developed a keen interest in farming and country matters, and in the history of the machinery and equipment used in the past. Knightscote was not the only farm to engage his attention, and on which to focus his sketching; with friends with similar interests he visited many farms around the country.

> I have met some owners of large farms who have private collections of tractors, farm machinery and old farm tools in wonderful old farm buildings two or three hundred years old, and they would like me to make plates of some of their favourite exhibits. There are some larger organised County Commissions who are spreading the interest of these farm open days to the public. My friend's (Townsend) Open Days attract over 2000 people in one day, and the larger farms 10,000 in one day. There is a big revival in the interest of our countryside, and people from cities and towns visit for educational purposes. I could spend all my time just in helping to arrange these shows.

His interest was pervasive. He was helping to collect, restore, renovate and conserve antique machinery and tools. He would disassemble and reassemble machinery and metal tools having cleaned and polished all the parts: he would repair and re-varnish wooden articles; and — having consulted old catalogues, photographs and other available evidence — repaint items in their original colours and designs. He researched the origin and history of some items, moved by the danger of their imminent disappearance. He helped to display them in barns or other settings, and to identify, catalogue and label them. He helped to prepare and organise events when the artefacts could be displayed to the public. But most importantly, in the midst of all of these activities, he was making prolific detailed sketches and notes of everything he handled and observed. Later, in the quiet privacy of his studio, he designed the images and engraved the plates which expressed all his interest in an artistic form. His preoccupation with old agricultural machinery and tools and other objects was to dominate the remainder of his life, and artistic output. The hundreds of machines, tools and objects affected by his love and attention are directly recorded in the following line engravings, made between 1974 and 1985:

'Shandy Barrow, Maize Kibbler and Butter Churn' (114)
'Breast Plough and Barley Hummeller' (115)
'The Plough' (116)
'Dick Taylor and Yoke' (117)
'Surrey Drill, Dog Rose, and Chaff Cutter' (118)
'Fiddle Bow Seed Broadcaster' (119)
'Cheese Press' (120)
'Welsh Cart' (121)
'Scotch Cart' (122)
'Bramble and Plough' (123)
'Snowdrops and Mowing Machine' (124)
'Turnip Seed Drill' (125)
'Light Carriage' (126)
'Jinty Cart' (130)
'Hop Pole Tug' (131)
'Milk, Butter, Cheese' (132), and
'The Banham Waggon' (136)

These, together with the earlier 'Going for a Song' (110) 1969, and 'Put out to Grass' (111) 1970, constitute a remarkable record of antique country items, where every detail — including the sometimes strange names identified in the titles — is faithfully and accurately portrayed. A close study of these images, and reading of the artist's notes to each plate, also reveal a host of other detailed items surrounding the main subject matter of each print, from tools to rare plants, from special grasses to domestic paraphernalia, each item lovingly recorded and named. The backgrounds and distance detail are often not of Knightscote Farm itself, but of some other — more artistically suitable — location retrieved from the artist's sketches and notes. All of these prints were exhibited at RE Annual Exhibitions, but only six of them were exhibited at RA Summer Exhibitions. It is not known whether others were submitted but rejected, or not hung, or whether Chaplin chose not to submit them to the RA. He seems to have sensed that the style of the RA was

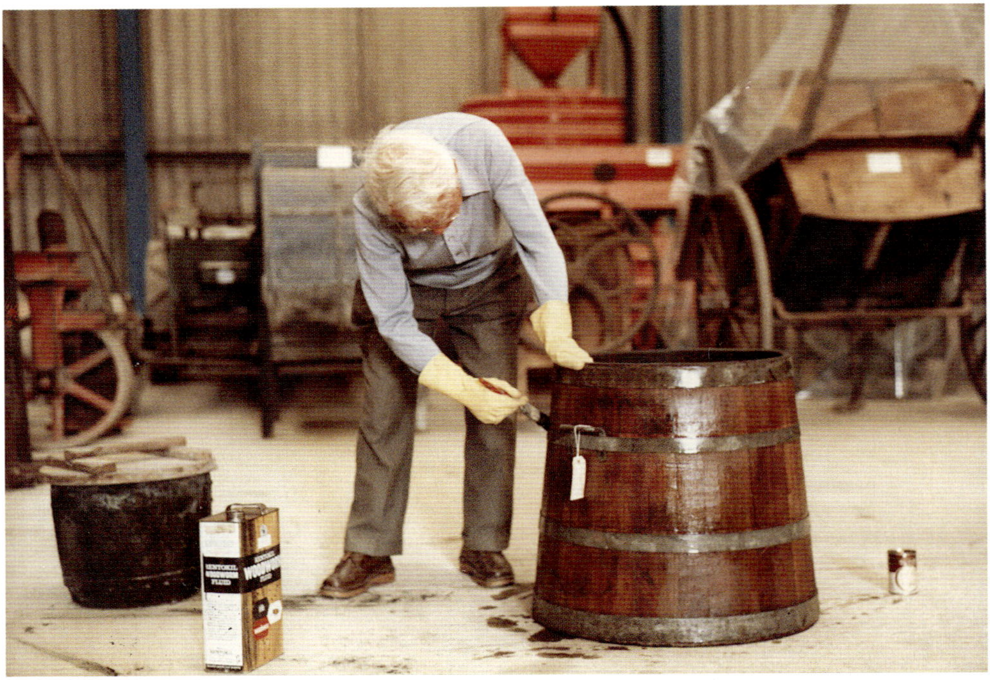

Chaplin refurbishing a barrel at Knightscote Farm, c. 1975

changing, and that his own style of engraving did not fit into the changing trends. However, his prints were now seen and bought by a wider public, who included people interested in, and who shared his enthusiasm for, the rural subjects of his prints. A number of admirers began to build up their own collections of his work, and he and May would spend many hours entertaining visitors at their home and in his studio.

Chaplin and Townsend had become close friends, and with Townsend's initiative and enthusiasm and Chaplin's support the ever expanding collection of agricultural machinery and tools was gradually formalised into a country museum. Open days were held to which the public was invited. The GLC became more interested and started to use the museum in an educational programme for schools. The collection improved when it was moved into the new barn that the GLC had built for it. In 1976 the farm tenancy changed again, Townsend left and a new tenant took over the farm. The GLC purchased all the farm antiquities, and developed the museum to which Chaplin had now become virtually an honorary curator, spending much time there during weekdays as well as weekends. But the situation was continually changing and in November 1977 Chaplin wrote to his Swedish friend, Lief Lundström:

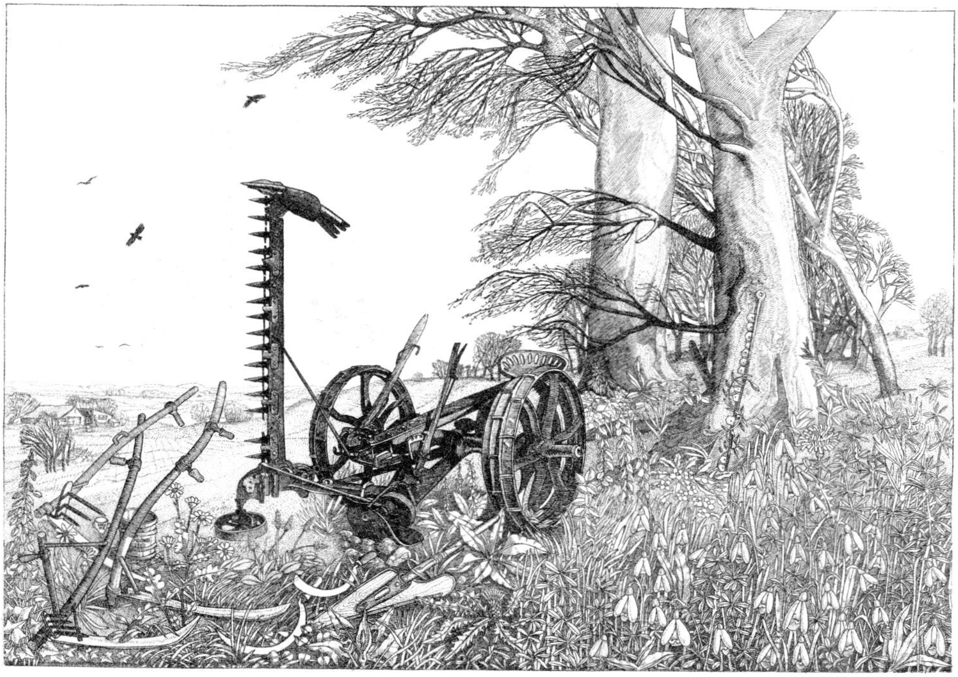

Snowdrops and Mowing Machine, line engraving, 173 x 233 mm, 1979

I still go over to the Museum, perhaps once a week with a friend now. The present farmer of Knightcote Farm is not in the least interested in the Museum side like the previous tenant, Frank Townsend, was. I miss him very much. It is the great variety of subjects at the Museum which keeps me engraving — not only the engraving of the plates, but the research and planning that goes into the making of the plates. The Greater London Council have not appointed a single man to look after the Exhibition, and have not touched the Exhibits in any way as regards repair and renovation. My friend who is a photographer, and I are doing all the small things. We rarely see anybody from the Council. They are doing major things like installing power, water, lighting and landscaping the surrounding area. I expect one day they will get down to the actual exhibits. With the new tenant the actual farm looks in a real mess — it is all rather disappointing.

The GLC were, however, interested enough in the museum collection to purchase in 1983 a set of 13 of Chaplin's prints of items housed in the museum. The GLC was famously abolished shortly afterwards, and the farm, the museum, and the collection of antique machinery were inherited by Hillingdon Borough Council. Today, the museum languishes, neglected and unloved, the remaining

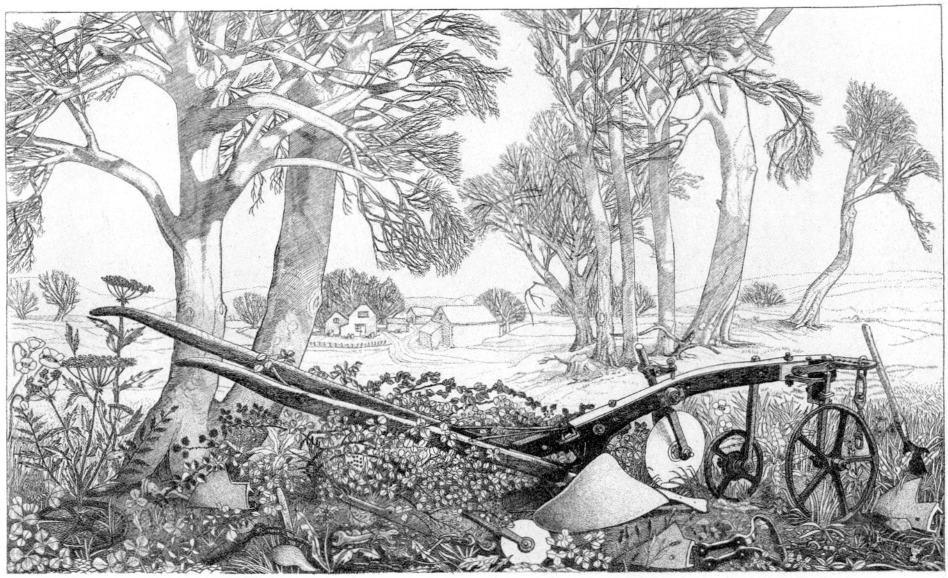

Brambles and Plough, line engraving, 165 x 265 mm, 1978

machines and artefacts rotting and rusting among undisturbed dust and debris. A few machines have been transferred to a museum at Park Lodge Farm, Harefield, which continues to show them to schools.

Contemporaneously with Chaplin's physical and artistic work at Knightscote, he and May were developing a close friendship with a Swedish family, the Lundströms, which became significant to Chaplin's art both in developing his confidence and in the organisation of his work; also in generating welcome sales. Lief Lundström was a Swedish businessman who travelled widely in Europe, including the UK, and who had a consuming love of art, particularly prints. Following the introduction by a mutual friend, Lundström had purchased a number of Chaplin's prints as early as 1964, and this was to be the basis of a comprehensive collection of his work. Following correspondence about that, they had first met Lief and Kerstin, with their children Per and Anders, in July 1967 when the family visited Highfield Way. More prints were purchased then, and further visits took place in 1969 and 1973. Lundström had established an arts society or association in Götene (Götene Konstförening) and was exhibiting Chaplin's work for sale at the art society's exhibitions. As in the UK, a number of persons became devoted collectors, and Lundström's appetite for Chaplin's work grew over the years. After much discussion and correspondence, Lundström arranged a solo exhibition of Chaplin's work in 1975, at which thirty prints covering the period 1939 to 1975 were offered. Later, Lundström told Chaplin of an incident at the library where the exhibition was held:

> During the exhibition our King, Carl XVI Gustaf was on a tour in Skaraborg, and he visited Centrumhuset where we had the exhibition. His visit was for the part of Centrumhuset which contains doctors and dentists. It is a new function here in Sweden having them all under the same roof. Our exhibition was in the library and the King was not expected to visit that part of the building, but he did. That day I was ill, feverish and cold, and had to visit the doctor in the same house. I came out from the doctor at the same time as the King arrived, but as I had investigated the day before, knew he was not expected to go into the library, and I went home to bed. Really I had in my mind to give the King one of your prints, but as I have said above, I missed it.

Even though Chaplin's work may not have appeared in the Royal Palace, his popularity grew over the years with Swedish collectors. Even for some years after Chaplin's death, May continued to despatch to Sweden work that he had printed and signed before his death.

Lundström gave Chaplin much encouragement and advice on how to organise his work. The artist had neglected to keep complete records of his work over the years. He wrote to Lundström after his visit in 1973:

> You have inspired me to make a record of all my works — my son has given me a very posh folder, and May will type out all the details and information I give her of all the plates I have made. I think at first glance they number over 100, so I really do not know where to start or in what order to do them.

The artist acknowledged the earlier advice of Lundström:

> It was only you, on your first visit, who prompted me to keep any detailed record of my efforts.

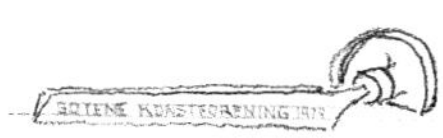

Chaplin did not devote himself exclusively to country subjects during his retirement. He engraved a small group of images of buildings — 'Christ Church, Chorleywood' (128), 'St Mary's Church, Rickmansworth', (129), and 'Oriel Window, The College, Marlborough' (134). These, with the earlier 'The Watergate' (78), are unusual in being the only 'architectural', (as opposed to indigenous or rural buildings) addressed by the artist, subjects which he was less comfortable with. He did not enjoy the symmetry and the angularity of these buildings, and their detail may have been quite demanding on his style of engraving. 'The Watergate' was a commission which he did not relish, and the others may have been the product of subtle pressures on him from friends and family to tackle subjects associated with them. A note on 'St Mary's' dismisses his subject shortly: 'This is my second church plate, and the last of my church efforts. They are too exacting and require too much research.' It is perhaps significant that earlier in his life he had ignored other opportunities to portray beautiful buildings, for example in the course of his trip to Spain or on his visits to Oxford or London. In spite of the artist's reservations as to his interest in such subjects they remain fine examples of his skill and sensitivity.

Throughout his retirement Chaplin's health was gradually deteriorating. He had been a heavy cigarette smoker all his life although in the later years, following his major operations, he had given up cigarettes in favour of his pipe, and in the last couple of years had stopped smoking altogether. Although he had had operations on his ear, his giddiness returned in the late 1970's , and he was frequently plagued by a dizzy head and sickness. The surrealist character of 'Floating Oak Leaf' (133) is a reflection of the feeling he had of floating on air as a result of the inner ear disease. There were some years of little or no output of engravings. In 1980 he suffered from shingles which was painful and depressing; he wrote: 'I regard the year 1980 as a lost one, sadly, over shingles.' However, referring to 'Two's Company' (127) he said in the following year: 'This was engraved at the insistence of my doctor, who said I must get out of my chair and forget the shingles!' Recovery was slow and in 1981 he wrote to a correspondent:

> My engraving efforts are slowing down considerably, for I find it difficult to use my press. With the actual engraving, I find it difficult to concentrate and worry that the results will not be up to my usual standard.

The following year he began to be troubled by a painful stomach disorder. His artistic work again suffered and, on his seventy-fifth birthday in January 1982, he wrote to his Swedish friends:

> It is the worst winter we have experienced for over 30 years, and has made going out very dangerous for us. Neither of us could keep our feet, and of course feel the cold. It was very cold and snowy on my birthday, but your [Lief Lundström] phone call and good wishes from you all [Kirsten, Anders & Per] made my day. I braved the weather, wrapped up well, went out and made two rough charcoal sketches round the lakes at Rickmansworth, and also started another plate.

His devotion to his sketching and his engraving was sustaining his life in increasingly difficult circumstances, providing the motivation to bear and overcome the discomfort of illness. In May 1983 he wrote again to Lundström:

> I find it is getting difficult to work on my plates, especially the proofing of them. In fact we both find it increasingly difficult to do all the usual things we used to do. My fear is that I

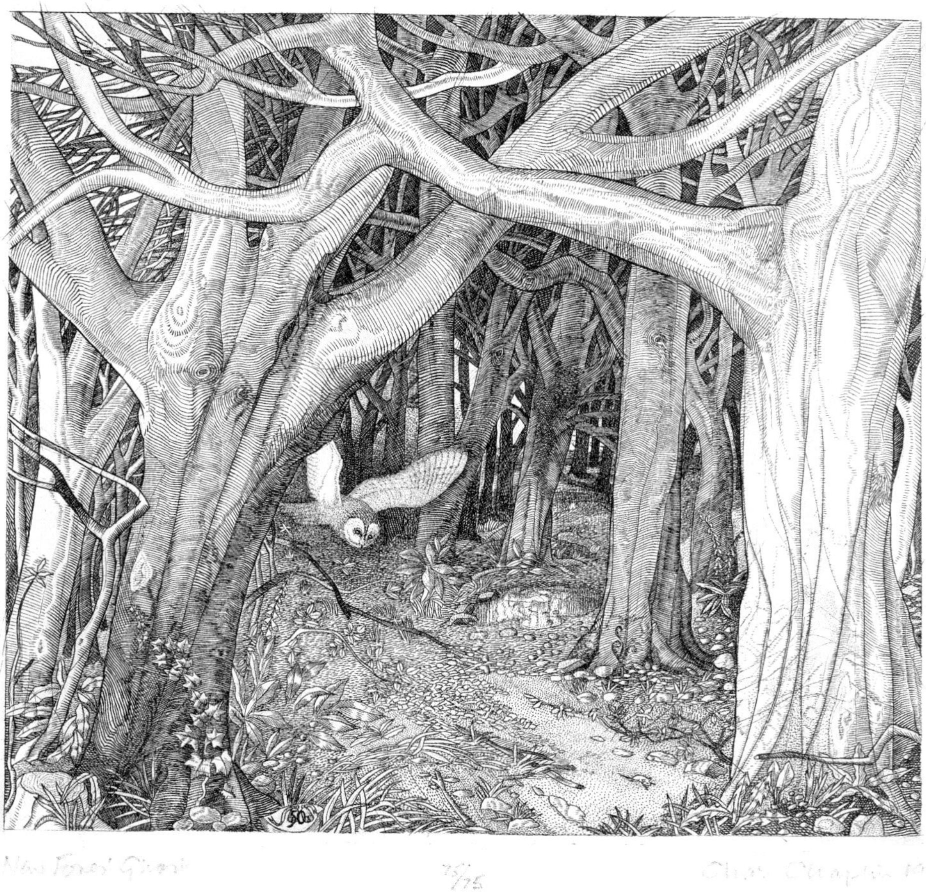

New Forest Ghost, 157 x 167 mm, 1984. The last engraving to be completed by C. H. A. Chaplin

shall loose the quality and technical side of my engraving. I am still working on two new plates, slowly and optimistically.

His correspondence at this time contains many references to the garden and the weather, indicating that the garden at Highfield Way was becoming increasingly difficult for May and himself to maintain.

He had managed to complete the line engraving 'New Forest Ghost' (135), and his good friend Hallbery had delivered the framed proof to the Royal Academy, when in the early Spring of 1984 he was once again admitted to hospital, on the face of it for a minor operation. This turned out to be a major operation from the effects of which he was never again really free. He was still in hospital when he heard from May that 'New Forest Ghost' had been accepted for hanging at the Summer

Exhibition. His son attended the Private View on his behalf; on arriving at Burlington House he made his way straight to the print room, and found the print, mounted in a comparatively small frame, completely covered in red stickers. Jon returned directly to the hospital to give his father this exciting news, only to find that he was not at all pleased! Chaplin had pulled only a few proofs before his hospitalisation, and he was clearly not now going to be able to print all those required for the Royal Academy sales. Fortunately a close artist friend, Corrie Graddon, stepped into the breach and undertook to print whatever was required; with the help of other friends, these were duly despatched to the buyers. This was the only edition of any of Chaplin's plates not printed by him personally. Although May had telephoned the RA office to ask them to stop sales after 50, there had been a misunderstanding, and the whole edition had been quickly sold before May's letter of confirmation arrived. Later he sat at the table behind his hospital bed carefully inspecting each proof, before signing the edition. He remained profoundly grateful to Graddon for relieving him of this worrying burden.

For some years Chaplin had been writing contemporaneous notes regarding each of his engravings, a habit encouraged by Lundström. He wrote his note on 'New Forest Ghost' whilst still in hospital:

> I usually make many sketches, large and small, for my copper plate engravings, but for this plate there are no sketches at all. I was making a large pastel drawing deep in the New Forest and decided to make a sketch direct on to a copper plate I had with me with a steel point — just a few guide lines. This was about twelve years ago.
>
> I did not stay on to finish the plate as whilst sketching I sensed that something was going on behind me. This often happens whilst sketching — people and children creep up behind to see what you are doing, and I can often sense their presence. This time, however, on looking back repeatedly over my shoulder, much to my surprise, I saw a large owl, silently flying around in wide circles behind me. At once I picked up all my sketching gear and moved away, thinking the owl must have a nest nearby and was objecting to my presence. It was only this year that I decided to engrave and finish the plate and this is the result — 'New Forest Ghost'. The little mouse was, of course an obvious addition to the plate.
>
> I was recovering from an operation in the Peace Memorial Hospital Watford, and decided to ring May. I was not happy as the news I had to tell was not good. However May told me to 'Keep quiet' and listen to her news, which was that this plate was hanging in the RA, very much to our surprise, I never expected it to be hung. I was going through a very bad time indeed and only sent it in as a gamble. It will be my last plate to be exhibited in the RA and the RE. The demand for proofs was greater than any previous plate I had exhibited there. I told May to ring the RA and cancel all sales as I had only a few proofs. However my good friends Frank Gutteridge, Corrie Graddon and Allan Bush decided otherwise. May as usual carried out all the paperwork. Corrie made the proofs, Frank and Alan helped with all the other work and I signed the proofs sitting by the hospital bed — the edition was finally sold out.

In 1983 Chaplin's friend, Paul Wigmore, had written a poem in the context of 'New Forest Ghost':

I sat and worked
But with the feeling someone, something, watched me there.
I knew it moved
Yet silently, and pressed the air about my ears
And nape of neck

All statuesque
New Forest trees held council in perspective's blackness
Some way away
Dear patient May (for fifty years she's waited thus)
Sat in the car

Now ill at ease
I turned about to see what haunting could be there.
A great white owl
Flew round in circles begging me to leave. At home
I sketched him in.

In July 1984, May and Charles celebrated their fiftieth wedding anniversary. He was still fragile and uncomfortable, having been out of hospital only a few months, and so their family arranged a quiet party in the afternoon in the garden at Highfield Way. A few close friends, some neighbours of fifty years, and all of their now extended family enjoyed the sunshine, tea and strawberries with them. Their family had grown with the births of their grandchildren in the early 1960s, and now the grandchildren had themselves grown up, and were on the threshold of their own lives. Elizabeth married Philip Brett that August — a happy ceremony at Christ Church, Chorleywood, which celebrated not only their wedding, but the Golden Wedding Anniversary of Charles and May, as well as the Silver Wedding Anniversary of their son Jon and Betty. There soon followed the wedding of Sara, and the birth of James to Elizabeth and Philip, Chaplin's first great-grandson whom he was able to see before his death. The many events taking place in, and the constant news of his extended family were a source of great pleasure to the artist as his health continued to deteriorate.

Early in 1985 Chaplin was working on an engraving of a banham wagon, a large wagon at Knightscote Farm which he and Hallbery had been repairing and painting. In his usual method he had made a large number of sketches of every detail of this cart, from every angle and perspective, an almost surgical analysis of the subject. He took many trial proofs of this engraving, seeking greater and greater

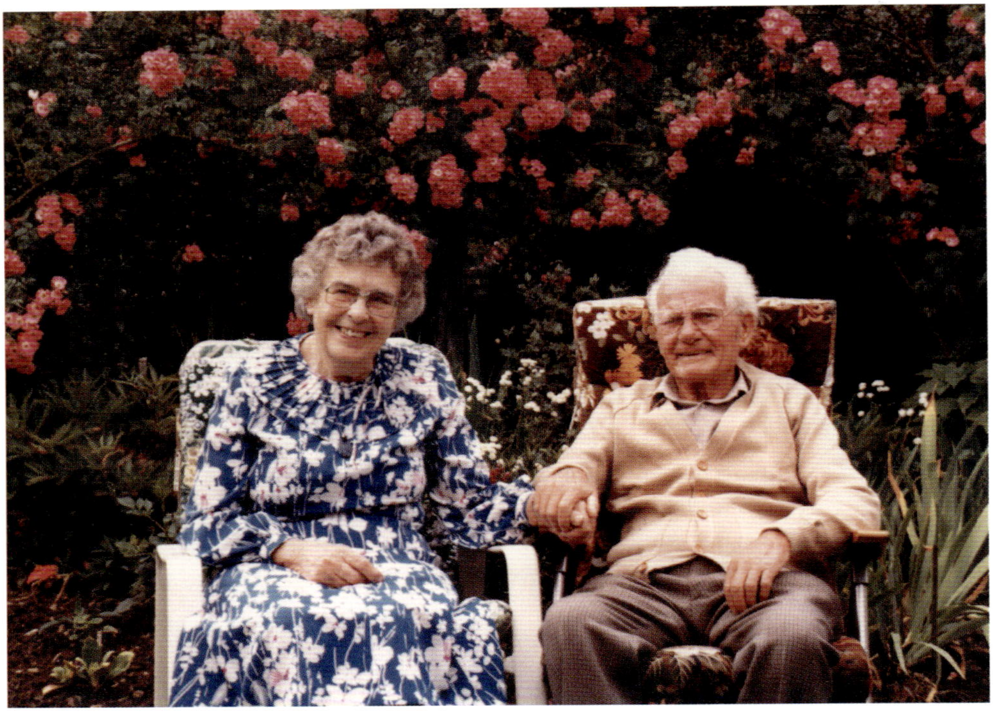

Charles with May in the garden of Highfield Way on their Golden Wedding Anniversary, 14 July 1984

perfection in his work. It was proving to be probably the best of his series of carts, and possibly one of the best of his series of antique agricultural machinery; but it was never finished. Following more abdominal pain he returned to hospital yet again for major surgery. He wrote to Lundström in July: 'I am still living in hope that they [the doctors] can do something to make life worth living again. We have decided we must find a smaller place quickly.' Within a period of only four days Charles and May had agreed to sell Highfield Way to the Christ Church Parochial Church Council, and to purchase a small maisonette in Rickmansworth on the banks of a River Colne tributary. The suddenness of their decision was remarkable, but a relief, and accomplished without worry or recrimination: indeed, the evening a group of PCC members came to survey the property at Highfield Way was largely spent by some Members of the Council in a friendly and sociable manner in the studio, reviewing proofs of his engravings. The weeks between agreement and completion (extended a little to facilitate a complete refurbishment of the maisonette) Charles and May were fully engaged in a somewhat frenetic sorting and disposal of an accumulation of over fifty years of domestic and artistic clutter, and the selection of a much reduced quantity of items to take to their new, much smaller, home.

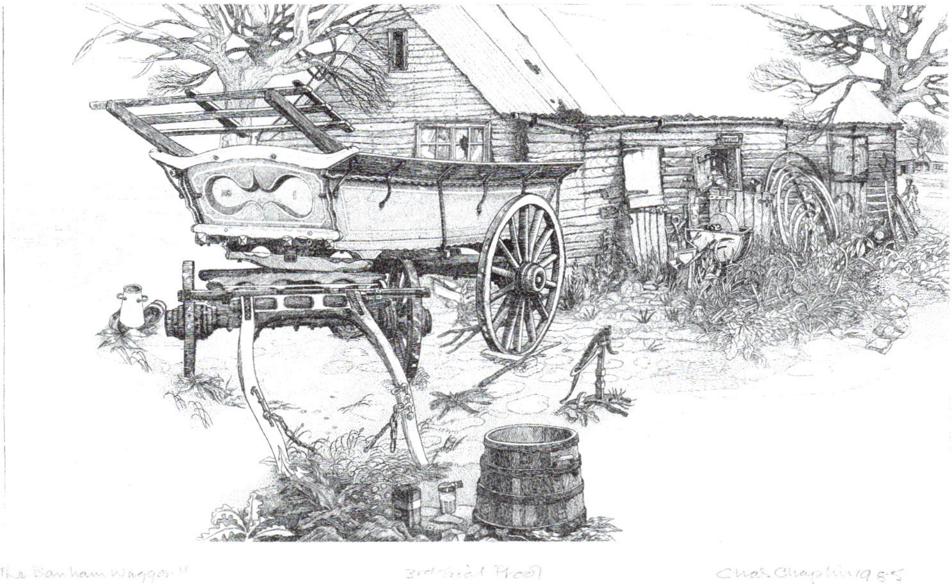

The Banham Wagon, line engraving, 152 x 257 mm, 1985. Not completed

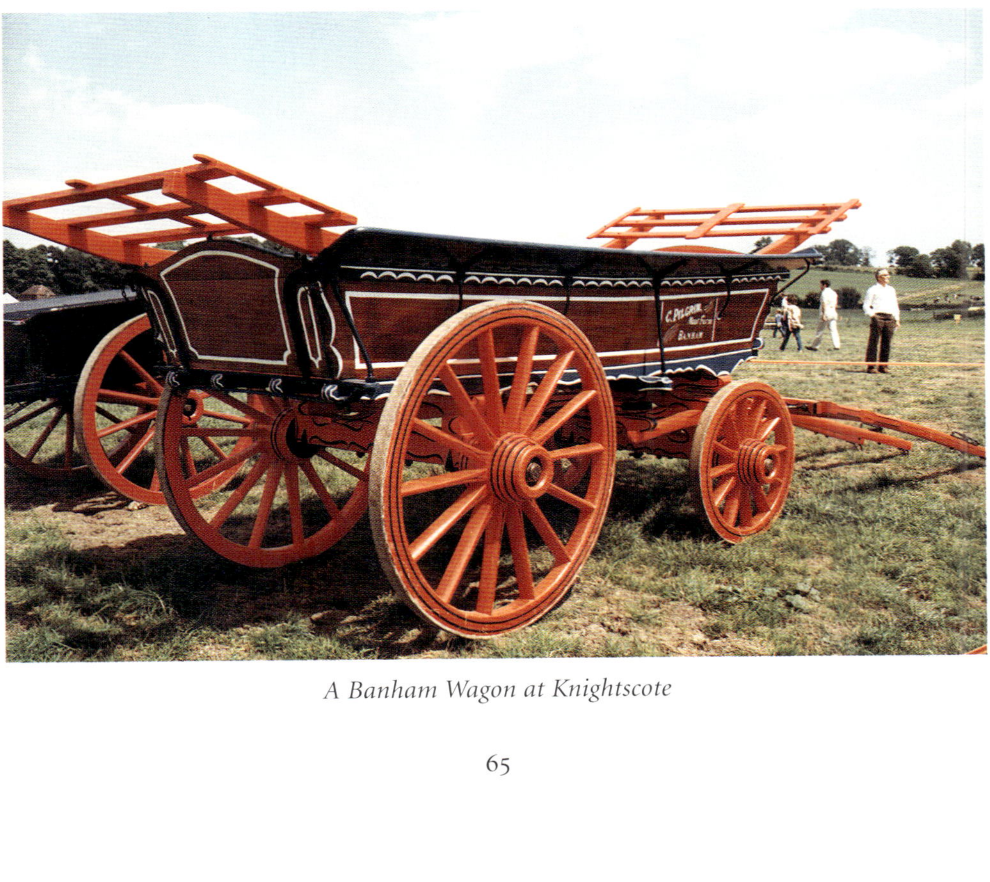

A Banham Wagon at Knightscote

During this time Chaplin gave away a large volume of his drawings, pastels, tools, collected rural antiquities and virtually all of his artistic and printing equipment and materials, including both his large and his small press. The move, which took place in the Autumn of 1985, involved giving up their garden, to which they had both devoted themselves, working lovingly to transform it from its original state as a rough field; and, for Chaplin, the loss of his studio and his printing press — which he described as like losing a close friend.

The maisonette in Bury Meadows in the centre of Rickmansworth town was adjacent to the lakes and the waterways which he loved and from which he had gained inspiration throughout his life. If there was any consolation in giving up his garden, his studio and his engravings on which his whole life had been focussed, it was that the familiar paths, open spaces of water, the rivers, weirs and tributaries, the willows and the teeming wildlife were now only a slow five minutes walk away. In his last two years at Bury Meadows he would walk again, every day that he was physically able to, through the many scenes of his own lifetime's pictures, invariably still accompanied by his sketchbook, pencils and box of pastels. During these walks he completed many beautiful pastels of small dimensions — about 250 x 300 mm — most of them completed in no more than fifteen to twenty minutes, and of great simplicity and charm. Despite his chronic pain and mobile disability, his creativity was irrepressible, even though it was no longer expressed with the meticulous and controlled graver, but with free and confident strokes of chalk.

He had to return to hospital a number of times in an attempt to control his condition. His sadness in having to let go of his art is clear from his last letter to Lundström in February 1987:

> It is nearly three years since I had my major operation, and I have been back in hospital three or four times since, but am still in the same position of not being able to sit down, and still suffer a lot of pain in spite of pain killers, sleeping tablets, and so on. I am told by the doctors that they cannot do any more for me, so I have to accept that. I'm afraid I don't do anything in the art line now, and have lost touch with the various exhibitions and galleries.

Charles Chaplin passed away at the age of eighty in the Watford General Hospital on 27th April, 1987; his funeral service took place at Christ Church, Chorleywood on 5th May, 1987.

The Whole Artist

PERHAPS THE FIRST IMPRESSION of a study of Chaplin's work is the extent of skill involved in his art. He started out with the solid skill base of a professional commercial engraver, and continued to practice this skill for many years in the course of his employment. The study of his art, through early life classes and later at the Royal College of Art, Department of Engraving, and through his exploration of methods and materials in drypoints, etching and finally line engraving, was built on this foundation of professionalism, which gave an essentially shy and modest artist the necessary confidence and authority to share his work with others. Perhaps it is not surprising therefore that the practical skill seen in his engraving extended to every task he undertook. For example, he made most of his own tools, including his extensive collection of gravers, some of which were fashioned from the points of old rapiers. Throughout his printing career he made all his own inks, grinding the powder and mixing with oils. His large collection of bottles of different shades of chalks and powders, pigments, oils, acids, and other chemicals was arranged on the shelves in his studio. Only towards the end of his artistic life did he find the manufactured ink product satisfactory for his purposes, and then welcomed its convenience. He wrote to Lundström in 1983:

> I have found an American firm in London who supply materials such as ink, oils, blankets and tools for engraving and etching ... So I am testing some of these ready made copper plate inks and oils — they are expensive, but I find them very good, so hope to have a new look, inkwise, to my future proofs. The inks already made up are certainly not so messy, and it saves time and labour in not having to grind and mix the powder and oils, as I have always done in the past.

His prints are executed in a wide variety of colours, and he continually experimented to find the best shade of colour for the mood of the work.

Chaplin also used a great variety of papers, all of them carefully prepared beforehand for printing. Family bathing at Highfield Way had to be carefully programmed since the bath was frequently filled with soaking papers. Only exceptionally did he made a note of the type of paper used, and generally it is not possible to identify precisely the type of paper used for a proof. He would not print an edition on one type of paper only, but invariably used several different types in a constant quest for improvement. He loved printing on antique paper, and used to keep a precious stock, much of it recovered from old books. Sometimes, particularly in the

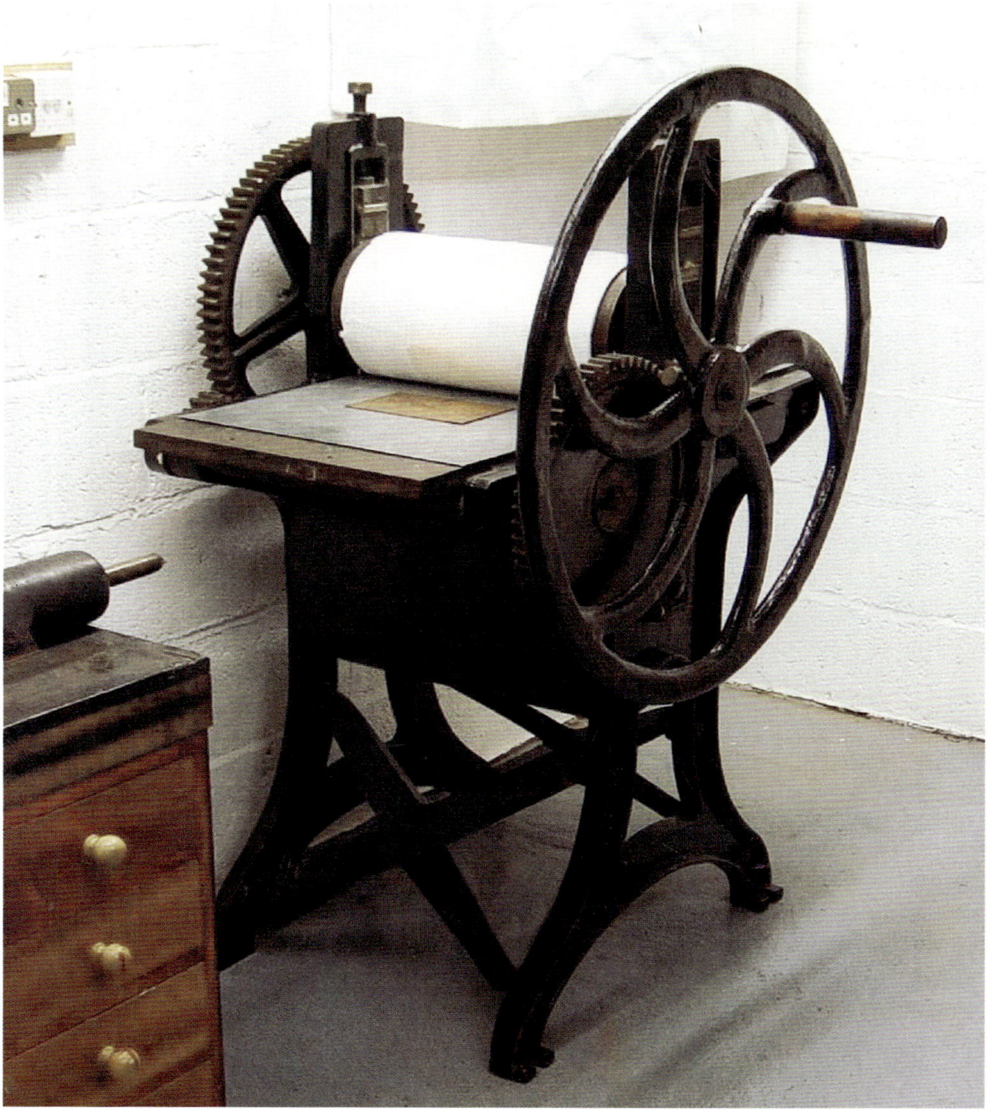

Chaplin's main printing press. By kind permission of David Cave. Photograph David Cave

early years, he used Japanese paper as an overlay. He was always most particular about the paper he used for his final prints: 'I find it especially difficult to get hand made paper for proofs in the weight that I want — thin lightweight paper does not suite my plates.'

Chaplin had two printing presses, one a smaller press resting on a bench which he used for quicker work such as trial proofing. His main press (above), a machine of great weight, with a cast-iron framework and 35-inch diameter wheel for turning the rollers, was used for all his finished work. According to the maker's plate, this press was manufactured by Wilfred C. Kimber, Maker, Cromer Street, London WC1. It is now in the possession of David Cave, together with the artist's detailed notes on assembly and disassembly. With the sole exception of his last completed work 'New Forest Ghost', the artist personally printed all of his own work. In the course of making a plate, Chaplin would take many trial proofs, usually at about four different stages of development, although sometimes there could be as many as eight different trial proofs. Where he regarded a trial proof as satisfactory he would sign and identify the proof thus: '3rd Trial Proof'. An unsatisfactory trial proof might be dismissed as 'NBG'! The sequence of these trial proofs, where they exist, provide a fascinating insight into the artists' method of working.

Occasionally, but not often, he would produce a plate in more than one state in order, after further reflection, to incorporate later and revised ideas into an earlier plate. In sending a proof of 'Snowdrops and Mowing Machine' (124) to Lundström in 1983 he wrote:

> This proof is a revised edition of a plate engraved in 1979, on which I have spent six weeks reworking; I have reproofed a second state, proofing the plate in different inks and in a different way, the result being a much better effort, I think.

The artist would never print a whole edition at one stretch; there might be several years between the first and the last proofs. The date he ascribed to a proof was the date of printing, not of the completion of the plate. All his printing was done in the evening — in the years prior to his retirement in 1970 it would be after his normal day's work; thus, no more than four or five proofs could be made in a single printing session.

Sketching was the basis of all Chaplin's work, and he designed and made, and constantly improved the design, and reconstructed his sketching stool and easel and other equipment. This was a folding device, light and strong, and adaptable for oil, watercolours, pastel or pencil drawing. It measured 20″ x 16″ x 2″, and was carried like an attaché case. It included a piece of card with a rectangular hole with cotton stretched across at regular intervals, which he used for finding subjects and determining just that part of the landscape needed for his design.

His studio at Highfield Way had been converted from the original integral garage to the house, with a large window facing east replacing the doors. It measured 18′ x 8′, and was completely packed with equipment. A high workbench, on which he did his engraving — perched on a stool — and on which rested a variety of adjustable lights, magnifying glasses and mirrors lay across the window. Other benches provided surfaces for the smaller press, and for ink making, heating and

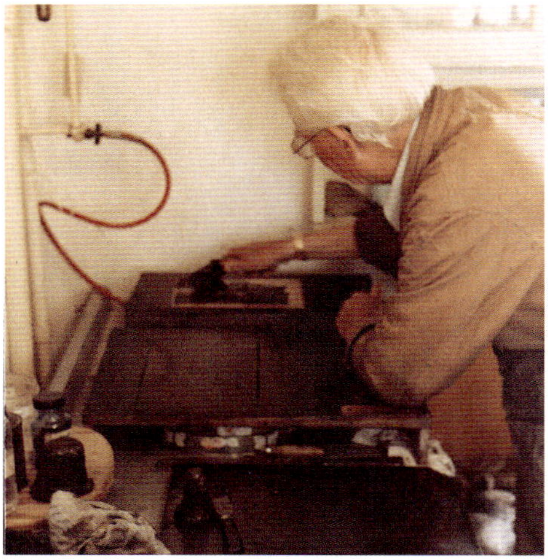

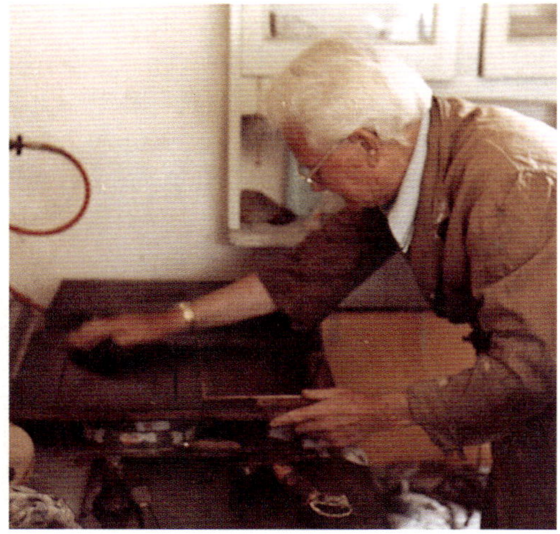

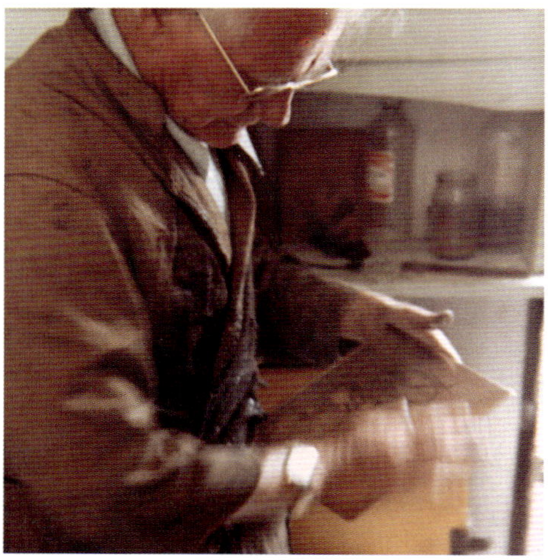

The artist printing in his studio, 1979: inking the plate and removing excess ink from the plate

ink-rolling the plates prior to printing. Wide shelves running down one wall contained his archive of prints, as well as stocks of paper and his collection of the prints of other artists. The large press stood in the middle of the studio, dominating the scene. Tools, equipment, books and often models or subjects littered all surfaces and hung from the walls and ceiling. Whatever the activity taking place the atmosphere was always exciting, pungent with the smell of oils, acids and chemicals. There was little room to move around, and when more than one collector visited they had to stand virtually in line down the centre of the studio. All the furniture and equipment in the studio, the benches, shelves, cupboards, and fittings were designed and made by the artist: it represented his burrow, alternative home, and escape from the world.

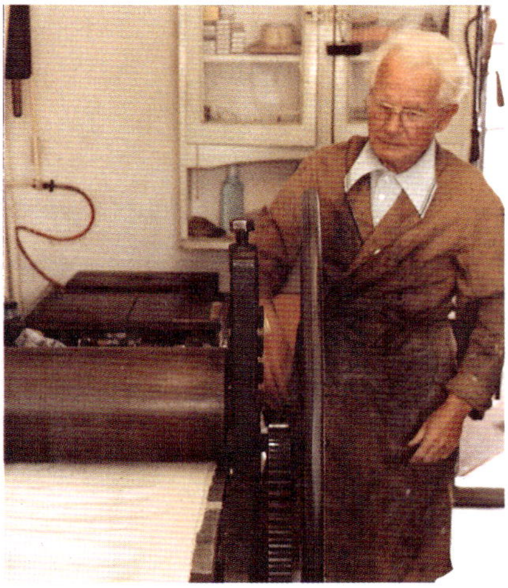

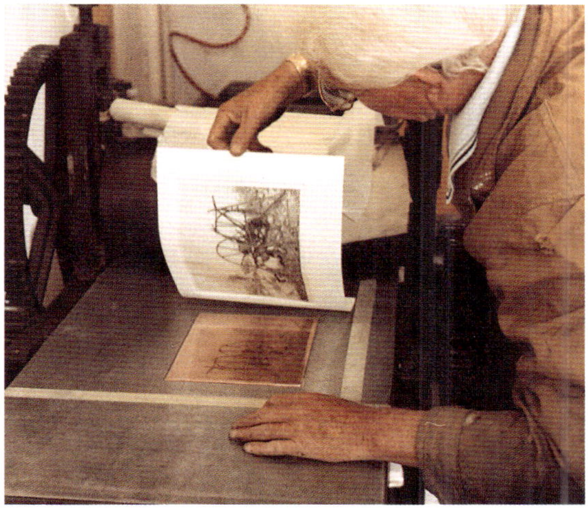

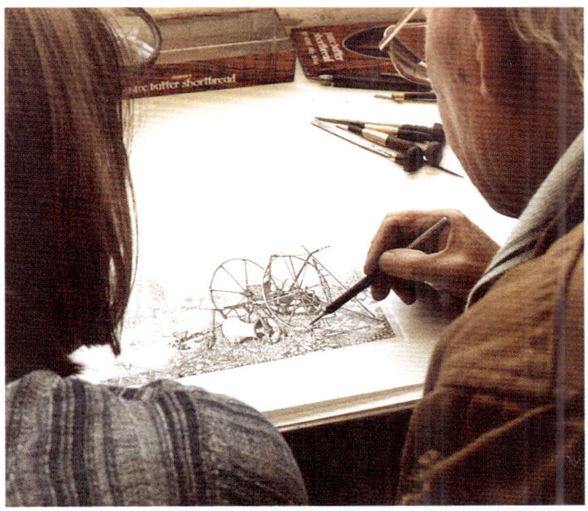

The artist printing in his studio, 1979: printing, lifting a proof from the press, and annotating the proof

Although in the early years Chaplin needed the proceeds of sales to fund what he regarded as his interest, or hobby, and in later years to maintain his lifestyle in retirement, his attitude towards selling his work was highly ambivalent, almost amounting to acute embarrassment. If he suspected that an enquirer was leading up to a request to purchase one of his works, he tended to disappear. The sales which he did make came principally through exhibitions (where dealing with the price was comfortably distant and objective), but also to some extent through private collectors. These, typically, would seek him out, visit his home and studio, and persuade him to sell them a print. He had many enquires from galleries over the years, which he invariably turned down. In practice he could sell prints of all he could produce — some two or three plates a year — privately to collectors. He was resigned to not making a living, or indeed a profit, from his engraving. 'I do not sell in large quantities or editions' he wrote.

> With my plates, which are very technical and very laboriously engraved, and very time-consuming, both in the making of the plate, and the personal proofing of each plate, it would not be possible to make any sort of living, unless of course they sold for a much higher price. Prints reproduced in litho, silk screen, woodblock and those where the camera and the mechanical printing were employed, of course become cheaper when making large editions.

Even so he appreciated the sales which he did make, as they reaffirmed to him the value of his artistic work. In 1978, recording a good year for exhibition sales at the RA and the RE, and in Canada and America, he wrote:

> I have sold locally also to collectors here, and have had many requests from shops, and galleries, etc. to display prints on a commercial basis from all over the country. However, I do not want to take on this task as I find that I have quite enough to do keeping up with private sales and exhibitions. It is gratifying to me to know that my prints are sought after.

He was always particularly uncomfortable when, having agreed to make a sale, he had eventually to discuss and agree a price. On one occasion, in quoting a price for which a collector had written to ask, he replied:

> Is this too much? My friends in the country are always urging me to increase my prices, but to me selling is an embarrassing question. Some people offer me much more than my asking price. I am not a happy salesman.

To Chaplin the most rewarding part of private sales was in meeting people with a like interest in art and in printing, and in the long conversations which followed. In 1974 he wrote:

> I still endeavour to sell personally, as meeting people who wish to buy is greatly to be enjoyed. I have now been in contact with some few hundreds of people who have shown interest in my work.

With a number of loyal collectors, who followed his work over the years, he developed a friendly correspondence which provided a continuous source of interest and amusement to the artist and to May. In 1979, a collector who had bought 'Light Carriage' following the earlier purchase of another print, wrote:

> I shall have them both by the phone. Don't laugh at the funny place to hang pictures! When I am holding on the line, I never cease to look at the pictures, and even after all this time I always find something else to admire.

Chaplin was also uncomfortable with publicity, and never took any action to promote himself or his works. *Who's Who in Art* sent the artist their c.v. forms many times, but he neglected to complete and return them.

Throughout his career Chaplin was a member of the Rickmansworth and District Art Society, and the Watford and Bushey Art Society, and would regularly exhibit one or two works at their Annual Exhibitions. In the case of the Watford Society he gave a number of talks over the years on engraving and pastels, and was acknowledged locally as an expert in these fields. Other local exhibitions included the Barnet Guild of Artists annual exhibitions in 1949 and 1951. Wider afield, outside London, his work was seen at a number of municipal galleries such as Liverpool, Harrogate, Folkestone and Rotherham, to which the RE sent collections from their annual London exhibition, and selections from the RA arranged by the Art Exhibitions Bureau.

Although Chaplin's principal artistic achievement clearly lay in his engraving and prints, there was hardly a medium in which he did not practice at some time. Perhaps the most important, and voluminous, of his artistic output, other than prints, was in pastels. His first pastel works were at life classes in the 1930s, and these were simple studies of the human form in two or three colours. Later he expanded his boxes of chalks to include scores of shades in order to enable him to tackle the subtle country and lakeside scenes around Rickmansworth. These pastels were on a larger scale than his plate-work, measuring approximately 16″ x 24″, and enabled him to express a freedom and simplicity of design, as well as a speed of completion not possible with engraving. Pastels facilitated an instant fulfilment, and almost a relief for his creative urges, which the slowness, physical effort and mental meticulousness of engraving denied him. His pastels disclose a fascination with colours as affected by different light conditions, and with the changing colours of weather. His many visits to the New Forest in the 1960s and 1970s inspired a large number of these works, and it was during these relaxed holidays that he experimented with different and less traditional styles of drawing, some of them impressionistic, and some almost cubist in character. An article on the New Forest by George Peterken in Tree News (Autumn/Winter 2003) is illustrated by a number of the artist's pastels, which represent his more traditional approach (page 49). Later in his career, particularly when ill-health was restricting his capabilities, he took to making smaller images in pastels. In 1975 he noted:

> I have not made any large pastel sketches for some time, but over the last 18 months I have made small pastels (10″ x 12″) of the evening light, sunshine and clouds, which make a

completely relaxing change from engraving. These little sketches in colour, when framed with a 2″ x 1″ moulding with only ¼″–⅜″ mount showing, look effective, and I find some people are more interested in these small pastels rather than the large.

Although comparatively few sales resulted, his pastel work excited much interest and acclaim whenever it was shown. One commentary in the West Herts Post of 21 May 1959 on a Watford and Bushey Art Society Exhibition stated:

We thought that the outstanding picture of the exhibition was a pastel by Charles Chaplin, 'Brill Windmill.'* It is an arresting work which provides a stimulating, emotional and intellectual shock as it hangs among the other pictures.

Chaplin also undertook a number of oil paintings over the years, particularly of subjects at Underhill Farm in Lyme Regis, and of the New Forest; however, he found the discipline of oils, whether of the brush or pallet-knife, too restrictive when compared to the freedom of pastels, and he acknowledged these to be less successful.

Somewhat surprisingly the prolific output of his sketching throughout his life did not lead to a comparable number of finished works, whether of pencil or pen-and-ink. He did have two wash drawings accepted by the War Artists Advisory Committee as part of the National Collection — 'Windsor Castle from Brunswick Tower', and 'Scene at St Albans Royal Observer Corps'. As referred to earlier, a series of four of his pen-and-ink drawings were published in an article in *Illustrated London News* on the Royal Observer Corps (page 29). Earlier reference has also been made to the large number of cartoons he produced during the wartime; these were executed in pencil or pen-and-ink with simple two or three colour watercolour washes. His sketches and drawings were, however, mainly used by him as practice studies and as a stock of subject material for his engravings. Further commentary on the artist's use of sketching follows.

Throughout his life, on his sketching expeditions, he would often take his watercolour equipment with him, returning with at least one or two watercolours in addition to much material drawn with pencils. Later in his career, for reasons similar to those which caused him to turn to smaller pastels, he turned again to simple watercolours. Writing in 1978:

Because of eye problems I have also been persuaded to start, after a lapse of many years, doing some watercolour painting in very free and open style. They are about 10½″ x 14″; I can complete them in a day, and they are such a pleasure to do. If I completely spoil one it does not matter. I wash the colour on and leave it — the results are sometimes good, others bad!

* Chaplin made a line engraving of the same subject (106)

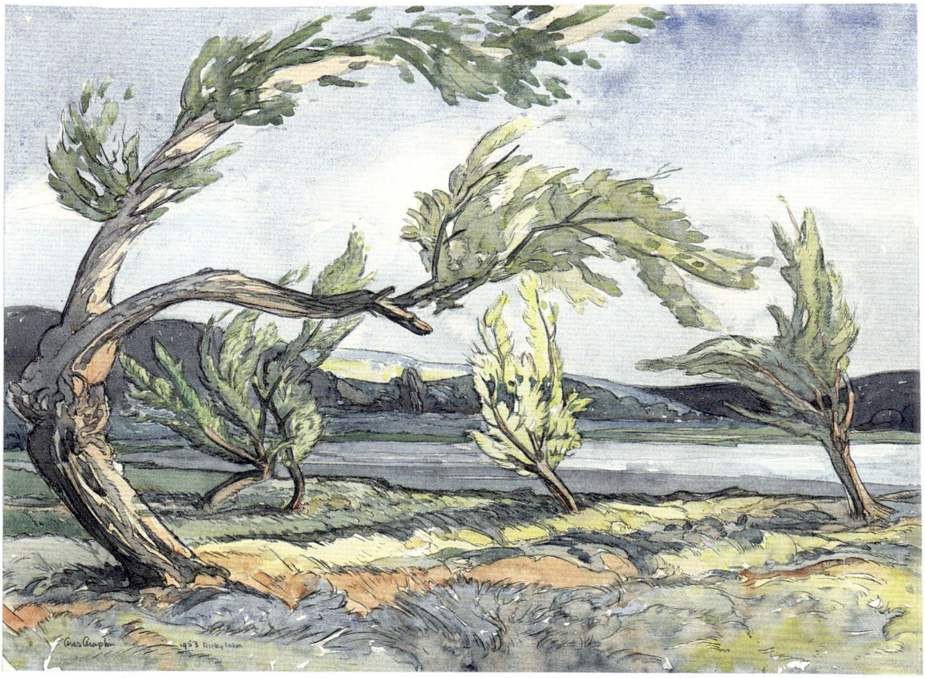

Batchworth Lakes, Rickmansworth, watercolour, 355 x 473 mm, 1953

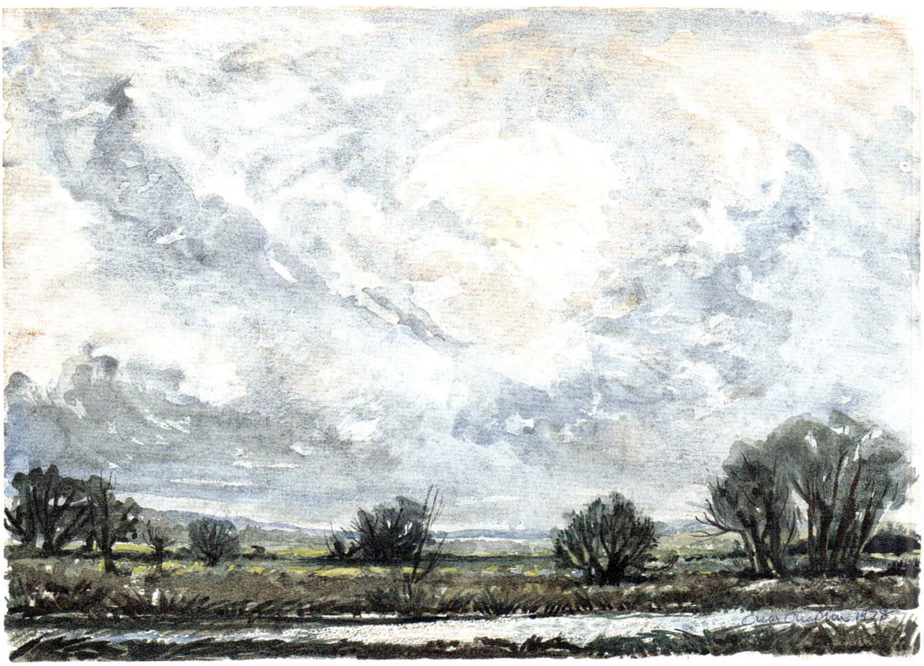

The Rickmansworth Lakes, watercolour, 350 x 480 mm, 1978

A letter to Joyce Taylor, a Canadian correspondent, in 1978 expressed the satisfaction he obtained from his watercolour work:

> I started watercolour again in July after 30 years. I am not a watercolour artist, but it gives me much pleasure to do them in a completely different style to my engravings, more full and much less detailed, and going entirely for an effect of light and atmosphere.

Chaplin was also an accomplished woodcarver, completing a number of small figures in different woods (page 12). One particular carving, some 470 x 385 x 70 mm, is a three-dimensional view of a beech wood, inspired by his love of the New Forest, and illustrating his fascination with the complex intertwining of branches and foliage of the forest, an effect so frequently portrayed two-dimensionally in his pastels, and in his engravings as well. His comment on his last woodcarving effort in 1975 is instructive:

> I have put my woodcarving tools away for, if anything, woodcarving is more time-consuming and exacting than engraving.

Earlier in his career he had also fashioned silverware into jewellery, exercising his engraving skills in bold, established and more formal patterns which nevertheless retained a delightful uniqueness.

Chaplin had a dry and gentle sense of humour, which could on occasion be sharp and witty, or mischievous, or sometimes a loving commentary on something dear to his heart. His demeanour was mostly serious, even severe, and his humour comparatively rare in appearance, although usually lurking quietly in the background, ready to surprise at the most unexpected time and place. His humour was often self-deprecating, displaying at the same time his own characteristic modesty, eccentricity or contrariness. Occasionally his humour is revealed in his prints. He described the information notes which he wrote for his engravings, of which he produced some forty-five, as 'blurbs', which underestimated their great interest to collectors, and indeed their scholarship. When the National Library of Wales purchased his 'Welsh Cart' (121), the Keeper of the Department of Prints, in acknowledging receipt of the print and the accompanying 'blurb', referred to the latter as a 'documentation of the circumstances of the picture's composition.' Referring to this comment in a letter to a friend, Chaplin responded: 'So you see I can at least improve on the description of my work, if not on the contents of the picture!' In 1964, in an interview article commenting on the RA's acceptance of 'Old Willows' (92), the *Watford and West Herts Post* reported: '"This is the twenty-first time I have been hung" was the rather strange comment from the very much alive and kicking

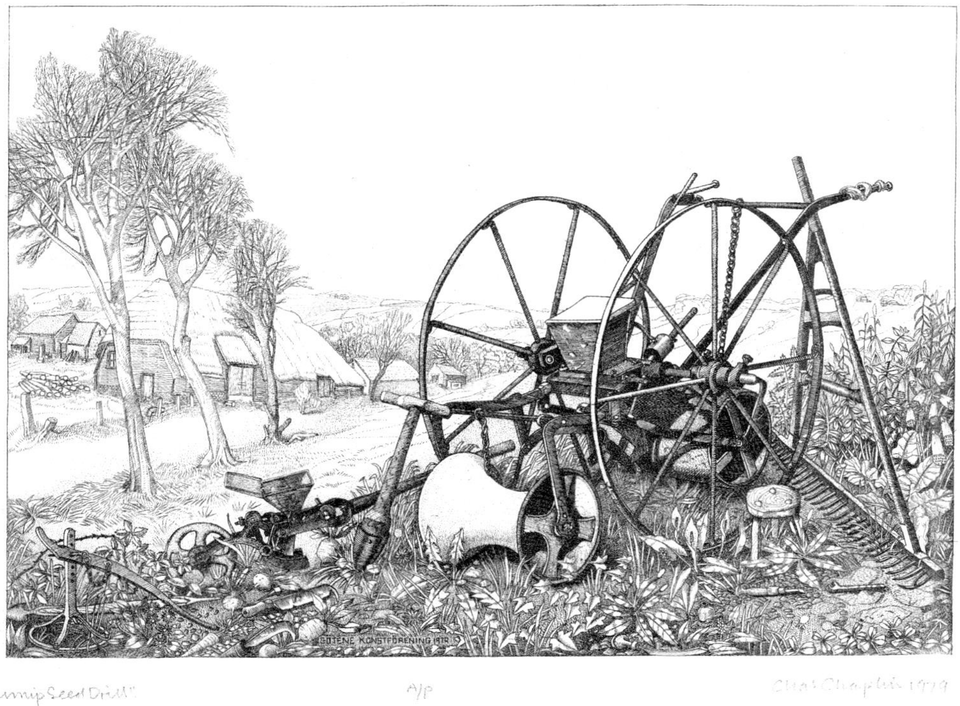

Turnip Seed Drill, line engraving, 162 x 222 mm, 1979

Charles Chaplin.' His attitude to criticism was sometimes amusingly contrary; in his Note to 'Brambles and Plough' (123) he records: 'It was pointed out to me that I had engraved a little group of blackberry fruits, which looked very odd — so many people remarked on them that I left them in.' Again, the artist's Notes on 'Surry Seed Drill, Dog Rose and Chaff Cutter' (118) reveal: 'When I first thought of engraving these two farm implements, I knew that I should be criticised for putting two subjects, making two pictures, in one plate. But, once having seen it in my mind, I continued!' Collectors as well found amusement in his prints. Ruth Bentley of Toronto wrote to the artist after she had received her print of 'Farm Corner' (107): 'The workmanship in the print itself is excellent. I find it a very humorous print.'

Perhaps the most frequent cause of merriment in Chaplin's prints is the little naked lady. This feature appears many times in later works where there are one, or sometimes two, naked ladies in different poses, so small as to be almost invisible without the use of a magnifying glass — they are well hidden in the undergrowth, under a leaf, or on the label of a bottle, and are so unexpected that they may escape the collector's attention for years unless pointed out. The catalogue identifies which

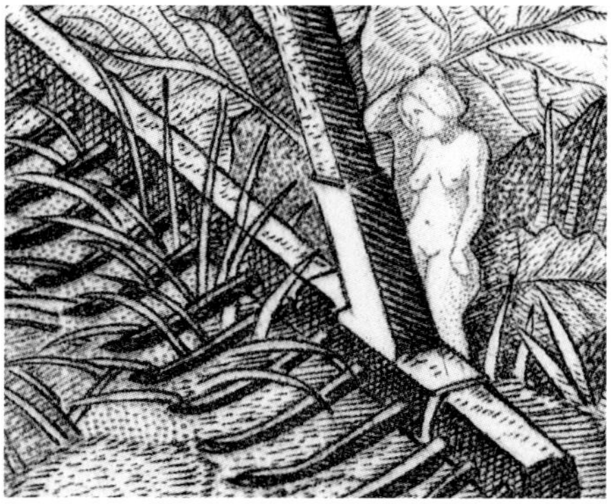

Magnified image of the naked lady, as she appears in 'Turnip Seed Drill' (overleaf). Also hidden in the picture are Chaplin's engraving tools and 'GK 1979'

images contain the little nude, but not where they can be found! One collector who had heard of the feature in 'Light Carriage' (126) wrote to Chaplin: 'I guess the little nude lady must have escaped, as we couldn't find her in our gardening books — only a naked crocus.' Chaplin replied:

> She is not the flower Colchiem, known as the 'naked lady', but exists as a very small person, residing in the end of a pipe which is in-between the whetstone grinding wheel and the old broken cartwheel leaning against the shed. I have often included a small naked lady in my recent engravings — just for fun.

Another correspondent observed: 'My son quickly found the nude lady!' The artist's correspondence was often engaged with bemused references to the little nude lady, and it was sometimes referred to as his 'trademark'. To take one final example of her fame: in 1979, in commissioning an engraving, the President of Götene Konstförening wrote to Chaplin:

> I hope you can manage to put 'GK 1979' somewhere in the picture with rather small letters. Also a very small nice nude woman, as otherwise people in Götene will be disappointed. Perhaps also one of the tools you are working with when engraving copper.

In his engraving 'Turnip Seed Drill' (125) all the requested features appear.

Chaplin came from a family and a background, and perhaps from a generation, which found some topics of conversation difficult and even taboo. He himself was of a shy and reserved character, not given to expressing personal opinions on every possible subject and occasion. Religion was one such topic, but although Chaplin never discussed spiritual matters, there are some clues as to his own faith. The only overtly religious subjects tackled by him were his very early drypoints 'Gerald and I' (1) and 'It is finished' (6), completed in his youth. These disclose a depth of feeling. However, he treasured other artist's religious work, particularly his own collection of Brangwyn's 'Stations of the Cross'. He spent much of his life outside in the countryside, close to nature, and a number of references in his notes disclose that he saw God in the creation around him. He was profoundly affected by church music, and his son recalls one occasion when, as a boy, after they had attended a choral evensong in St Albans Abbey (for some reason unrecollected!) he had asked his father whether he believed in God. After a long pause, Chaplin held out his hand, palm upwards, curling his fingers as if to hold something, and replied: 'Who else could have made this?'

Any account of Chaplin's life as man or artist would be misleading without reference to his wife, May's own life. She was the constant support and companion without whom, it is no exaggeration to say, his artistic life would not have been possible. He was eccentric and bohemian in nature, and for himself he never demanded nor expected a comfortable or well-ordered lifestyle: he rarely contributed anything towards domestic chores, never went shopping, never undertook the ordinary responsibilities of life beyond that of earning a living for his family. Yet May provided him with a disciplined framework to domestic affairs, and all the security of a comfortable and tidy home. As a frugal housekeeper and as an excellent cook she served him the best of food that he could enjoy. She looked after their son, dealing with schools and all the necessary educational requirements, including help with homework, with unremitting patience. For herself May was an accomplished needlewoman, at times turning cotton sheets sides-to-middle to economise on expenditure, at other times making delicate and exquisite lace and crochet tablecloths, embroidering or sewing tapestry chair covers, cushions and fire screens. She attended flower arranging classes, and their home was constantly decorated with beautiful arrangements of flowers from the garden. In a house dominated by art these were May's own personal artistic expressions. She was an active member of the Rickmansworth Horticultural Society and year after year won prizes for her conserves, preserves, jellies and cakes. After May's death a thick pile of prize cards, many of them Firsts, was found secreted in one of her drawers. In 1982 Chaplin recorded: 'May has been very busy with raspberries, runner beans, apples, making jams and conserve of quinces.' Indeed the garden at Highfield Way was a joy of both their lives. May laboured strenuously throughout the year to provide a never-ending succession of blooms, tidily arranged in neat borders, whilst Chaplin looked after the heavier tasks such as tending the softfruits, mowing the lawn, digging and sowing vegetables, and pruning the hedges, roses and trees. He readily acknowledged May's work in the garden. In a letter bemoaning his illness shortly after he retired he wrote: 'However, I have enjoyed myself with May who does all the work in the garden, home and shopping and keeping our affairs in order.' Again, in a later letter to Sweden:

I have this year stood and looked at all the roses and flowers which have been absolutely marvellous again — thanks to May's efforts. You will remember our garden very well, and would have liked to see the front this year. First it was daffodils and bulbs, then irises, followed by the roses and — May's new adventure — large begonias. It has been our best show ever in the garden, despite the very changeable weather.

(At May's request, Chaplin painted some of her bright red and yellow begonias in watercolour).

As far as his art was concerned, May was Chaplin's personal assistant and confidante. She filled in all the exhibition forms on time, paid the fees, and packed the items for delivery. She recorded and acknowledged sales, accounted for the proceeds, and carefully packed and posted the prints to the buyers. Frequently buyers would gratefully acknowledge safe receipt and her careful and secure packing. She wrote in longhand, or typed on an ancient Imperial typewriter, all Chaplin's correspondence with collectors, friends and enquirers, sometimes by dictation and sometimes through interpretation of his scrawling notes. His handwriting was reasonably legible, but his spelling and punctuation were quite curious: throughout his life, for example for the pronoun 'I' he would write 'i', and 'trial proof' was rendered 'trail proof'. She would help him write his letters — indeed he said that if it were not for May he would not write at all — and May would add items of interest to herself. Apart from the mounting and framing of prints, Chaplin himself had virtually nothing to do with this necessary process of administration, finding it an intolerable distraction to his work. In 1982 he wrote:

As success with sales at the RA grows over the years it becomes increasingly burdensome with correspondence, printing, mounting, framing, packing and posting of prints and general administration.

— not that he did any of this, he was probably referring to the burden on May! As with the art, on the domestic front May kept all the accounts, and paid all the bills; Chaplin never wrote a cheque in his life, though he signed without demur the hundreds of cheques made out by May.

With the demands of his employment and his enthusiastic and single-minded focus on his art, it may be a little surprising that Chaplin had any time at all for family affairs. Yet his son recalls much time spent walking the surrounding countryside as a family, or perhaps more often on father-and-son expeditions which involved a continuous learning process about countryside matters. Hours were spent in the neighbouring fields and woods gathering mushrooms, wild blackberries, raspberries and strawberries for tea. Other activities recollected by his son include visits to the Royal Opera House in Convent Garden with May's sister, Muriel, a balletomane, to marvel at the Royal Ballet. Muriel later recalled:

My memories of him will chiefly be those wonderful evenings up in the 'Gods' at Covent Garden watching an altogether different kind of art, and seeing him alight with pleasure as he got the same kind of exhilaration from it as I did.

There were trips to St Albans to sail a large model schooner, or a model steam launch both of which he had made; to numerous local art exhibitions, without May, to listen to the local art gossip; to the Sun factory at Watford on a Saturday morning to meet the production crew and watch the giant printing machines running; to the Royal Observer Corps post at night, well past any kind of bedtime, to share the tensions of watching for enemy aircraft and hobnobbing with male comrades; to rivers and lakes for endless sketching trips, observations and discourses on nature and birdwatching. Chaplin had planned that his only son could follow him into the Sun Engraving Company as an apprentice printer. Unfortunately his son had no artistic talent or skill, and when he became fifteen, Chaplin and May were summoned to their son's school to be told that his teachers felt that he should try for University. Whether this was a disappointment or a relief to Chaplin himself is not known, but in any event, his son went on to gain a state scholarship, and to attend Magdalen College, Oxford, to study law. This was certainly a source of pride to the couple and there are a number of references in the prints to events in their son's life and subsequent career.

When, eventually, grandchildren arrived, the artist was drawn into a fresh new cycle of family life. He was involved, with May, in much babysitting, his particular role being as a storyteller: his stories of Mr Haberjammer, and the twin pigeons, Percy and Percival, absorbed the new young grandchildren. He would also spend many patient hours teaching them to draw and paint, rewarding their efforts by carefully mounting and displaying their work, and later dating and storing it for posterity alongside his own print collection. Most weekends in the 1960s and 1970s he would take his grandchildren to Knightscote Farm to teach them about country matters, to inspire their subsequent love of the country, and simply to play in the barns and fields. Chaplin's art reflects much of his delight in his family and pride in their achievements, and many of the family references to be found in his engravings are explained in the catalogue notes. In his own notes to 'Forest Glade, New Forest' (103) Chaplin wrote

Studies of this plate were made whilst on holiday in Brockenhurst with Betty and Jon, and Elizabeth then aged three. Elizabeth insisted, whenever I unloaded my sketching equipment from the car, that she should help, and placed my stool down somewhere for me. She did not like me to wander away out of her sight, so, wherever the stool was placed I used to sketch, often with her help: of course Elizabeth had her teddy bear to keep us company. One day in the forest, Elizabeth insisted in taking off her clothes, and wandered about with her small potty in her hand. I sat down to sketch while the others went off to explore the forest

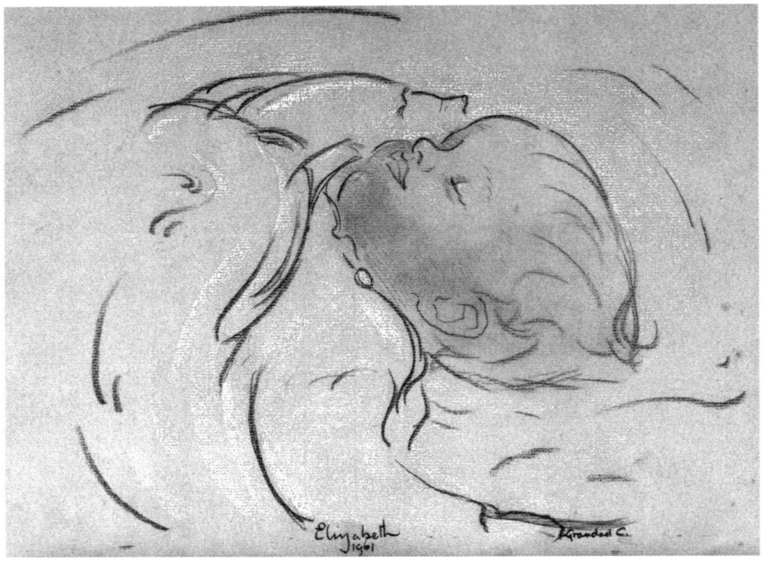

glade, little Elizabeth holding on to her potty and trailing somewhat behind! Instead of the potty I engraved her small teddy bear to remind us of those happy days.

About 'The Windmill, Brill' (106) Chaplin wrote

I have made many black-and-white sketches and many pastel sketches of this windmill. My granddaughter's name, 'Sara 1966', is engraved on the beam supporting the mill as she was with me and it was her fourth birthday when we visited Brill. Jon my son drove the car as I was too giddy suffering from Meuniere's disease at the time; I had to kneel on the sloping mound to make the sketch for this plate.

In 'Snow Drops and Mowing Machine' (124) there is a reference to Sara winning the Art cup at the Arts Educational School, Tring Park, an indication of inherited talent that was to emerge much later, after Chaplin's death.

'Oriel Window — the College, Marlborough' (134) was Chaplin's penultimate plate, completed shortly before his death. A letter to his grandson, Jon Edward, explained the background to the line engraving:

I usually write a note referring to the main detailed objects in my engraved plates. However, with this plate, which is a very personal one, there are not many detailed objects. Nevertheless, Jon, I expect you would like a note. You will remember that one beautiful sunny day last summer you escorted Grandma and me around the college — we enjoyed it very much indeed looking at the old and the new buildings. I was very impressed with it all, especially the window, the subject of my plate, so much so that on arriving back home I made some small rough sketches on tracing paper. I always do this for my plates. Your plate was started. I collected all the references I could, selected a small sheet of copper, and started the

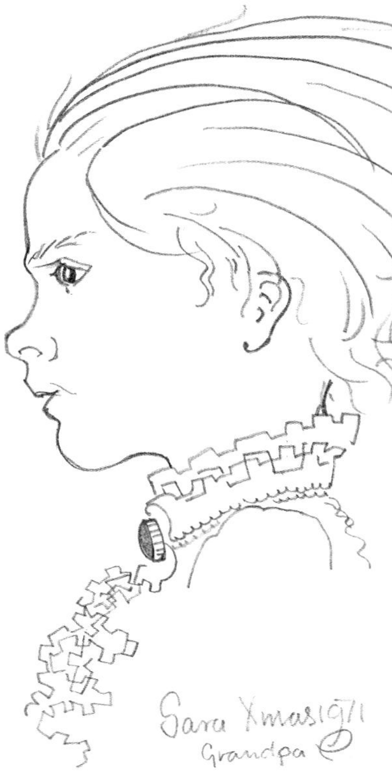

Chaplin's sketches of his grandchildren:
OPPOSITE: *Elizabeth (1961)*
THIS PAGE: *Sara (1971) and Jon (1972)*

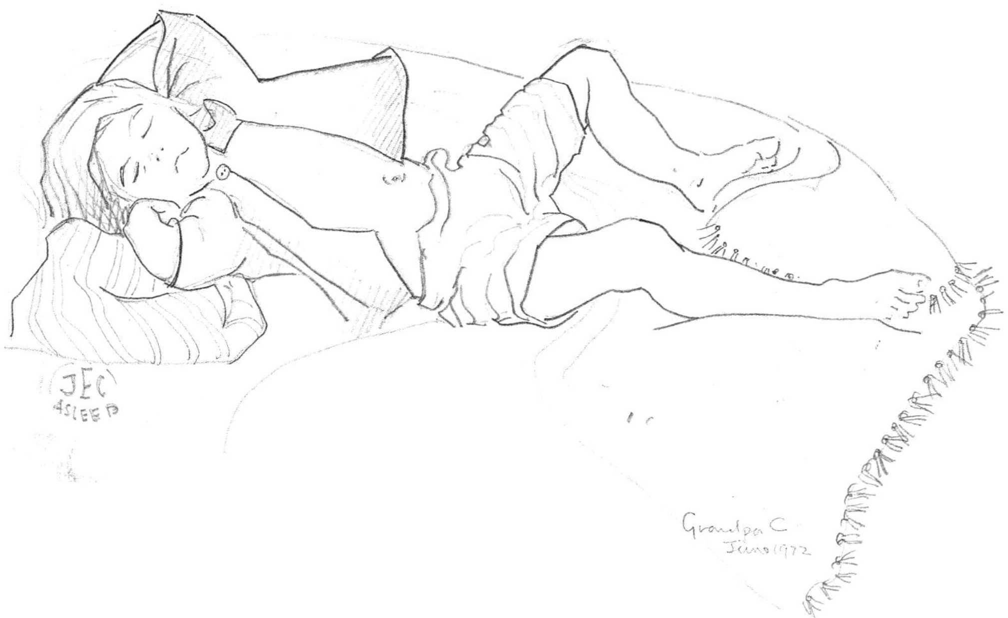

engraving side of it all. More interest was created next term, when you moved into the room with this Oriel Window — which I believe was sometimes called the 'goldfish bowl'. Hence a goldfish bowl in the side window, used for propping the sash windows open. The cat, by the way, did stroll across the quadrangle, just as cats do. As you know, at one time I did not think I could ever finish the plate, let alone pull these proofs. However, I did it, and here it is — not an exact rendering, but an impression of what I saw and concocted up. By the way, Jon, there is no little nude lady in this plate.

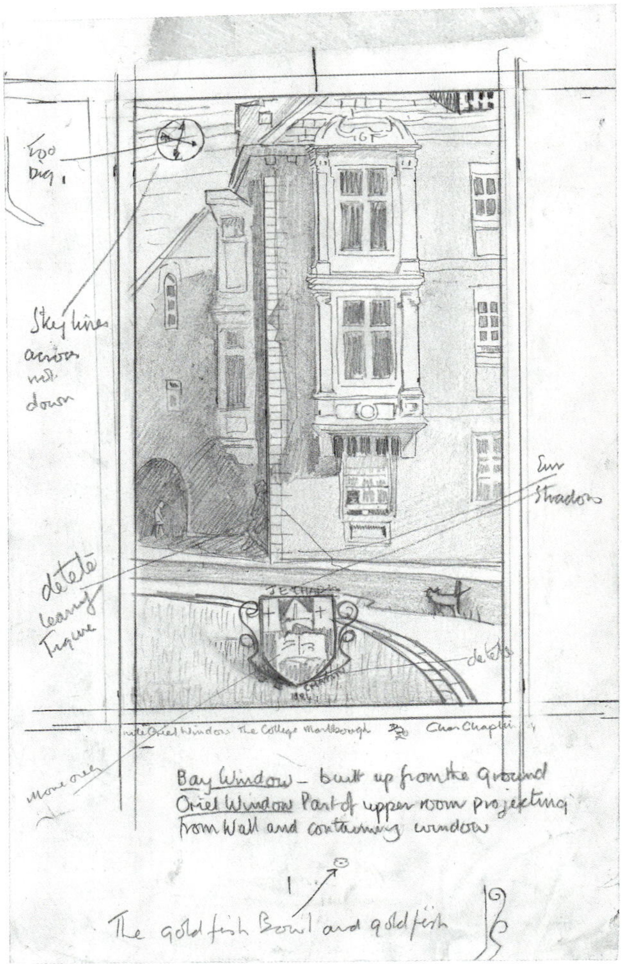

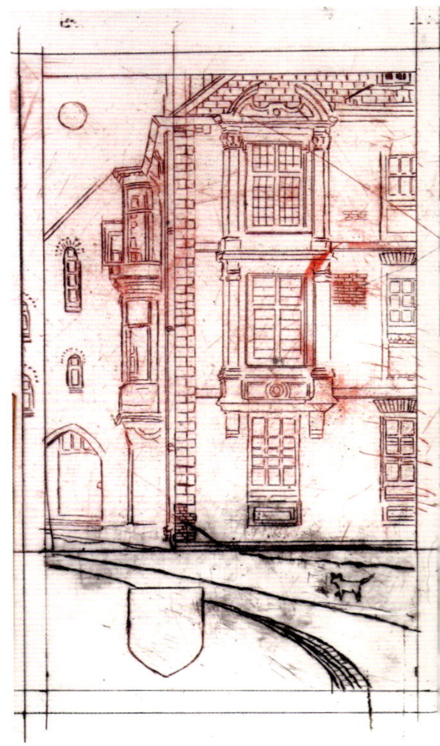

Oriel Window, The College, Marlborough, line engraving, 182 x 105 mm, 1984.
The illustrations show stages from a sketch on tracing paper, transferred to the copper plate by means of an incised acetate sheet rubbed with red chalk (this page), through three stages of proof (opposite page from top left), to the final print (opposite page bottom right).

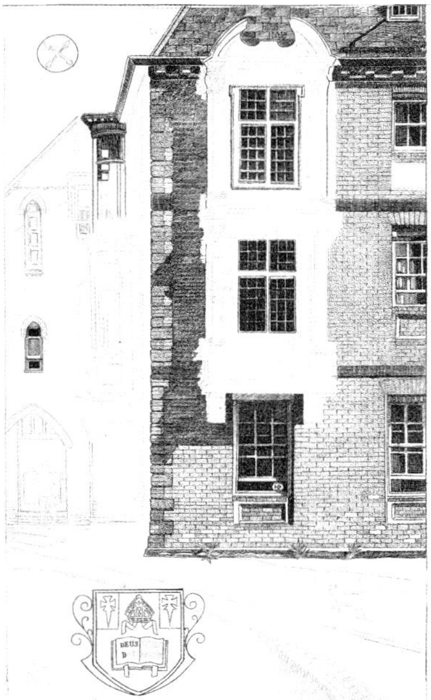

2 Trial Proof   Chas Chaplin 1984

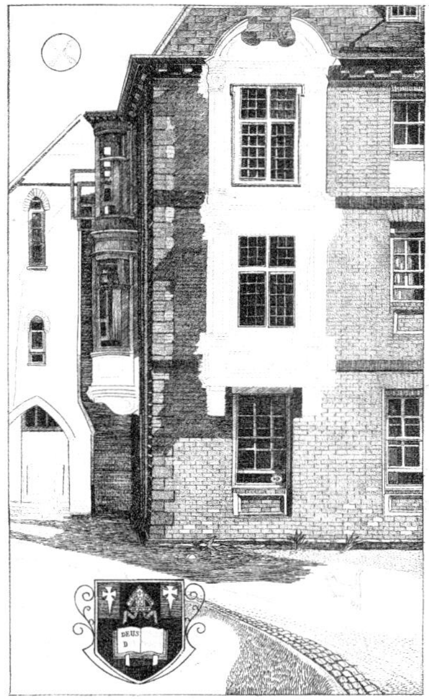

3rd Trial Proof   Chas Chaplin 1984

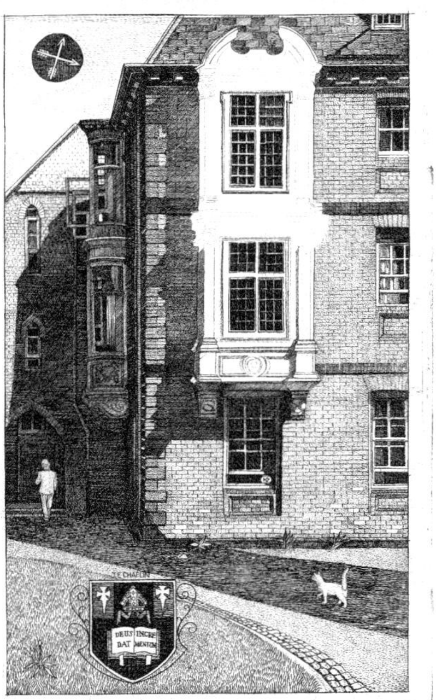

5th Trial Proof   Chas Chaplin 1984

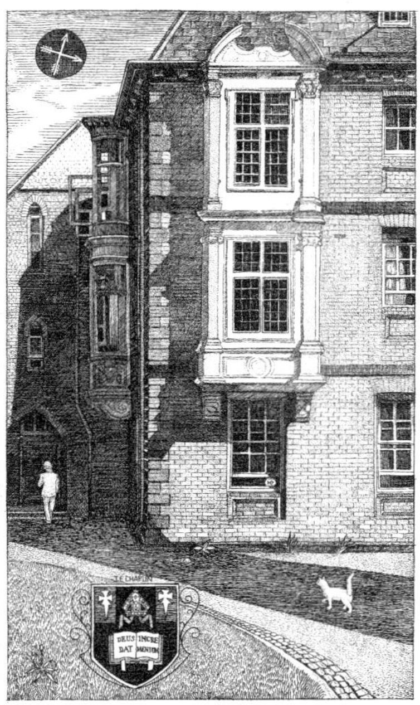

"Oriel Window"   The College. Marlborough
19/75 Chas Chaplin 1984

His Own View

CHAPLIN'S PHILOSOPHY OF ART was simple and was expressed succinctly in his own commentary on his engravings in *The Journal* (No. 7, 1985, p. 35): 'I have no theories about my own work — I just do what I want.' He was driven by a constant urge to reproduce his observations of nature as accurately and as perfectly as he could. The inauspicious start to his artistic career in loosing an eye, which contributed to his shyness almost to the point of self-effacement, presented a challenge which, however, never overcame his desire for artistic expression, which was itself simple, direct and unaffected by theory: 'I hold no brief for any style or type of art, academic or modern, or any school or group.' His view of his own work was overlaid with an utter modesty. He described his early work as 'blind excursions of the heart, rather than of art', and in 1978 he wrote: 'I am what is called a 'Sunday painter', chiefly working as an engraver and etcher, but also doing pastels.' As an engraver he felt a certain artistic loneliness, regarding himself as one of a dying breed. 'Engraving — it is the most technical and exacting of arts, and why I continue to spend my time at it I could not say.' (1970)

At the heart of Chaplin's drawings is a highly developed power of detailed observation.

I like to know my subject thoroughly inside and out. I break off a small twig from a poplar tree and observe how thin and pliable it is, and how each leaf is joined to the twig by a long, slender stalk, which allows the slightest breeze to set it moving. I see that this twig foretells the shape and character of the tree. The poplar tree is tall and graceful — the slightest breeze will move all the leaves, it is rarely still.

In 'Surrey Drill, Dog Rose and Chaff Cutter' (118) the background is of Stockers Farm in Rickmansworth. On one of the detailed pencil sketches of this scene Chaplin's notes record:

Stockers Farm from across the canal. Made this rough sketch of Stockers Farm some 10–15 years ago, then went back July 1975. Since that earlier visit alterations had been made to it all. The film 'Black Beauty' was made on this location. All the old lean-to sheds were pulled down, all barns had grey plastic gutters, a number of fake plastic sheets were made into windows, and the main house was completely renovated and repaired, with windows and beams to suit the period of the film. I could not get to the position I made this rough sketch — and they charged me 30p to park the car.

The sketch is covered with annotations of the changes observed by him over the period since it was made. His powers of observation could be constantly regenerated at the same location.

For three consecutive years prints of mine which were made direct onto the copper plate, and which were exhibited at the RA, were made while I stood on the identical spot looking in different directions for each subject. The spot was a tree stump, which formed a most comfortable seat.

Chaplin's engravings were basically compositions, where one or more carefully chosen subjects were set against a background of more or less detail. He never made a complete drawing for a plate, but would collate all the details from his rough sketches and notes.

It is not wise to make an etching or an engraving from a completely finished drawing, for the danger is that you tend just to reproduce the drawing, and in so doing lose the qualities and interest that an engraving can give when created originally as an engraving. Good pencil drawing must go hand in hand with repeated sketches and gaining of knowledge and observation on every subject.

This approach affirms the constant freshness of his engravings, even where detail is at its most dense. The result also is sometimes an image where the subject matter, with backgrounds and other subsidiary features, are from sketches recorded in a number of different locations; in 'Light Carriage' (126), for example, there are scenes taken from Northamptonshire, Hertfordshire and Sussex.

Sketching, combined with observation and imagination, was thus the technical key to Chaplin's creativity in engraving. In 1952 he wrote a series of six 1600-word articles on drawing for the 'The Artist' which in the event were not published. In these articles Chaplin reveals much of his approach to engraving, and the few extracts which follow may give some insight into his methodology:

Besides enthusiasm and the wish to create, we [artists] must have some knowledge and technical ability, and this can be acquired by study and practical effort, and the unceasing will to analyse one's own work.

No sketch need be perfect to be of immense value.

I am to be master of my materials, and not let my materials master me. To be able to master pencil and paper is the artist's greatest asset.

I was thrilled and delighted with the wonderful effects before me. To me, this is sufficient reason to wish to record it. Apart from the exercise, the usefulness of the sketch lies in the fact that it may later become the basis for a larger watercolour, or oil, or engraving. Until many such sketches have been collected in the artist's own style, method and approach, their usefulness will not become apparent.

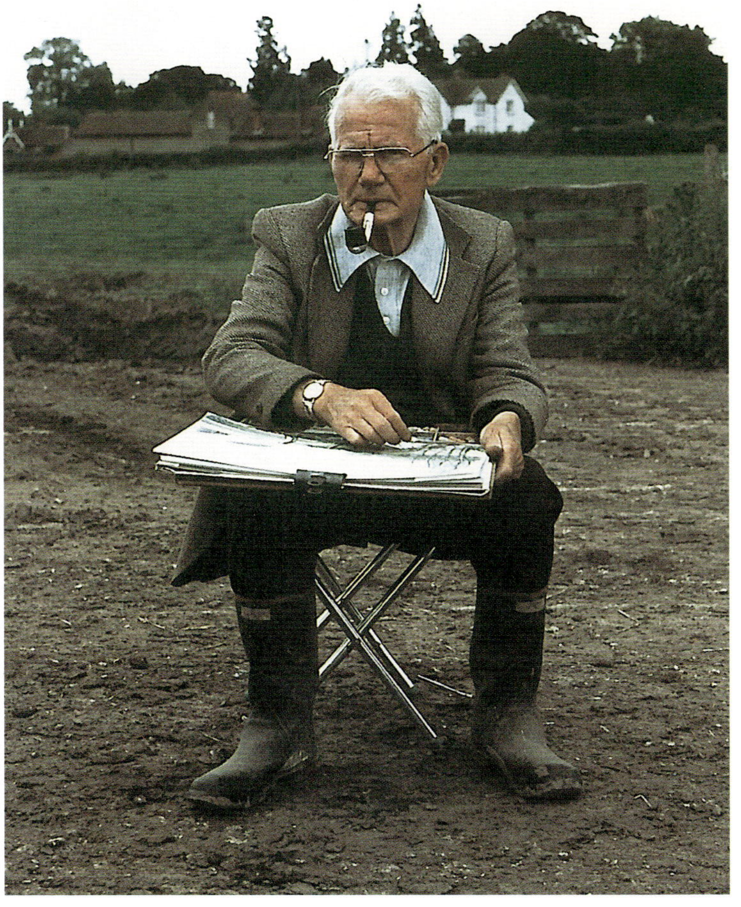

Chaplin with his sketchboard, c. 1980. Photograph D. Hallbery

Almost all of my pencil drawings are executed with the idea of further development in the studio as engravings, as many as 10 or 15 drawings being used for one engraving.

Craftmanship, while not in itself an art, is the basis of all art, and pencil drawing can convey the meaning swiftly, with ease and simplicity.

I have found it most instructive and inspiring, on being given the opportunity to see the preliminary studies and drawings of other artists' work. However, I have found it wise not to allow the public in general to see preliminary studies for my own work — but only the mounted and framed work, and under the best light conditions. The efforts and struggles experienced by the artist to produce his finished work belong to him alone.

A pencil note on paper is of far greater value than any mental note.

I have found it useful to make a written note on the actual sketch as to the details of texture, etc, what some few quick lines actually represent. I find this saves time and reminds me later of the true character of what I had seen, and allows my memory to concentrate on other aspects of what I wish to remember.

In some ways a commentary on Chaplin's art is a tale of the minutiae of life. The many drawings which preceded his engravings, and the trial proofs which accompanied every stage of his engravings, are covered with copious notes relating to the objects, machinery or plants featured, as well as instructions and suggestions to himself regarding further development of the plate. A few examples of his interest in the detail, and indeed the scholarship sometimes involved, can be seen in manuscript notes on a trial proof of 'Fiddle Bow Seed Broadcaster' (119): 'Some seeds from Mum's Christmas present of dried grasses'; again, 'Grasses gathered on farm during the Summer — these mostly fell apart by the time this engraving started'; again, 'Winter Bere Barley — see *Standard Cyclopaedia of Modern Agriculture,* Vol. 2, page 52.'

Throughout his life Chaplin rarely went outside without his sketchbook, and he thus amassed a huge collection of images of the objects of his observations, regarded by him almost as stock-in-trade for the composition of his engravings. In a letter to Lundström in 1976 he explained his technique of incorporating material from these sketches into his engravings:

You ask how it is I do not make pen-and-ink or pencil drawings. I do make lots and lots of pencil sketches and drawings and notes for every plate I do. I have rough pencil drawings of all the tools and machines featured in my engravings, but never any completed or completely finished pencil-and-ink drawings. I have lots of pencil tracings, one on top of each other, and lots of references on the flowers and trees included in my plates, and for some of the large pieces of machinery and implements, I took prints of photographs. It takes me weeks to decide what to include, what is to be in the main design, and to scale some of the drawings down to plate size. The final tracing is made on celluloid. Sometimes I use 2, 3 or 4 of these. I do all the things you expect should be done, but do not ever work from a completed drawing. Much is left to be worked out with the actual engraving tool and steel point on the copper plate, often changing details from the original drawings. I

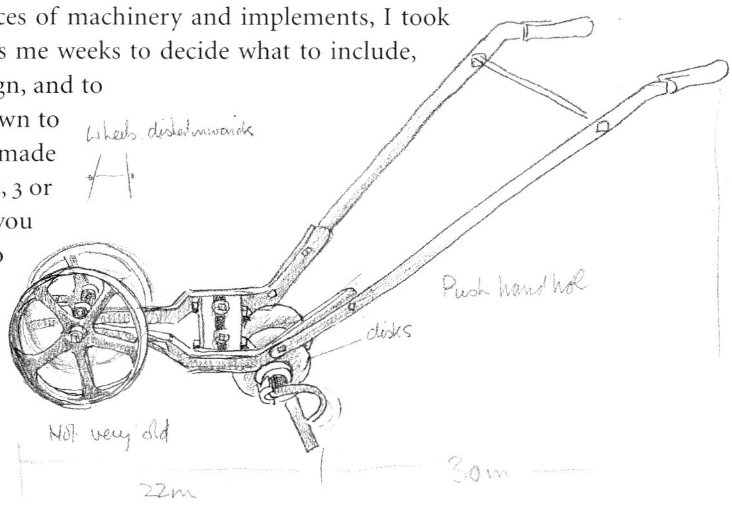

do not show anybody, other than other artists, my preparations that go into the making of a plate. After the trial proofs that I sometimes make when I have completed a plate, I generally destroy my notes, sketches and tracings.

(In spite of this last statement, fortunately a large number of Chaplin's plates are still represented by a considerable file of drawings, tracing and notes.)

We have earlier noted Chaplin's obsession with paper for printing his plates; a similar concern regarding paper for sketching also applied.

I have never sketched on pads or in sketch books because there you only have a single choice of paper. In my sketch box I always have at least six kinds of paper each giving different effects, each being slightly different in colour and tone. A paper I always use a great deal of is tracing paper. Also good hand made paper, good quality cartridge, toned ingress, and sheets of antique paper torn out of old books (some over 200 years old), linen surfaced paper, and paper with a china clay coating. I like to feel I have on hand just the paper for the effect I want.

As we have seen, Chaplin's retiring nature and natural diffidence led him to take a simple and modest view of his own work. He wrote to a correspondent in 1978:

I can only complete two plates a year with some effort, when I feel like it. These two plates enable me to show at the two London exhibitions [RA and RE] and a few local ones, but mostly, what I like best of all, is to show to collectors who write or call on me for prints. They are most interesting to meet and to talk to, and they help to make me feel that I am doing something in some little way worthwhile, and dare I say, something artistic. I cannot, in any way, assess the artistic side of my work, but if people continue to phone or call on me I suppose there is some little achievement there.

He gained much personal encouragement from conversations with people, both friends and strangers, interested in his art, and from his correspondence. He told of one such very early encounter:

Many years ago [he was writing in 1950] I took advantage of the Queries Department of the 'The Artist' and sent along to the editor some of my work. The reply was short — two words — that have encouraged me ever since: 'Go ahead'.'

He lacked the inclination and the small-talk to enable him to mix easily with the artistic establishment, even in his own specialist field. As he said to Lundström in 1982: 'I do not seem to have been a very sociable artist.' His files contain many unused invitations to RA soirées and similar functions specifying 'evening dress with decorations'. His drive and his focus in life was reserved for creating his art, the constant striving for perfection in observation, execution and design, and the eager anticipation of his next undertaking. In 1978 he wrote to Joyce Taylor in Canada:

I must say I always expect and hope that my next engraving will be the best. Once I have engraved a plate it is in the past, and it is the next one that is interesting to me.

Chaplin's life, with its joys and sorrows, and his art, with its constant striving for perfection and renewal, were inextricably entwined, and his optimistic outlook embraced all aspects. In 1982, during one of the increasingly frequent periods of illness, he wrote to a friend in a manner which can probably be taken to sum up his simple philosophy of life:

Doctors can't cure old age, and that is really the trouble. To sit in the sun in the garden, with all the colours of the flowers, or to sit engraving away at my plates, or visiting the farm museum with my friend each weekend is a joy, so I am really very lucky.

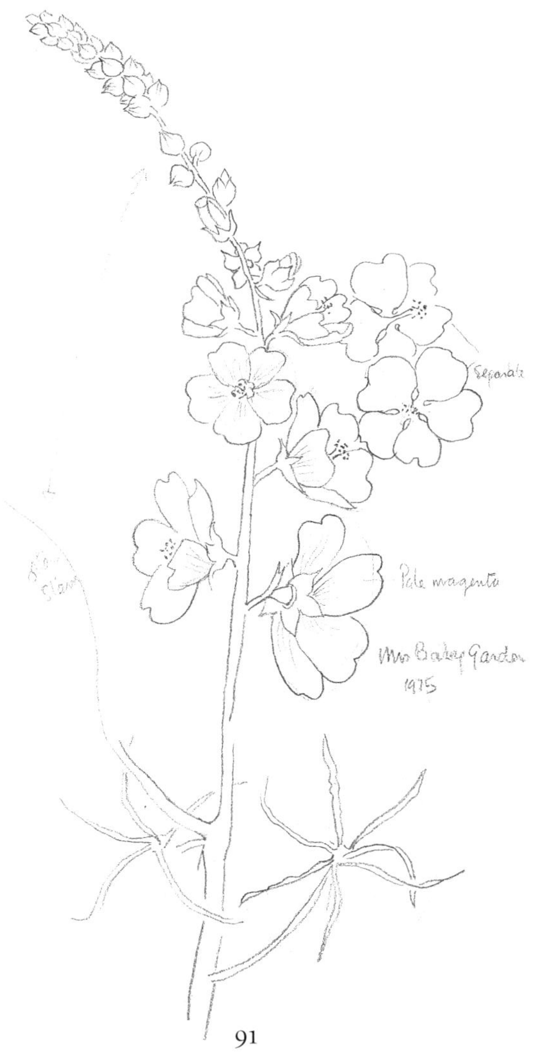

References

The Artist
Commended 'Winter Sun' 1938 (30)

Illustrated London News, 1 May 1943, pp. 492–493
Illus: 4 pen-and-ink drawings of ROC posts

Daily Telegraph, 2 May 1949
T. W. Earp, Arts Correspondent, critique of RA Summer Exhibition
Reference: 'Frog' (72)

Picture Post, 28 May 1949, Vol. 43, No. 9
Illus: 'Dragonfly and Passionflower' (70)

Leader Magazine, 28 May 1949,Vol. 6, No. 30, p. 3
'How old are trees?'
Illus: 'Sweet Chestnut' (1940) (33)

Everybody's Weekly, 20 October 1951, p. 17
Article on 'Four feet on canvas'
Illus: 'Squirrel' (79)

The Collector, July 1953, Vol. 1, No. 1, p. 18
Review of RA Summer Exhibition
Reference: 'Melting Snow' (31)

Knitwear & Stocking, May 1966, Vol. 20, No. 5
Illus: 'Allotment Hut' (105)

The Royal Academy Illustrated, 1974, p. 32
Illus: 'Shandy Barrow, Maize Kibbler, and Butter Churn' (114) [wrongly described as an etching]

Yorkshire Post, 4 June 1977
Ref 'Cheese Press' (120)
(Harrogate RE Exhibition)

Journal of the Royal Society of Painter-Etchers and Engravers, 1985, No. 7, pp. 19, 20, 35
'CHA Chaplin R.E. discusses his engravings'
Illus: 'Cheese Press' (120), 'New Forest Ghost' (135), 'Hop Pole Tug' (131)

Tree News, Autumn/Winter 2003, pp. 38–39, Felix Publishing
'CHA Chaplin: Artist of the New Forest — Passionate Pastels of the Ancient and Ornamental Woods'
Illus: 8 pastels and 'In the New Forest' (with pheasant) (99) 1960 [wrongly described as an etching]

Chronology

1907 12 January: Charles Herbert Arthur Chaplin born in Watford, Hertfordshire.

1914 First expressions of interest in drawing.

1919 Looses right eye in street accident.

1925 Joins The Sun Engraving Co. Ltd, Watford, as an apprentice engraver
Produced first plate, a drypoint, 'Gerald and I'.
First recognition of work; Hertfordshire Art Society highly commends 'After Rain'.

1930 Attends figure drawing classes at Watford School of Art.

1934 Marries Else May Howick. Moves to Highfield Way, Rickmansworth.

1935 December, son born, Jon Howick.

1939 October, war service with Royal Observer Corps begins.
First engraving, 'Melting Snow', accepted and hung in Royal Academy Summer Exhibition.

1946 September, enrols as a student in the Etching and Engraving Department at the Royal College of Art. Studies under Malcolm Osborne and Robert Austin 1946/7 and 1947/8.

1950 Made Associate of the Royal Society of Painter-Etchers and Engravers, with engraving of 'Stoat' as diploma plate and presentation print.
Made Associate of Canadian Society of Painter-Etchers and Engravers, with 'Early Spring' as diploma plate and presentation print.

1951 Visits Spain with friends.

1952 G. A. Reid Silver Memorial Award of CPE awarded for 'Underhill Farm, Lyme Regis' in Toronto, Canada.

1954 Son goes to Oxford University.

1959 August, son marries Elizabeth Ann Cave at Christ Church, Chorleywood.

1960 August, granddaughter Elizabeth Louise born.

1962 Fellowship of RE with diploma plate 'Forest Glade'.
October, granddaughter Sara Ann born.

1966 September, grandson Jon Edward born.

1967 Summer, meets Lief and Kirstin Lundström, and association with Sweden begins.

1970 Retires from full time employment after nearly fifty years' service with Sun Printers of Watford.
Engraves 'Put out to Grass'.

1972 Granddaughter Sara to Arts Educational School, Tring Park.

1975 Solo exhibition of work in Götene, Sweden.
Knightscote Farm museum established.

1977 'Cheese Press' celebrates seventy years of artist's life.

1978 CPE acquire for its archive collection 'Farm Corner', 'Early Spring' and 'Underhill Farm Lyme Regis'.
The GLC acquires Knightscote Farm Museum.
Granddaughter Elizabeth goes to Exeter University.

1979 Sketching tour in Sussex with friends.

1980 Grandson Jon goes to Marlborough College

1982 Granddaughter Elizabeth to Oxford University (Magdalen College) as a post-graduate student.

1983 GLC purchases collection of thirteen prints of rural and agricultural subjects.

1984 August, celebrates Golden Wedding Anniversary together with son's Silver Wedding Anniversary, granddaughter Elizabeth's wedding, and grandson Jon's coming of age!
Exhibits at RA Summer Exhibition for the last time, 'New Forest Ghost'.

1985 After fifty-one years moves from Highfield Way to Bury Meadows in Rickmansworth.
Gives up studio and printing press.
Article in *RE Journal* 'CHA Chaplin discusses his engravings'.
Granddaughter Sara marries.
First great-grandson, James Harold, born to Elizabeth.

1987 8 April, elected Honorary Retired Member RE.
28 April, dies at Watford General Hospital, funeral at Christ Church, Chorleywood on 5 May.

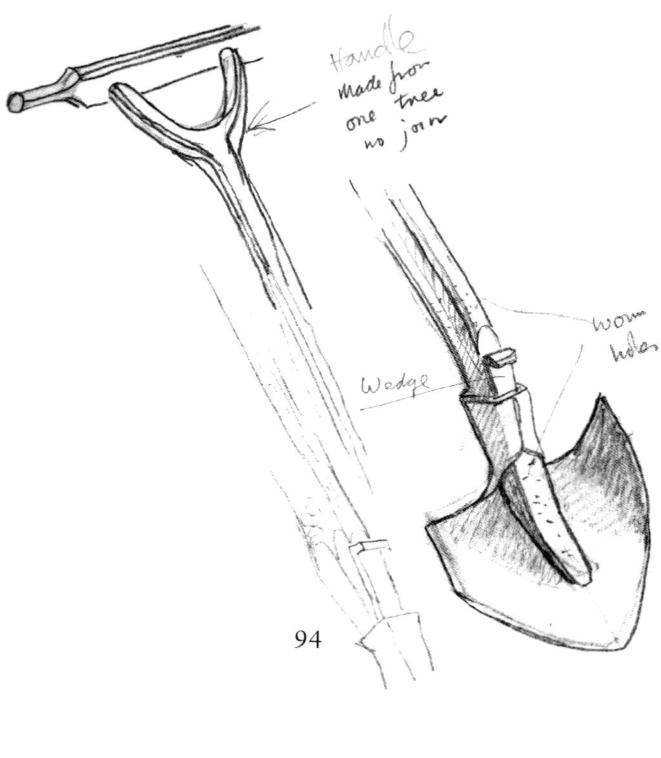

Catalogue Raisonné of the Prints

Notes on Printmaking Techniques Used by Chaplin

THE FOLLOWING NOTES on drypoint, etching, aquatint, colour linocut and mezzotint, are intended to help the print enthusiast or collector with little knowledge of the techniques and skills in these artistic processes. The explanations here are brief (though I hope accurate) but do not attempt to explore the subjects in any depth. They are, as it were, a commentary by an amateur for an amateur. For an excellent and professional exposition of these media see E. S. Lumsden, *The Art of Etching* (the New Library, 1924, 1962) or Walter Chamberlain, *Manual of Etching and Engraving* (Thames and Hudson, 1984).

Line Engraving

Line engraving is an art medium where the lines of the image are individually cut into the surface of a flat metal sheet, usually copper or zinc, using a simple hand tool. The metal sheet, or 'plate', is then inked and printed on paper to reproduce the image. Chaplin used copperplate for most of his work.

The copper plate is usually around $1/16$ inch thick, flat and highly polished. The edges are bevelled, in order both to protect the blankets during printing and to prevent the paper from splitting, and to render the plate safer to handle during the engraving and inking processes.

The basic tool for cutting the lines into the copper plate is known as a 'graver' or 'burin'. This consists of a straight piece of square or lozenge section ($1/10''$ to $1/8''$) steel some four inches long with one end fitted into a partially rounded handle. The point, or cutting facet, at the opposite end to the handle, is shaped in various ways designed to cut different kinds of line. Differences in the cut line produce different receptacles for the ink which in turn produce different effects when printed, for example, sharp or soft lines. The steel of the graver needs to be very hard and carefully tempered; the cutting tip is constantly polished on all surfaces and sharpened on an oilstone. Examples of other tools used in line engraving are needles, callipers, burnishers (for smoothing a rough surface), scribers, scorpers (for broad textured lines), scrapers (to remove burr), rockers (for mezzotinting), leather sandbags, hammers and punches (for repoussage and erasing engraved lines from the reverse of a plate) and lead blocks.

The engraver may work directly on to a fresh plate with nothing but his memory or imagination, or perhaps an adjacent model, as a guide. Alternatively, his graver may follow an impression of an image which has been previously transferred to the plate. Such an image, usually a pencil sketch by the artist, may be traced on to tissue with a soft pencil, and transferred to the plate by placing the tracing on the plate and burnishing, or running through the press, to impress the pencil lines on to the surface of the plate. Or a strong transparent acetate may be used; in this case the image is scratched on the acetate and coloured chalk used to fill the scratched lines before burnishing the image on to the plate. This method has the advantage that, if some of the feint lines of the transferred image on the plate are rubbed off during the engraving process, the acetate can be replaced on to the plate in the correct position so that fresh lines can be burnished on.

The graver is held with the handle resting in the palm of the hand, well back towards the wrist. The plate rests on a round leather pad and is fully mobile, being held in position with the other hand. The top of the graver is pressed into the surface of the copper and slowly and smoothly pushed forward at a slight angle to the plate to cut the line, flicking upwards at the end of the cut to prevent the formation of a burr. Curved lines are achieved by revolving the plate on the pad whilst cutting. The engraved line is a V-shaped incision on the surface of the plate, the depth of the incision governing the amount of ink to be held, and thus the boldness of the eventual printed line. Great skill, discipline and patience is demanded of the artist in controlling the graver to produce the type of line required. The engraving process is very different from pencil drawing on paper, or drawing a line through a ground on a plate to be etched, where the surfaces worked yield virtually no resistance.

The copper plate is inked with a dabber or roller to force the ink into the full depth of all of the engraved lines. The whole surface of the plate is covered with ink, which is then removed by lightly wiping the surface in circular movements with a muslin pack, until only the ink remaining in the lines is left; the inking process is finished by careful wiping with the base of the palm of the hand, rubbed over whitening and dusted off to free the skin from sweat. The plate is then warmed before being placed on the press for printing.

The printing of a copper plate is itself a fine art. There is a huge variety of type, weight and tone of paper, and great care is needed in the choice of the most appropriate paper and inks in order to express the particular image envisaged by the artist. Paper improves with age and antique paper is much sought after. The paper to be printed is dampened before printing to a limp, but not wet, state. The dampening process, depending on the characteristics of the paper may take anything from a few hours to a few days. As referred to more fully in the text, for most of his artistic life Chaplin mixed his own inks achieving, in his view, the best results from freshly made ink, which allowed him the greatest flexibility in type, thickness, colour and tone. Only in the last two years of his career did he use manufactured inks, considering these to be just as satisfactory.

The printing press works on a similar principle to that of the old clothes mangle or wringer, except that the rollers are steel. The copper plate to be printed is placed face upwards on a large flat steel plate or bed which passes between the rollers, all of which are supported on a heavy cast iron frame. The paper on which the image is to be reproduced is placed face down on the engraved surface of the plate, followed by a number of felt blankets. The large steel plate is then passed slowly through the rollers by manually revolving a large wheel attached by gears to an upper roller made of solid steel; by means of this gearing considerable pressure can be applied smoothly and with relatively little effort. The lower roller, usually a large hollow drum or cylinder, turns freely on bearings to support the bed plate. Pressure must be even over the whole copper plate, and is adjusted by means of a screw mechanism bearing on the hub of the upper roller. Pressure is necessary in intaglio (or incised) printing in order to press the paper into the inked lines.

After printing, the blankets are rolled back and the paper removed with the image imprinted on it. The print is then flattened and dried. Working proofs are printed at various stages of engraving the plate both as a progress report and in order to assist the artist in developing the image as he requires. The final print is the culmination of the artistic process, and key to its success. With the exception of his last plate, Chaplin printed all his work himself.

Drypoint

In this technique the line on the copperplate is produced by drawing on the surface with a strong steel 'needle', or point'; no cutting or acid is used. This produces a burr at the side of the incision, the strength of the burr increasing with the depth of the line. The ink is held in the line and clings to the burr, producing on the printed image a line which is more blurred than the clear-cut line of an engraving. Drypoint plates are more vulnerable to the pressure of printing and the wear-and-tear of inking and wiping, and the editions of satisfactory prints taken from them are necessarily less than in line engraving. The term 'drypoint' also refers to the printed impression.

Mezzotint

The mezzotinting process involves roughening the smooth surface of the plate with a serrated steel tool, or 'rocker', to create an area of cuts and burrs. When printed the area so treated appears as a rich and consistent black, with tonal graduation and lights achieved by scraping and burnishing the mezzotint ground. In mezzotint the artist is working from dark to light, the opposite of etching and engraving.

Etching

From the Dutch, *etzen*, to eat. Etching involves a 'biting' process in which acid is used to eat away the surface of the copperplate to form an indented line. The word 'etching' applies to the impression or proof of the image itself, and not to the etched metal; every proof is original, and not a 'copy'.

The working surface of the copper plate is covered thinly and evenly with a waxed acid-resistant coating, or 'ground'; the back of the plate is coated with varnish. In drawing on this waxed surface the ground is removed with a point which does not, however, scratch the surface of the metal. After the image is thus drawn, the plate is submerged in a bath of acid solution which eats the lines where they are drawn through the waxed ground, the depth of the lines so etched depending on the strength of the acid solution and the length of time the plate is exposed to the acid. The ground is then cleaned off with a solvent. The inking and printing process is virtually the same as that described under 'line engraving' above. The many recipes and formulas, and the preparation and mixing of ingredients for both the waxed ground and the mordants (etching acids), reflect the personal style and skill of the artist.

Soft ground etching is a technique, sometimes combined with line engraving, which can reproduce the effect of pencil or crayon drawing on a plate.

Aquatint

This process involves the use of acid to produce dots on the surface of a copper plate, similar to etching, in order to create areas of pure tone. The technique is sometimes combined with line engraving.

Colour Linocut

The only example of a relief form of printmaking used by the artist (i.e. the printing lines stand in relief and are not incised) and the unusual use of colour. The design is drawn on a block of soft linoleum. The areas around the design are cut away. These upstanding areas are inked and printed on to a sheet of paper. To add a colour, another block is cut with the area to be printed in colour left upstanding; this is then inked and printed over the original design on the same sheet. Further blocks have to be made and overprinted if further colours are required.

Notes to the Catalogue

Dates

The date ascribed to an image in the catalogue and text is the year in which the plate was completed, or, if there are more than one states of the plate the year in which that state was completed. Chaplin usually, but not invariably, dated his proofs, and this date would be the year of printing the proof, which may or may not be that of completion of the plate itself.

Dimensions

Dimensions are of the image size, not the plate size, and are in millimetres, height before width.

Editioning

Chaplin would usually, but not always, ascribe an edition to a plate, and the numbers of proofs taken from that plate are limited to the edition number plus several 'artist's proofs' for his own use. The numbers of the edition varied, in the earlier years being in the region of 20 or 30, and in later years 50 or 75. Artist's proofs were usually identified by the artist as 'A/P'.

Abbreviations

RA Royal Academy of Arts
RE Royal Society of Painter-Etchers and Engravers, now Royal Society of Painter-Printmakers.
CPE Society of Canadian Painter-Etchers and Engravers
RCA Royal College of Art, London
ROC Royal Observer Corps
GLC Greater London Council

Identification of Works

Nearly all of Chaplin's work was titled by him. However, partly due to the sometimes extended time over which a work was proofed, and partly due to the fact that he was foremost an artist rather than an administrator, occasionally more than one title is associated with a work. Where this has occurred the known alternatives are identified. The titles of his works, particularly where they are the same or similar to another work, are sometimes accompanied by a subsidiary phrase, for example, a location or a feature of the work, to assist in identification. Most of his studies are not titled. The Index of Titles of Prints and Alternatives which follow, lists all the known titles.

Illustrations

Except where noted, the illustrations in this book have been reproduced from the original proofs in the author's collection, or that of the artist's grandson.

The Prints

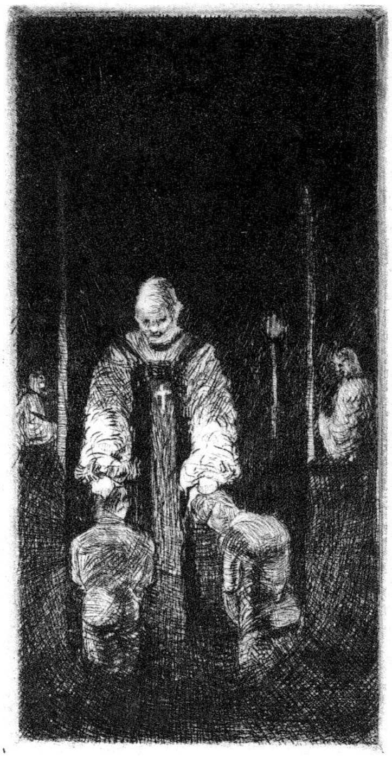

1 GERALD AND I 1925

DRYPOINT 110 x 52 mm

EDITION 30

This is the first plate of the artist produced when he was 18. The bishop of St Albans, Dr Furze is laying hands on the artist and his friend Gerald at their baptism and confirmation at St John's Church, Watford.

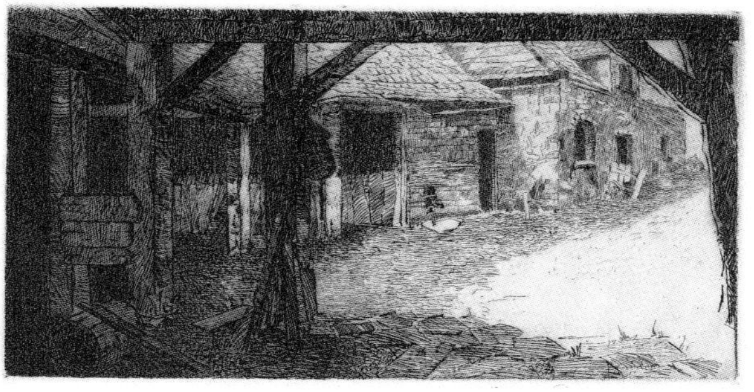

2 OLD BARNS or SHEDS 1925

ETCHING 105 x 198 mm

EDITION 30 *Printed in brown ink. Some printed in 1931*

A view of old barns at Leavesden from inside one of them. The artist's first etched plate.

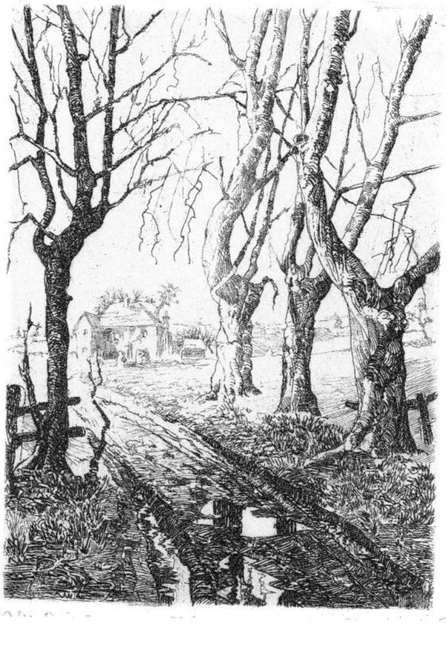

3 AFTER RAIN 1925

ETCHING 155 x 108 mm

EDITION 30 *Printed in brown inks*

Trees in winter bordering a muddy track leading to a farmhouse. This early print was highly commended by the Hertfordshire Art Society — the first public recognition of the artist.

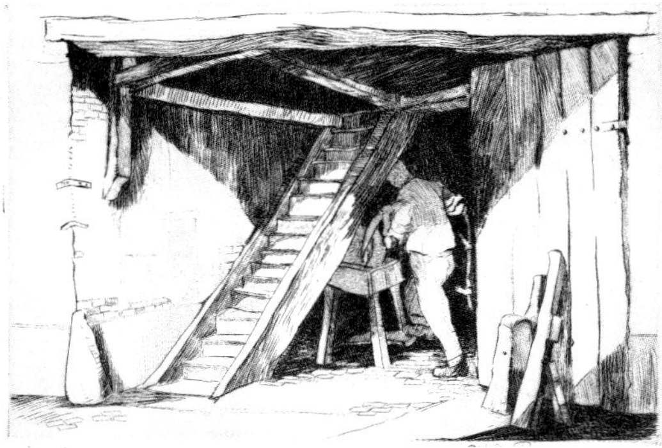

4 FARM WORKER 1926

Drypoint 165 x 240 mm

Not editioned *Apparently incomplete*

A farm worker is sharpening the blade of a scythe on a pedal-driven stone in a barn in Ware, Hertfordshire. An early indication of Chaplin's fascination with rural artifacts which was developed in his later work.

5 THE CLEARING 1927

Etching 273 x 176 mm

Not editioned *Printed in brown as well as black inks*

A clearing in woodland (probably Whippendell Woods, Watford) with a Romany Caravan and tent, and a figure gathering firewood. The etching was made while Chaplin was a student at the Watford School of Art, principal Mr A. Scott. The artist's first attempt at a large plate.

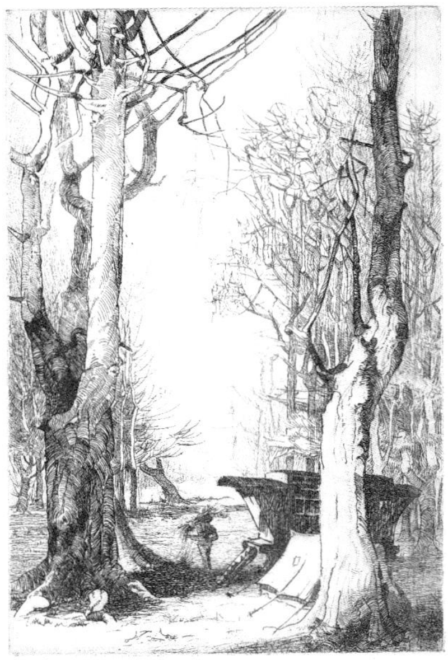

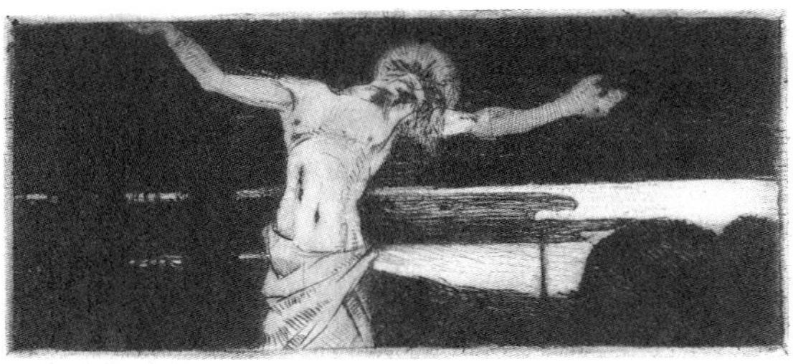

6 IT IS FINISHED 1927

Drypoint 58 x 132 mm

Edition 30 *Believed to be only 2 prints made*

Representation of Christ crucified against a black sky. Chaplin wrote in his notes: 'It was drawn direct onto the copper with the point of a dart. I borrowed the copper for the plate from the Sun Engraving Co. Ltd (his employer). The management found this out and suggested I helped myself in the future — which I did.'

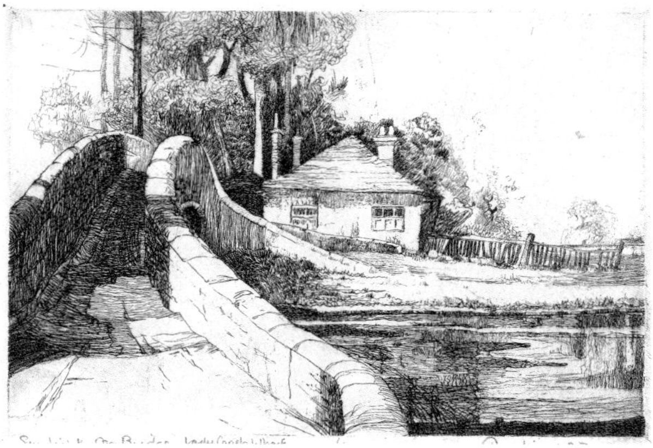

7 SUNLIGHT ON BRIDGE 1927

ETCHING 145 x 215 mm

EDITION 30

Dappled sunlight illuminates a humpback bridge over the Grand Union canal at Lady Capel's Wharf, Cassiobury Park, Watford.

8 HILLTOP 1928

DRYPOINT 122 x 253 mm

NOT EDITIONED

A male figure rests on a tree trunk, accompanied by a standing female figure, looking from their hilltop position to the far horizon.

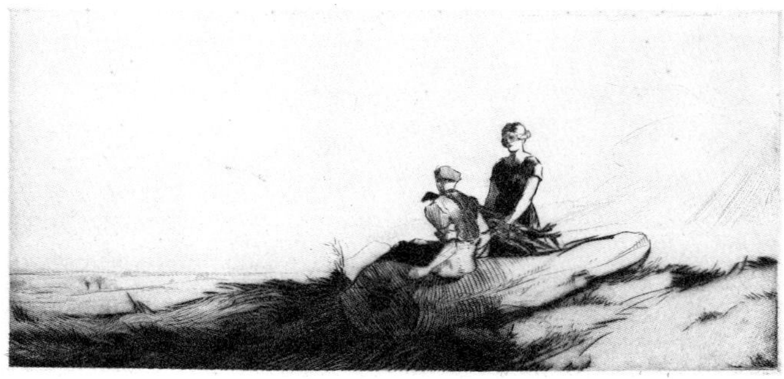

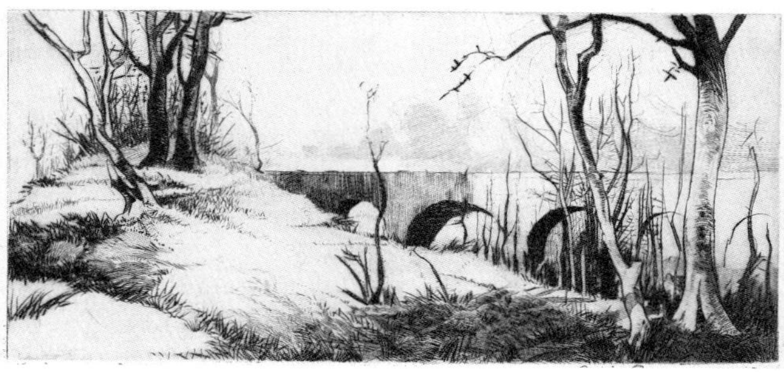

9 THE ARCHES AT BUSHEY 1929

DRYPOINT 146 x 310 mm

NOT EDITIONED *Only two prints extant*

A dry point direct on thin copper plate which, the artist records, was subsequently cut up for doing odd jobs.

10 HILLSIDE 1929

DRYPOINT 124 x 300 mm

NOT EDITIONED

Romany caravans rest beside a hill, while several gypsy figures tend a fire.

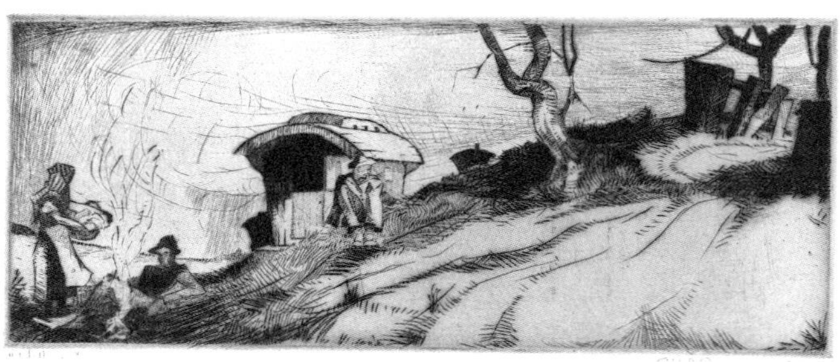

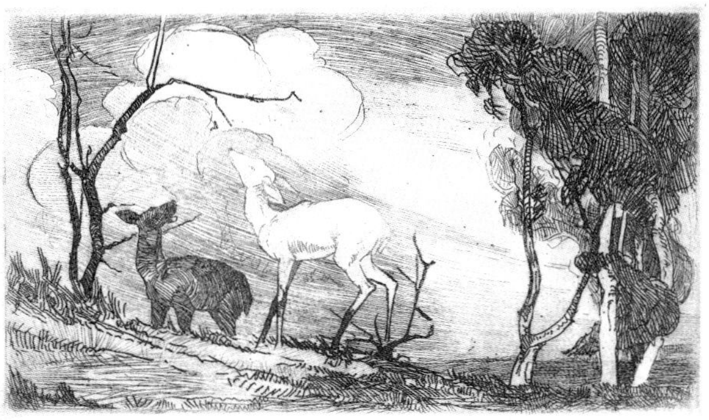

11 TOPSY AND EVA 1929

ETCHING 105 x 175 mm

NOT EDITIONED *Some printed in 1931*

Two deer. Chaplin wrote: 'My father was seriously ill when this plate was etched. He was delighted when he saw it, and at once gave it the title "Topsy and Eva".'

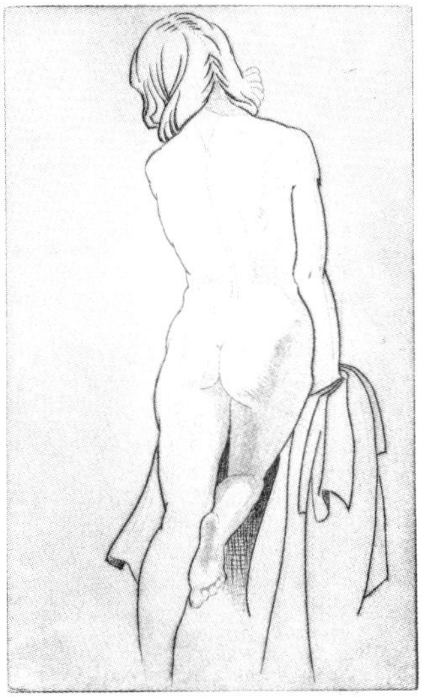

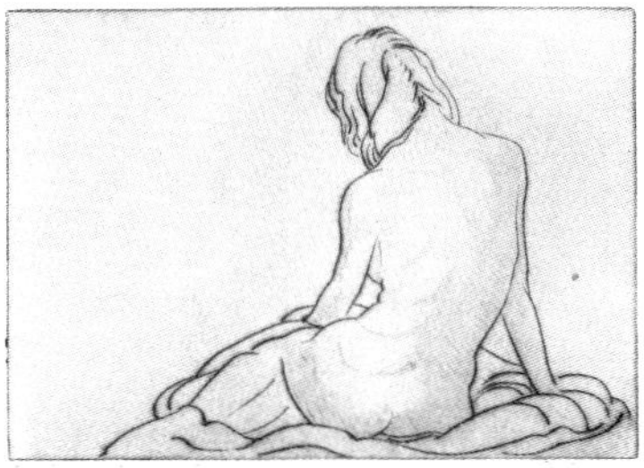

13 (Untitled) NUDE FIGURE (B) *c.* 1930

DRYPOINT 152 x 204 mm NOT EDITIONED

Study of a seated female nude facing away from the artist supported by her right arm. Life study needled direct onto copper.

12 (Untitled) NUDE FIGURE (A) *c.* 1930

DRYPOINT 248 x 145 mm

NOT EDITIONED

The standing female model faces away from the artist, her right knee in a resting position. Life study needled direct onto copper.

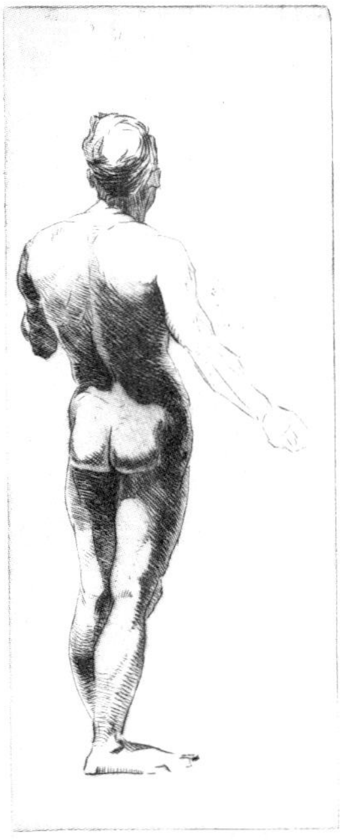

14 (Untitled) NUDE FIGURE (C) *c.* 1930

DRYPOINT 293 x 112 mm

NOT EDITIONED *Brown ink*

The standing male nude figure faces away from the artist, his right arm extended. Life study needled direct onto copper.

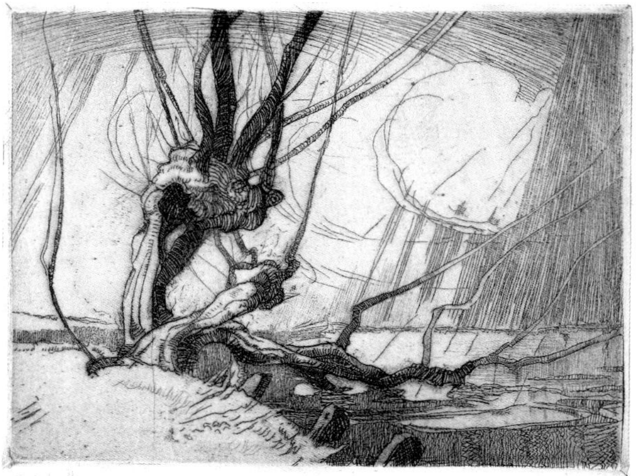

15 OLD WILLOWS *c.* 1930

Etching on zinc plate
123 x 165 mm

Not editioned

Gnarled old willow trees lean into February floodwaters as the storm passes.

16 FEBRUARY FLOODS or OLD WILLOW 1930

Etching on zinc plate
148 x 190 mm

Not editioned

A broken old willow dips into winter floodwater.

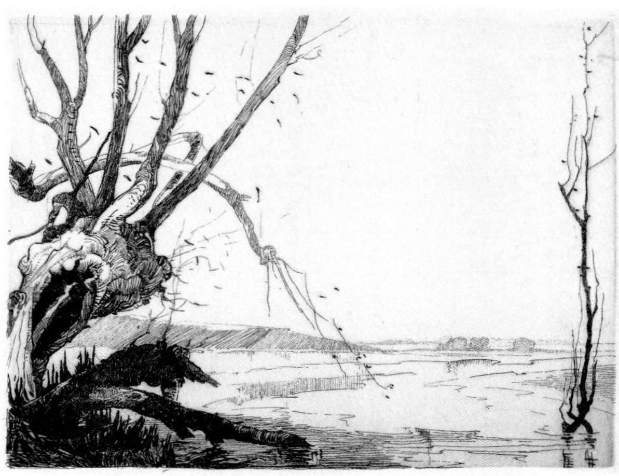

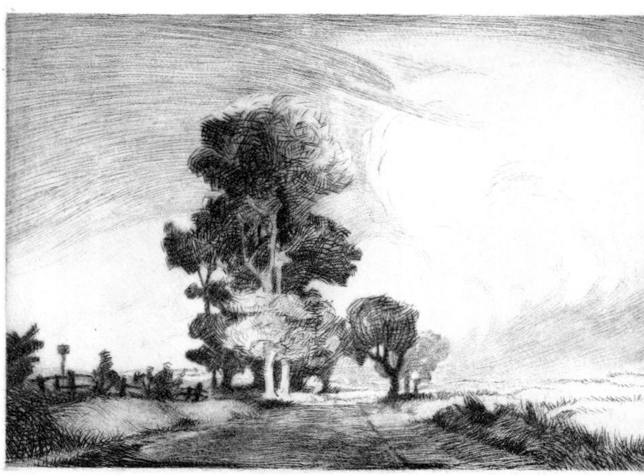

17 THE LANE 1930

Drypoint 145 x 197 mm

Not editioned *Printed on David Cox paper. Some printed 1938*

A group of tall trees tower over a remote country lane on a windy day in Summer. Needled direct onto copper.

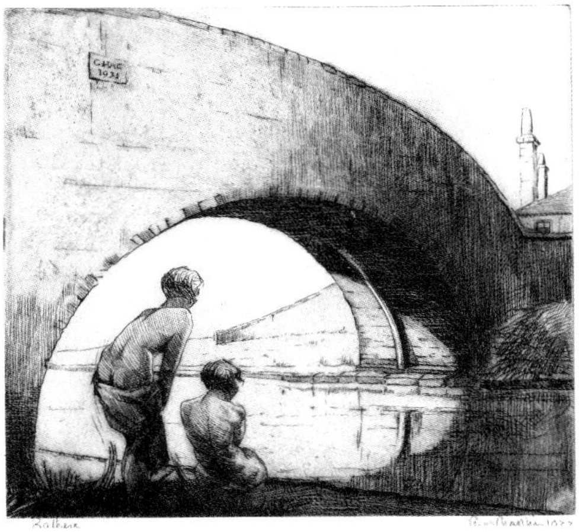

18 THE BATHERS 1931

Drypoint 189 x 207 mm

Not editioned *Brown ink. Some printed 1932*

Two naked female bathers rest on the edge of the Grand Union Canal under the arch of the bridge at Lady Capel's Wharf. The initials 'CHAC' appear on a plaque on the bridge.

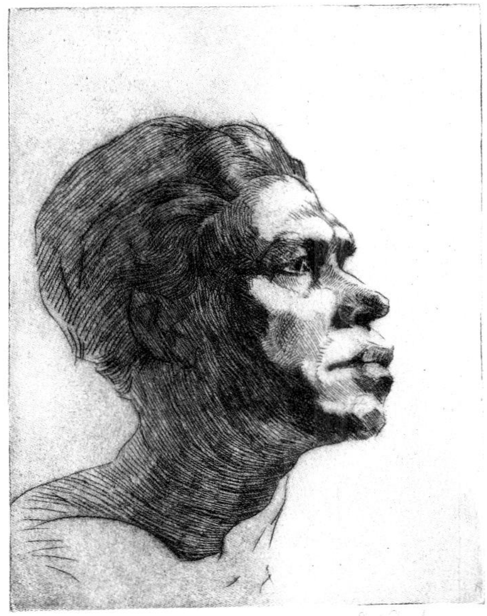

19 (Untitled) HEAD FROM LIFE 1931

Drypoint 220 x 168 mm

Not editioned

The head of a black man, drawn from life at the Watford School of Art. Needled direct onto thin copper.

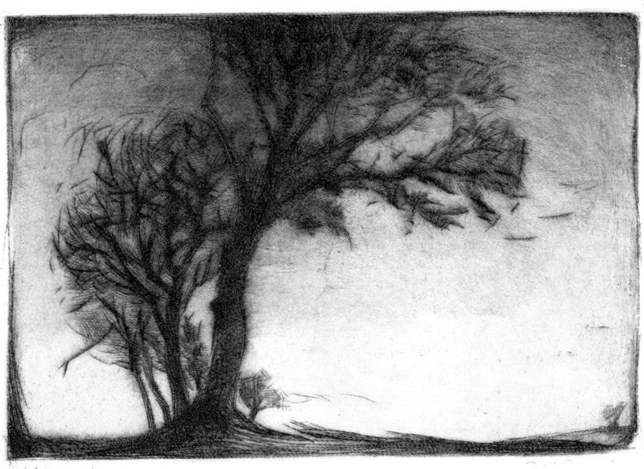

20 WINTER or TREES 1931

Drypoint 108 x 150 mm

Not editioned *Brown ink, some printed on Japanese paper*

A clump of trees needled direct onto the plate on location.

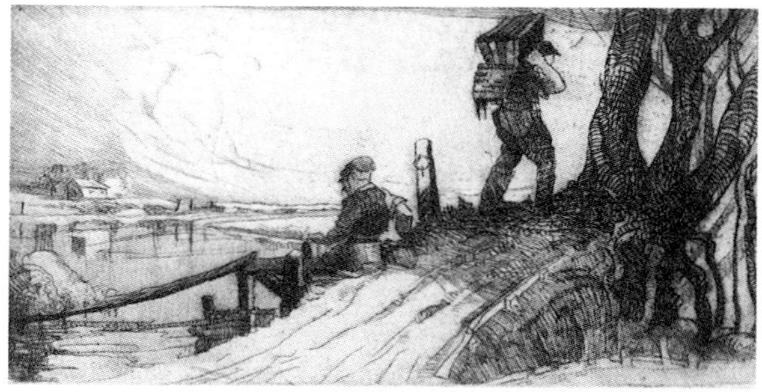

21 GATHERING WATERCRESS 1932

ETCHING 105 x 200 mm

(No print was available and the image is taken from Hilary Chapman Fine Prints, 20th Century Gallery, Exhibition Catalogue, April 2003)

A figure overlooks watercress beds to the left, whilst another figure carries baskets of watercress up a bank towards trees to the right.

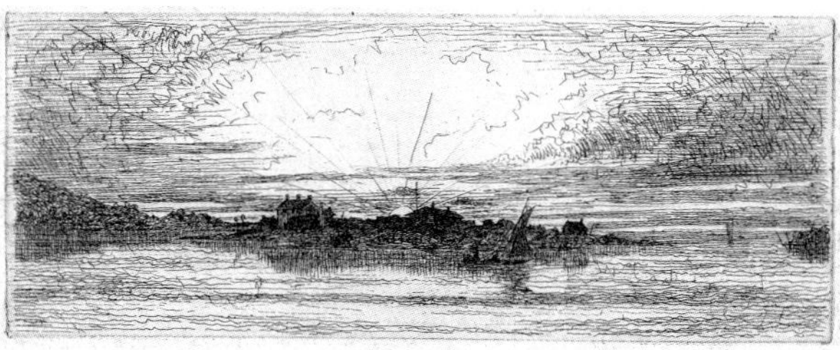

22 ST IVES 1932

ETCHING

No print can be identified with certainty. The illustration is of a small untitled work (51 x 125 mm) believed to be by the artist and which may correspond with the title 'St. Ives' recorded by him.

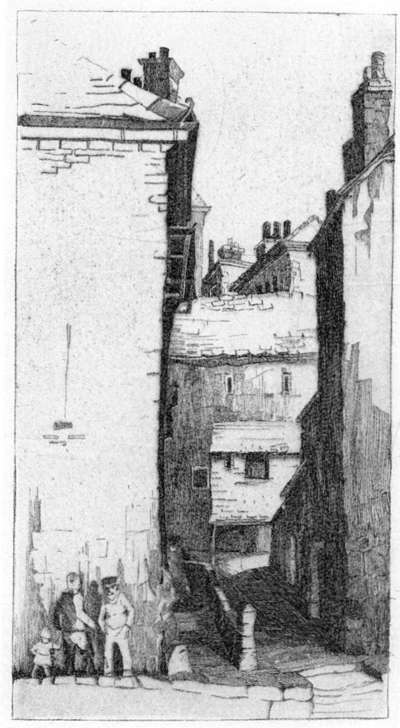

23 POLPERRO 1933

LINE ENGRAVING 195 x 100 mm

NOT EDITIONED

An alleyway between buildings in Polperro, Cornwall, with two figures and a child.

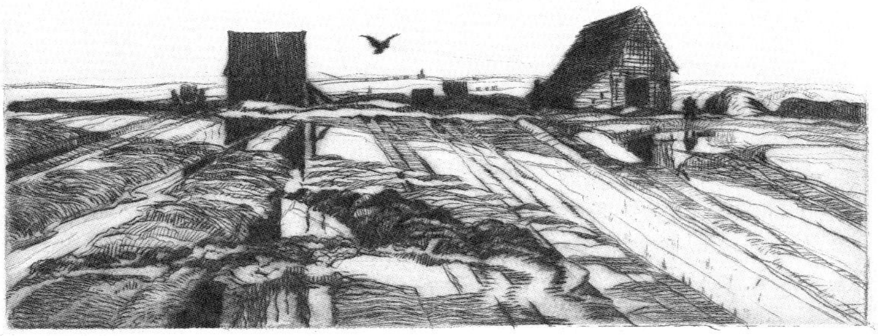

24 SEWER FARM, WATFORD 1936

Drypoint 86 x 220 mm

Not editioned *Brown ink*

A view over the sewer farm, Watford, with two buildings and a bird of prey hovering. The work done on the spot direct onto copper.

25 SEWER FARM *c.* 1936

Drypoint 167 x 248 mm

Not editioned *Brown ink*

Another view of the sewer farm, Watford, with the Sun Engraving Co. printing factory in the background

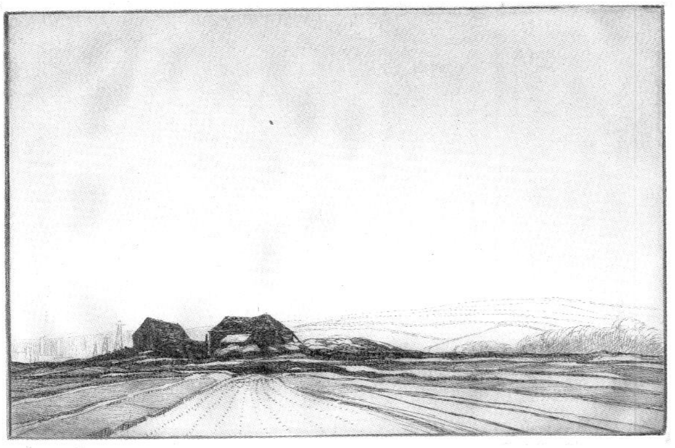

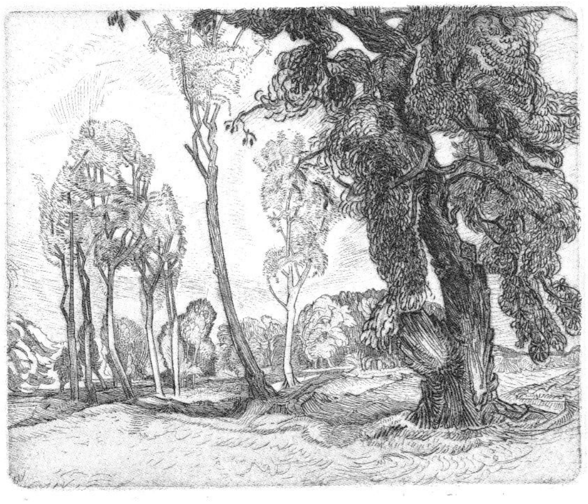

26 CASSIOBURY PARK, WATFORD 1937

Etching and engraving 147 x 175 mm

Not editioned *Printed in brown ink*

A scene of trees in the park which, the artist noted, started as a sketch direct onto the copper, later finished with a graver.

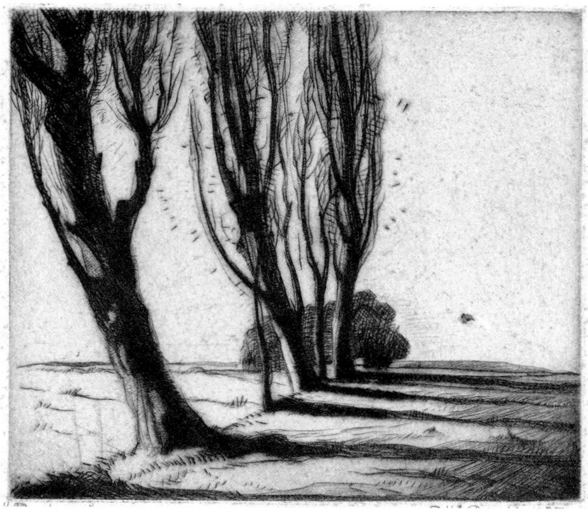

27 POPLARS 1937

DRYPOINT 156 x 175 mm

NOT EDITIONED *Printed in brown ink*

A row of poplar trees, with a wooded copse behind.

28 BRIDGE 1937

LINE ENGRAVING 98 x 112 mm

NOT EDITIONED *1st state view only, illustrated. 2nd state engraved 'Christmas Greetings from Mr and Mrs C H A Chaplin and Jon, Xmas 1937, 19 Highfield Way, Rickmansworth, Herts', and including birds, telephone wires and additional working of fields and trees.*

A small plate showing the bridge in Moor Lane, Rickmansworth, near the former isolation hospital.

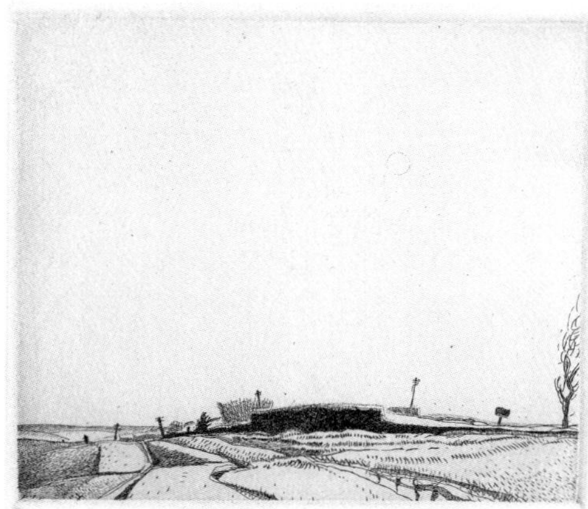

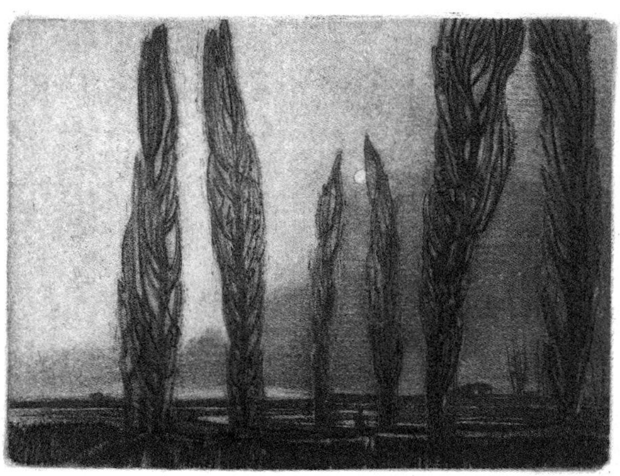

29 PEEPING MOON 1938

SOFT GROUND ETCHING 167 x 220 mm

NOT EDITIONED

The moon peeps through a row of poplar trees in a lakeside setting.

30 WINTER SUN or CASSIOBURY PARK BRIDGE 1938

LINE ENGRAVING 90 x 182 mm

EDITION 30 *Printed in brown inks, and blue*

EXHIBITED CPE Toronto, 1951, No. 22

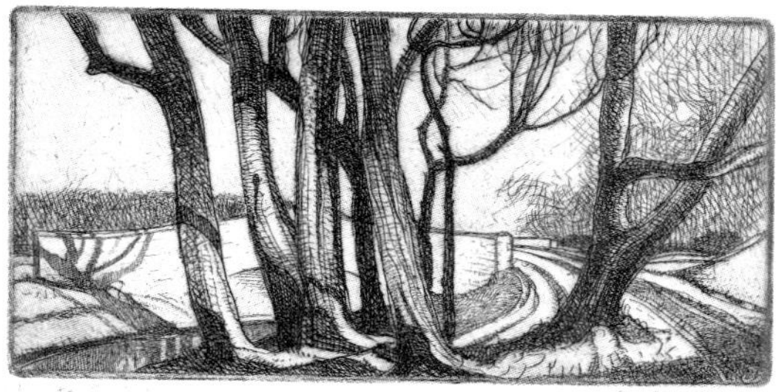

Trees in the foreground throw shadows in the winter sun onto the bridge over the Grand Union Canal in Cassiobury Park, Watford. This plate was commended in *The Artist*, 1938.

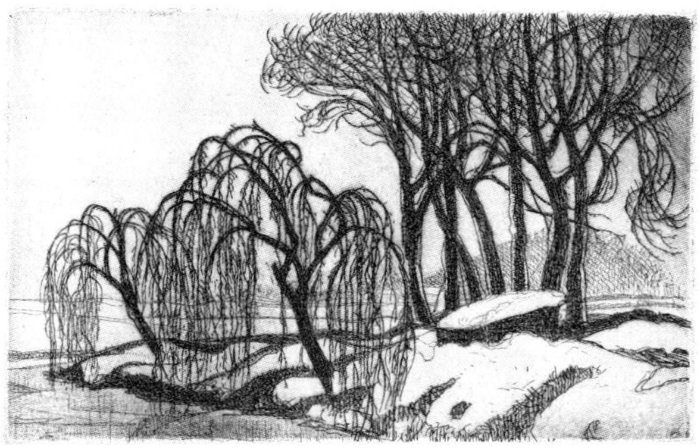

31 MELTING SNOW 1939

ETCHING AND AQUATINT 112 x 172 mm

EDITION 30 *Some Printed in blue ink*

EXHIBITED Royal Academy, 1939, No. 947

Willow and other trees in deep snow in Cassiobury Park, Watford. This plate was the first by the artist to be accepted for the Summer Exhibition at the Royal Academy. In the subsequent years to 1984 a further 32 of the artist's prints were hung in the Summer Exhibition.

32 BINDING REEDS 1939

LINE ENGRAVING 162 x 146 mm

EDITION 30

EXHIBITED Götene, Sweden 1975

The title is engraved at the foot of the image.

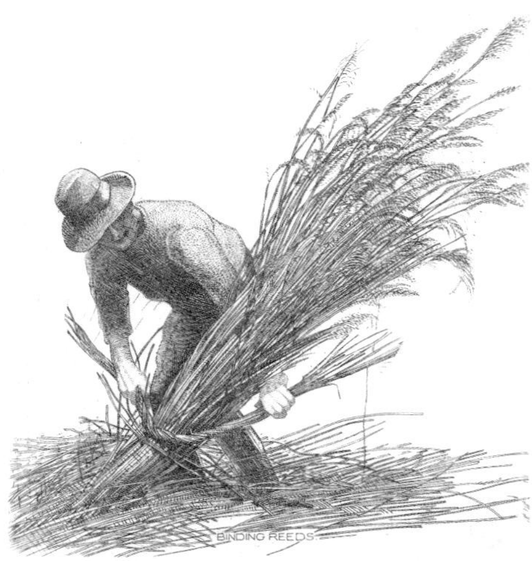

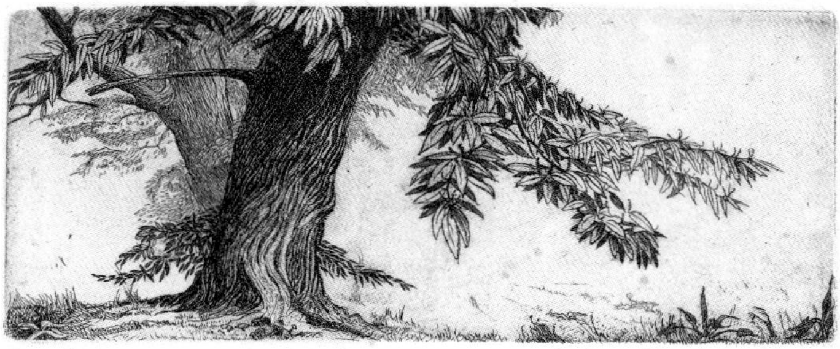

33 SWEET CHESTNUT or SPANISH CHESTNUT 1940

ETCHING AND ENGRAVING 90 x 216 mm

NOT EDITIONED *Printed in brown inks*

EXHIBITED Götene 1975

ILLUSTRATED *Leader Magazine*, 28 May 1949 Vol 6, No. 30, p. 3

The trunk of a sweet chestnut in bloom. The artist noted that a sketch was made on a waxed ground on copper on location, and engraved work added later.

34 RYE, SUSSEX 1940

ETCHING AND LINE ENGRAVING 94 x 275 mm

EDITION 30 *Some prints on 18th-century paper*

Barns and willow trees in Rye, Sussex.

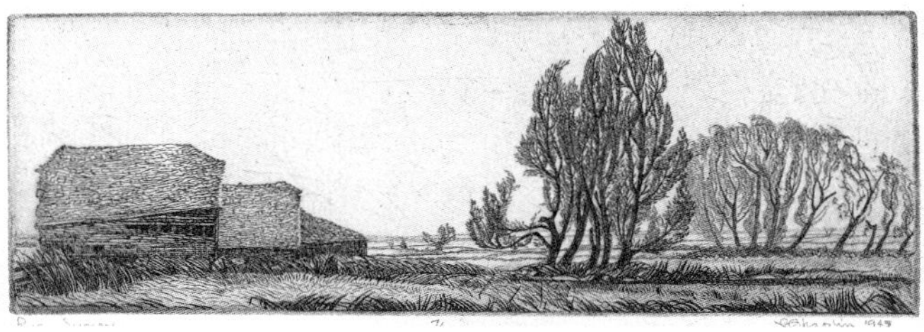

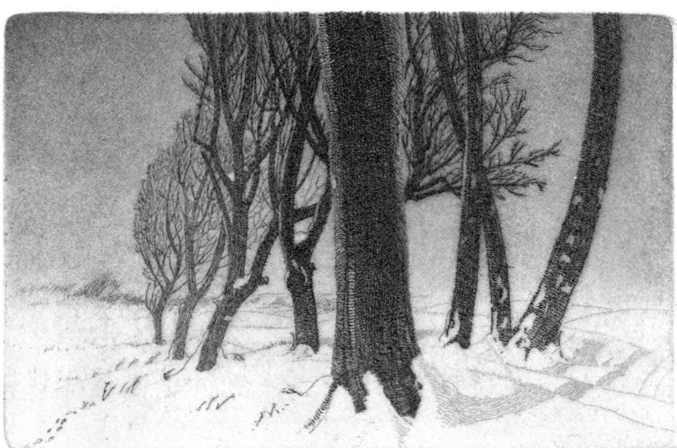

35 WINTER or WINTER SNOW, CASSIOBURY PARK 1940

ETCHING AND AQUATINT 138 x 206 mm

EDITION 30 *Some printed on 18th-century paper. Some printed on Japanese tissue*

EXHIBITED Royal Academy, 1940, No. 1373: CPE Toronto, 1950, No. 21: RE, 1951, No. 47

The trees in snow in Cassiobury Park, Watford were needled direct on waxed copper on location. The second print of the artist to be exhibited at the RA Summer Exhibition.

36 OLD JOE 1940

LINE ENGRAVING 160 x 147 mm (1st state 1940*)

EDITION 30 *The image illustrated is printed on Japanese paper*

ILLUSTRATED *West Herts Post*, 29 April 1943

An old farm worker in Chorleywood sharpens his scythe on a hard stone.

* In the final state the handle of the scythe has been completed, and the foliage has been developed and added to the right.

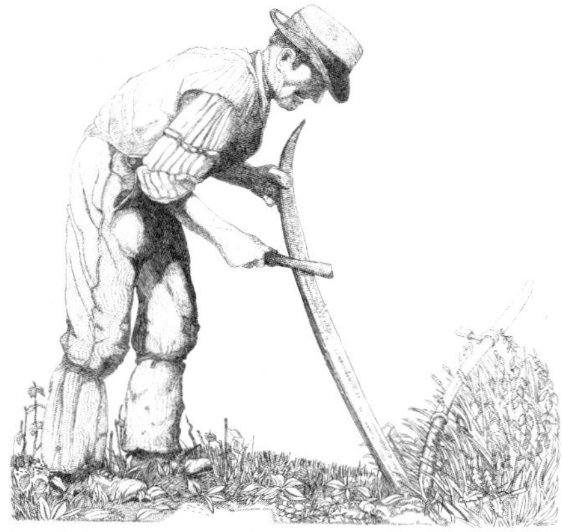

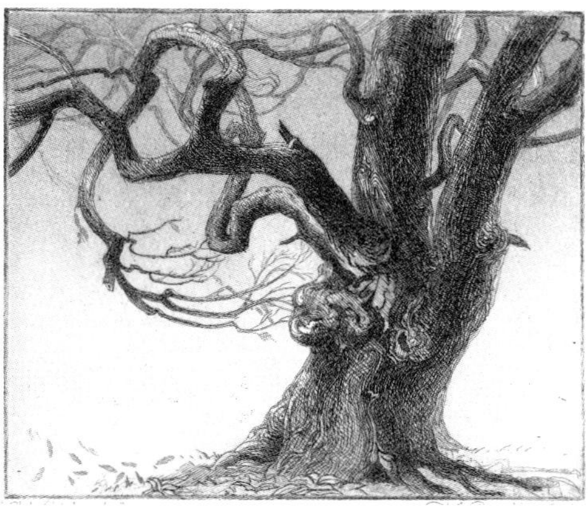

37 OLD CHESTNUT 1941

ETCHING 154 x 173 mm

EDITION 30

A chestnut tree in winter.

38 WATERY SUN 1942

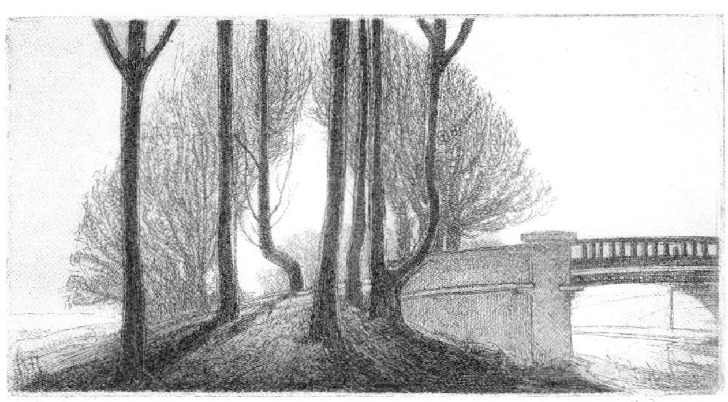

ETCHING 124 x 230 mm

NOT EDITIONED *Printed on duck egg blue paper in blue black ink*

Watery winter sunlight filters through trees around canal bridge no. 168 leading to Rousebarn Lane, Cassiobury Park, Watford. The image was needled direct onto waxed copper plate held in the hand whilst standing at the location, subsequently finished in the studio; the image is a 'mirror' image as it was not etched in reverse.

39 SILVER BIRCHES AND SNOW 1943

ETCHING AND AQUATINT
162 x 183 mm

NOT EDITIONED *Some prints on 18th-century paper*

Silver birches in a misty snow-covered wood.

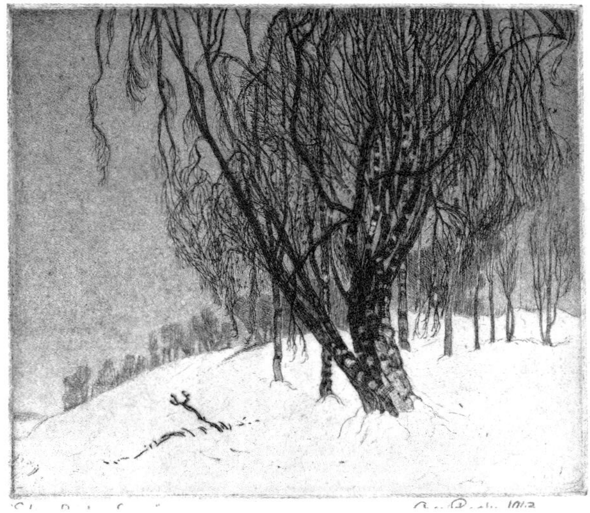

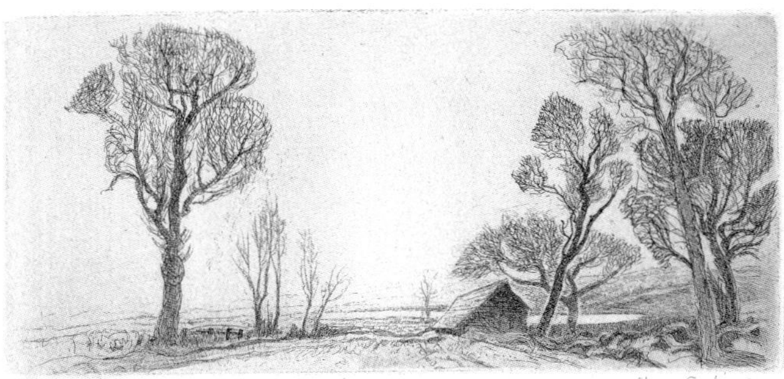

40 MISTY MORNING 1943

ETCHING, SKETCHED ON TO COPPER 120 x 248 mm

EDITION 30

EXHIBITED Royal Academy, 1943, No. 788

A barn set among trees by Brightwell's Farm, West Watford. A fellow artist described this as the most expressive plate the artist had done.

41 WILLOWS 1943

ETCHING WITH AQUATINT GROUND 143 x 215 mm

NOT EDITIONED *Some prints on 18th-century paper*

Five willow trees with misty sun.

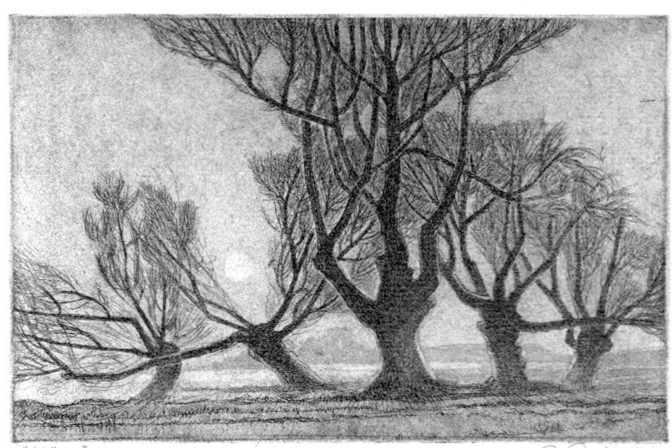

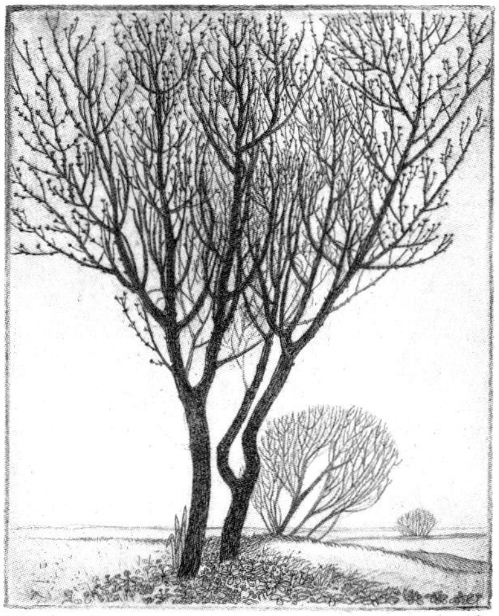

42 SPRING 1943

LINE ENGRAVING 200 x 155 mm

NOT EDITIONED *Printed in brown ink*

Two trees bursting into bud.

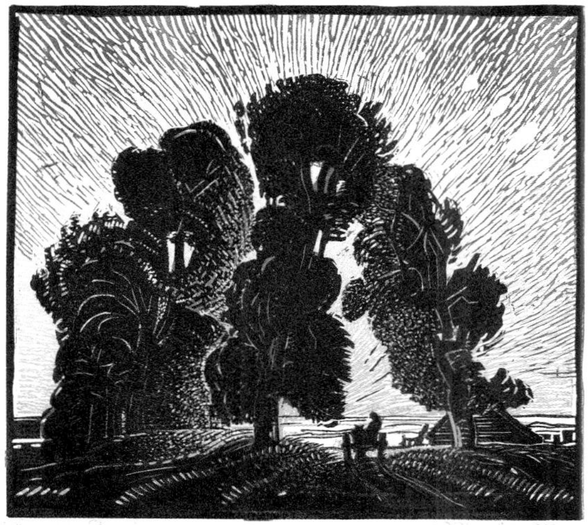

43 EVENING GLOW 1944

LINOCUT, 3 COLOURS 192 x 212 mm

NOT EDITIONED

The sun sets behind tall trees as a horsecart and driver wend their way home.

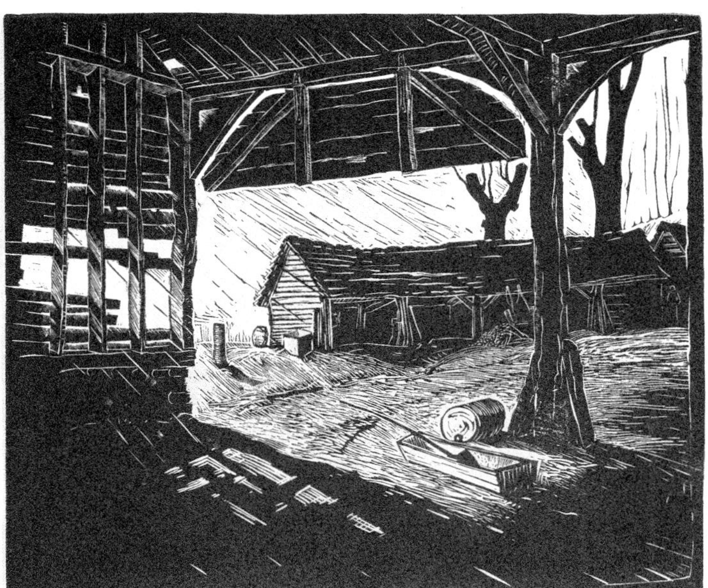

44 BARNS 1944

LINOCUT, 2 COLOURS 240 x 280 mm

NOT EDITIONED

Some wooden barns seen from the inside at Brightwell's Farm, West Watford.

45 THE WAY HOME 1944

ETCHING 134 x 177 mm

EDITION 30 *Grey ink on blue paper*

Trees surrounding a canal bridge in Cassiobury park, Watford, the same bridge as that portrayed in 'Cassiobury Park Bridge' (30).

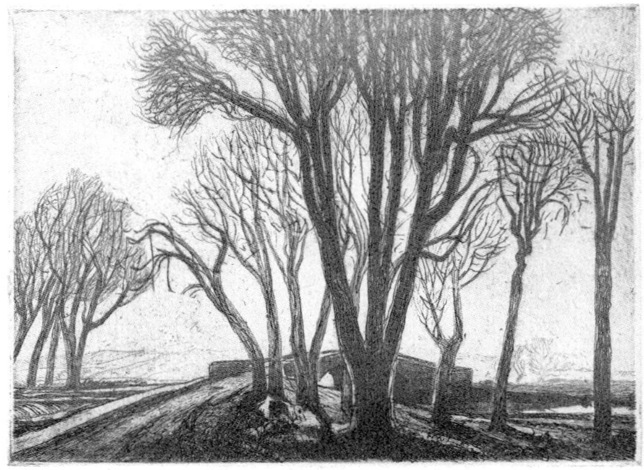

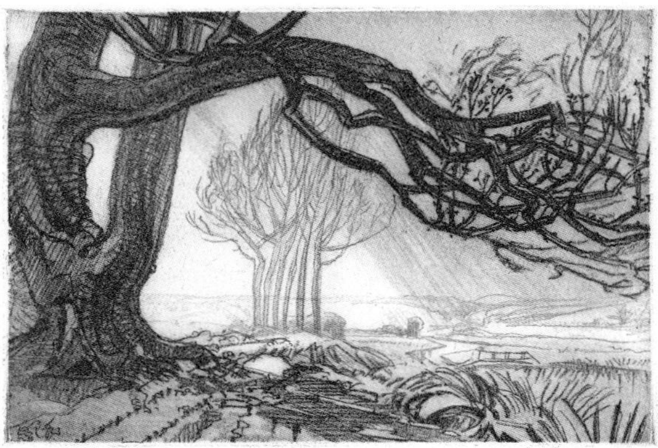

46 SUNSHINE WIND AND RAIN 1945

SOFT GROUND ETCHING AND AQUATINT 143 x 208 mm

NOT EDITIONED

A large tree overlooks the river, with a footbridge over the River Colne in North Watford. Sunshine emerges after a heavy rainfall. The image was drawn direct onto the waxed plate through tissue paper with a pencil.

47 HOAR FROST 1945

ETCHING AND ENGRAVING 173 x 135 mm

EDITION 30

A tree in frosty weather.

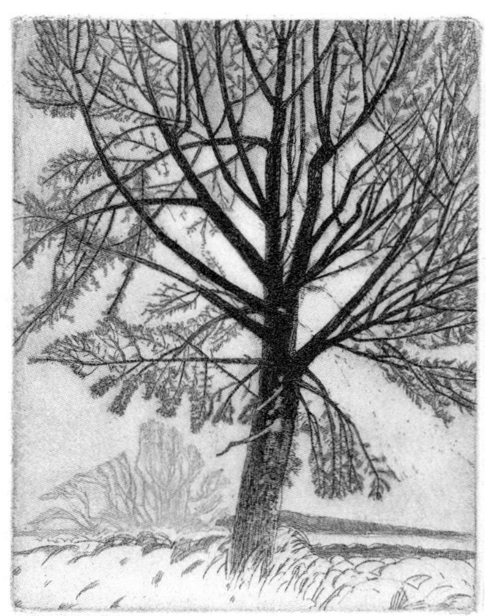

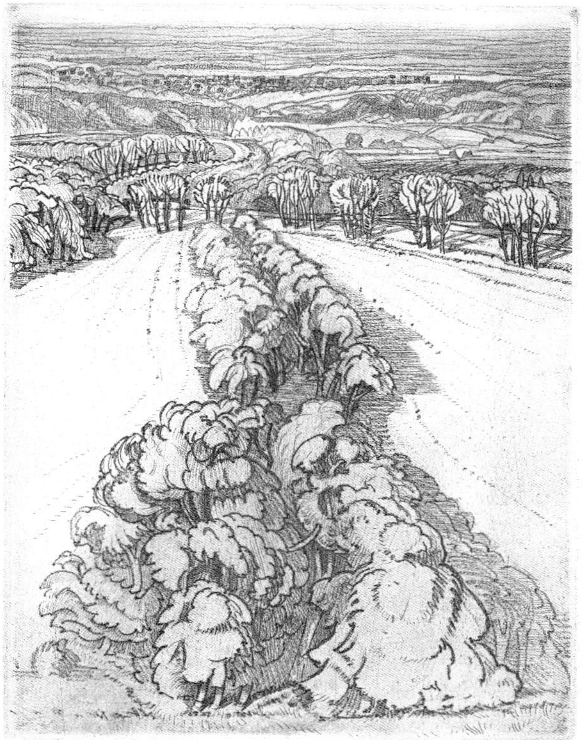

48 VIEW FROM BRUNSWICK TOWER
1945

Soft ground etching and engraving 200 x 150 mm

Not editioned

The view from Brunswick Tower, Windsor Castle, was drawn whilst the artist was on duty there for the Royal Observer Corps during the war.

49 STOCKERS FARM or BARNS 1945

Etching direct on copper 140 x 195 mm

Not editioned

Mirror image of group of barns at Stockers Farm, Rickmansworth.

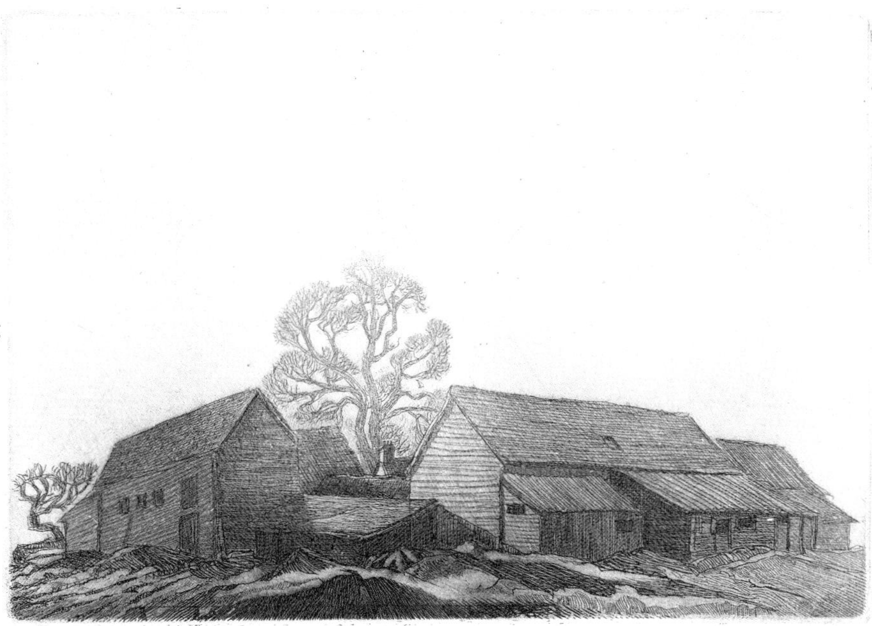

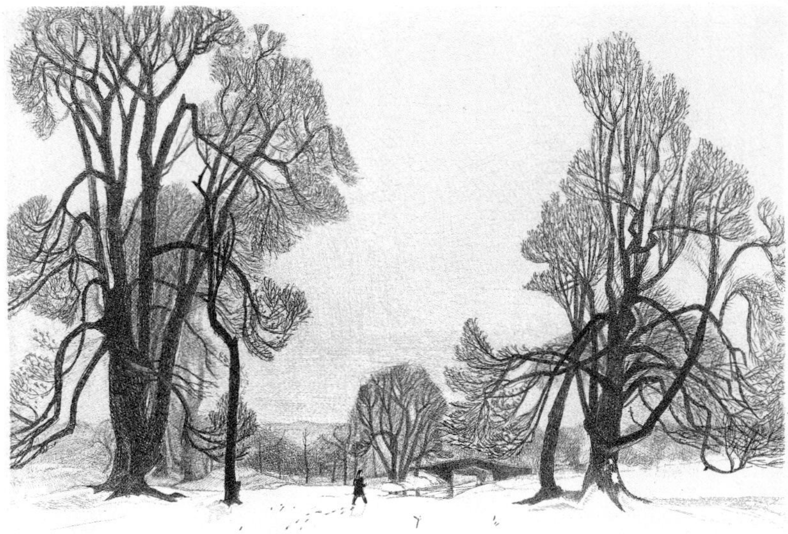

50 WINTER, CASSIOBURY PARK BRIDGE 1945

ETCHING 1st state 173 x 322 mm:* final 173 x 248 mm (illustrated)

NOT EDITIONED *Printed in different colours. Some printed in 1951*

Exhibited Götene, 1975

Cassiobury Park, Watford in deep snow, with large trees to left and right and a bridge in the distance, centre. A small figure of a woman approaches the bridge leaving footprints in the snow.

* In the final state the copper plate has been reduced by 54 mm on the left and 20 mm on the right, curtailing branches of the trees on either side.

51 TREE TOPS AND SNOW OR RICKY PARK 1945

ETCHING AND AQUATINT 147 x 200 mm

NOT EDITIONED

Trees laden with snow in Rickmansworth Park.

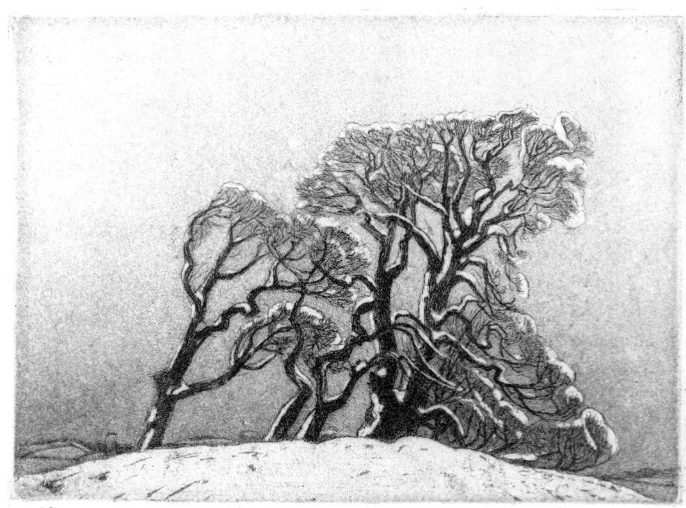

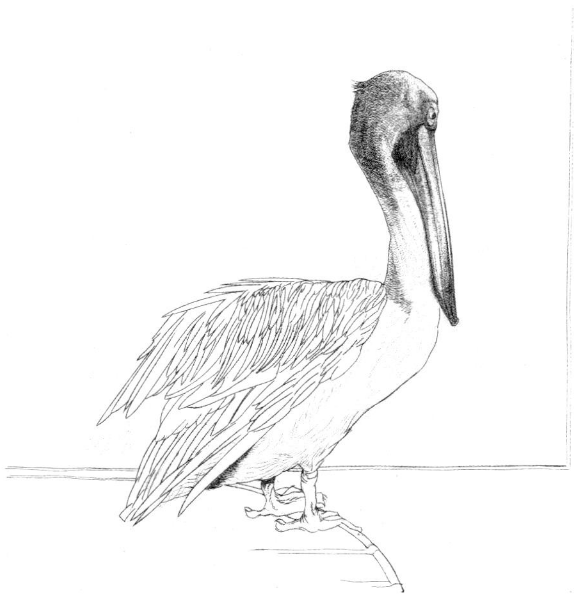

52 PELICAN 1946

LINE ENGRAVING 188 x 170 mm

EDITION 30

The subject, the first of a number of animal, bird and insect studies undertaken following his enrolment at the Royal College of Art, appears not to have been completed, although the artist signed all copies of the limited edition.

53 Untitled 1946

SOFT GROUND ETCHING
167 x 220 mm

NOT EDITIONED

The moon shines through cloud onto a group of poplar trees along a river bank.

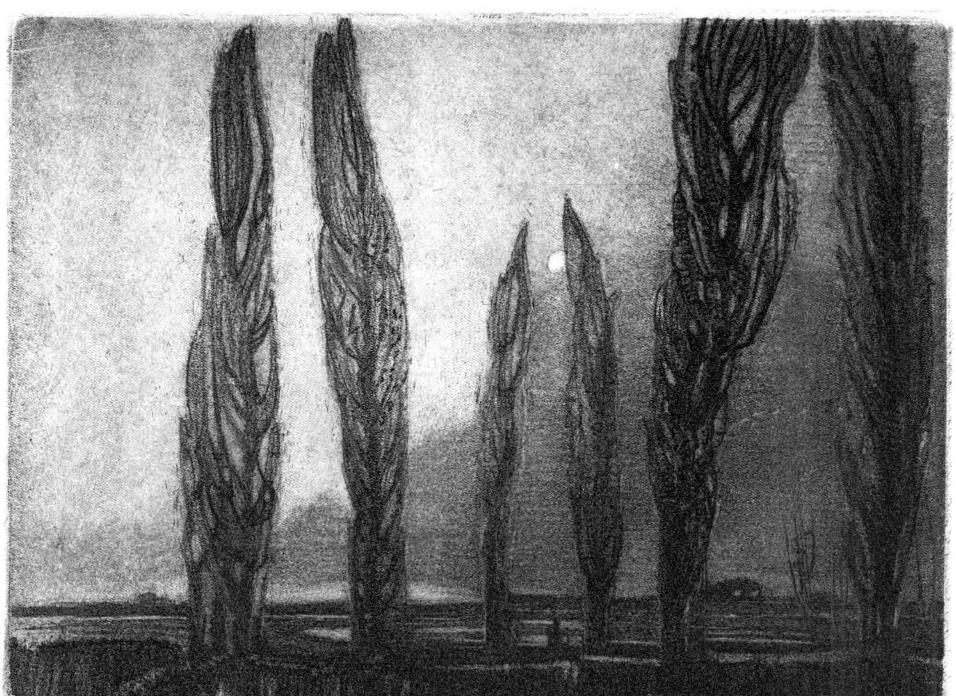

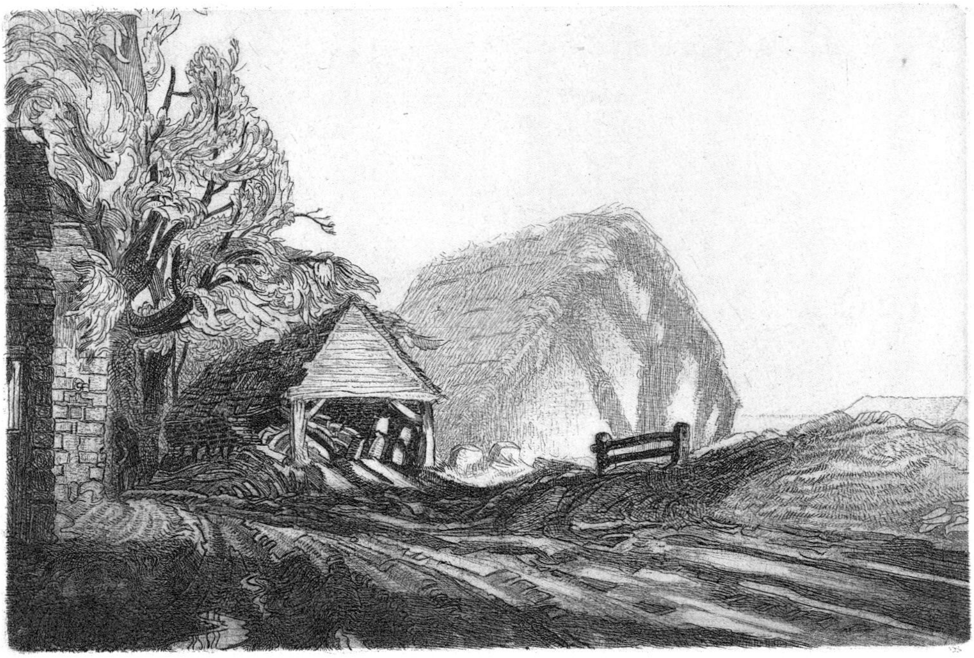

54 EVENING 1946

LINE ENGRAVING 185 x 266 mm

EDITION 30 *Printed in red/brown inks. Print illustrated is printed on Japanese tissue*

Long evening shadows over farm buildings and a haystack at Gough's Farm in Northchapel, near Petworth, Sussex. A plate rich in personal memories of the artist recorded on the back of a proof.

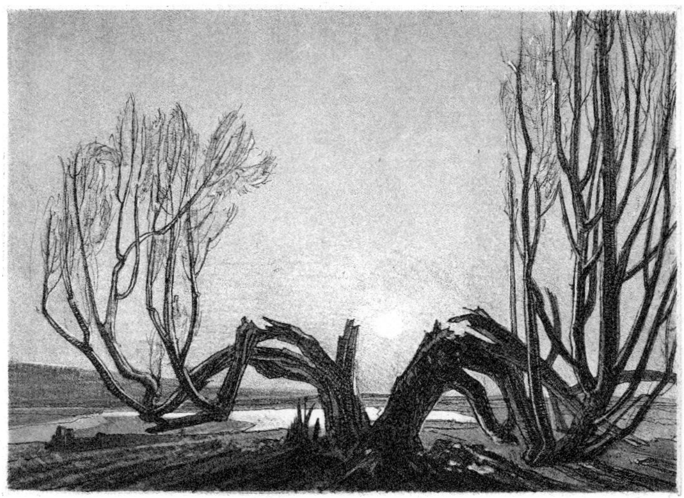

55 SPLIT WILLOW 1946

SOFT GROUND ETCHING 173 x 237 mm

NOT EDITIONED

EXHIBITED CPE, Toronto, 1950, No. 17

The misty morning sun peers through the boughs of a split willow near Moor Lane, Rickmansworth.

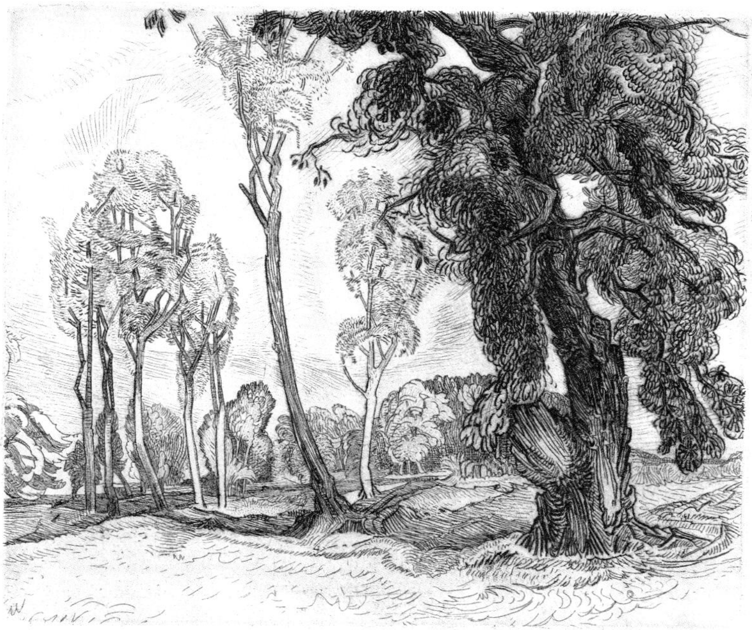

56 TREES IN SUMMER

1946

Line engraving

152 x 176 mm

Edition 30

Printed in brown inks

A view of trees in a park.

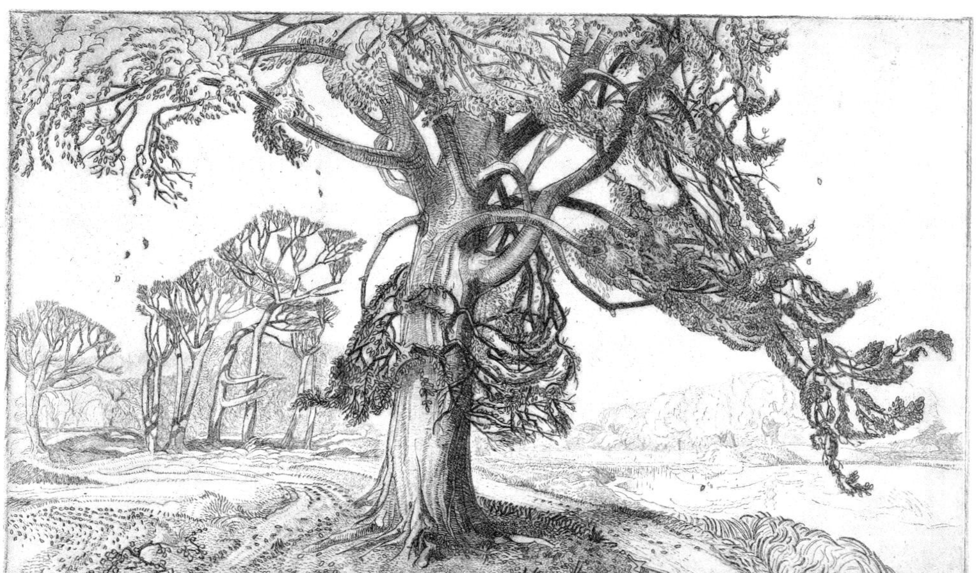

57 EARLY AUTUMN 1946

Engraving 204 x 337 mm

Edition 20

A large tree in Cassiobury Park, Watford.

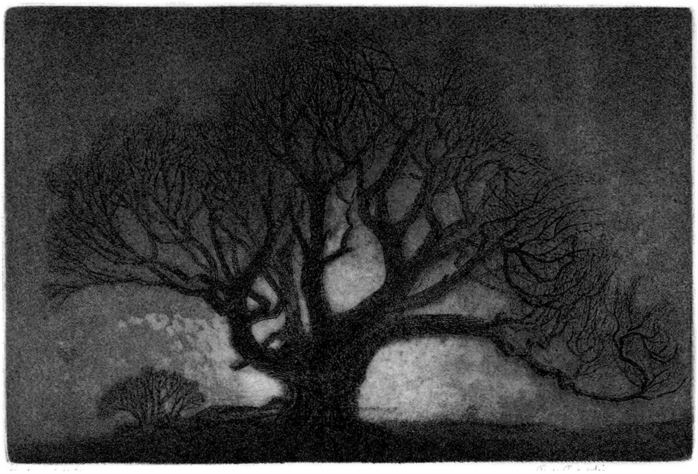

58 MYSTERY OF NIGHT *c.* 1947

ETCHING AND AQUATINT 183 x 265 mm NOT EDITIONED

EXHIBITED CPE, Toronto, 1950, No. 18

An old chestnut tree silhouetted against the moon's light in Cassionbury Park, Watford. The etching was needled direct onto copper, aquatint ground added later, with a few touches with a graver.

59 COLESHILL POND 1947

ETCHING AND LINE ENGRAVING

EDITION 30 *(No print of this plate was available for illustration but see sketch on p. 38)*

EXHIBITED Royal Academy, 1947, No. 1009: CPE Toronto, 1951, No. 23

Coleshill pond, Amersham. Completed whilst studying at the Royal College of Art.

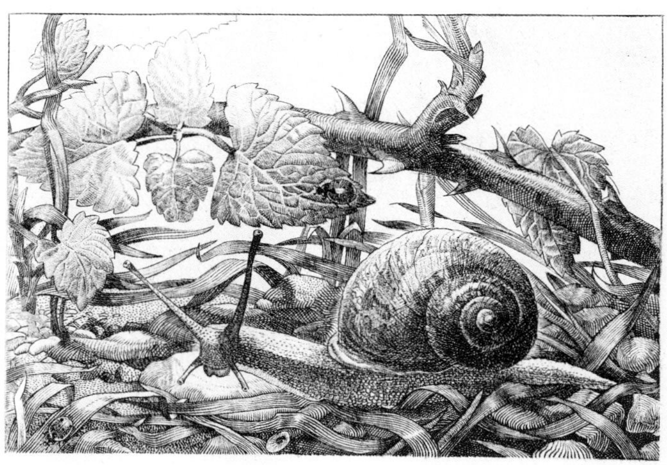

60 GARDEN SNAIL 1947

LINE ENGRAVING

65 x 94 mm

EDITION 75 *Some printed 1950*

EXHIBITED RE, 1950, No. 231

A snail makes its way past a bramble, with ladybirds.

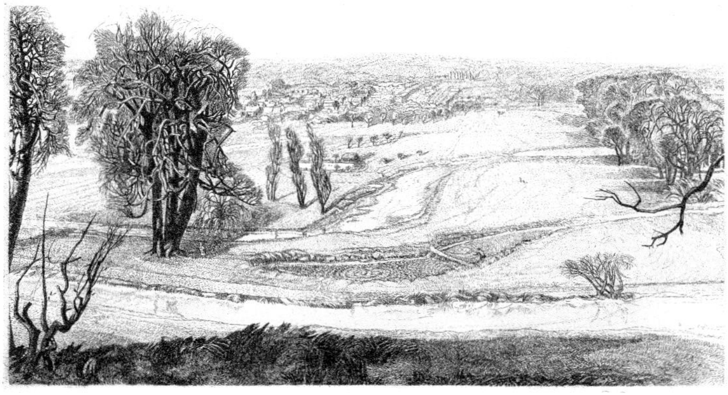

61 CASSIOBURY PARK, VIEW FROM GOLF COURSE 1947

LINE ENGRAVING 173 x 317 mm

EDITION 30

Behind the canal in Cassiobury Park, Watford lies the river Gade, and the paddling pool in the park. A group of horse chestnut trees dominates the left of the image. A number of tiny figures can be found in this landscape, a feature which was to develop in later work. Mr Sampson works on his watercress beds. The plate was completed while a student at the RCA.

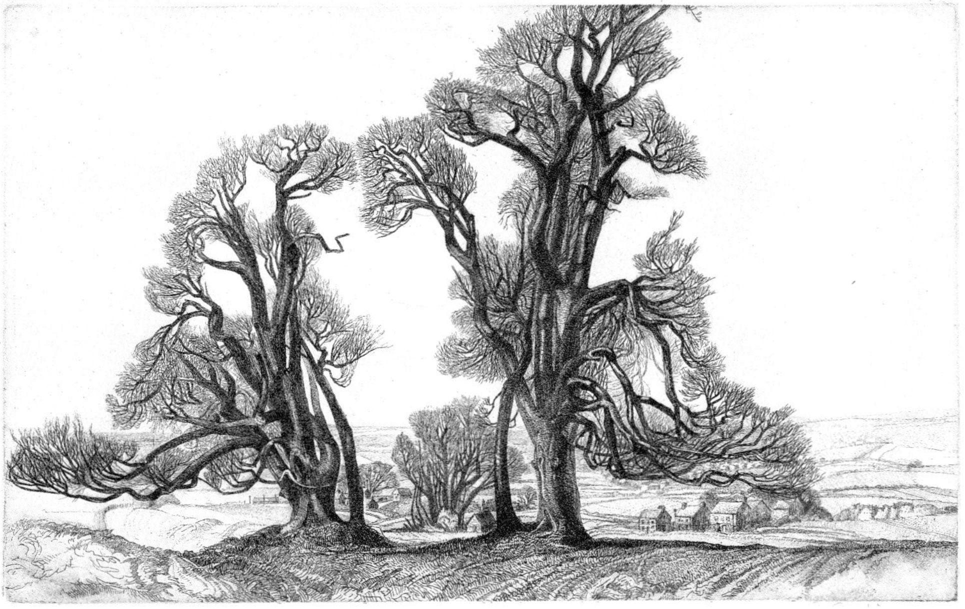

62 CLOSE FRIENDS 1948

ETCHING 196 x 300 mm

EDITION 10 *Further edition of 30*

Two large trees on Kings Langley Common seem to be in conversation.

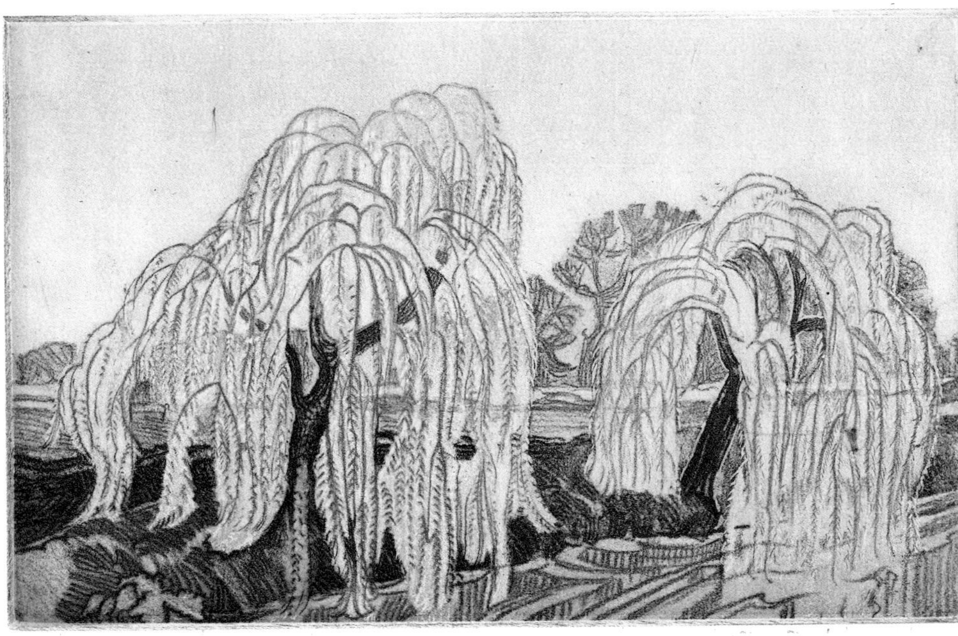

63 WILLOWS, CASSIOBURY 1948

SOFT GROUND ETCHING AND AQUATINT 155 x 235 mm NOT EDITIONED

Willow trees weep into the river in Cassiobury Park, Watford.

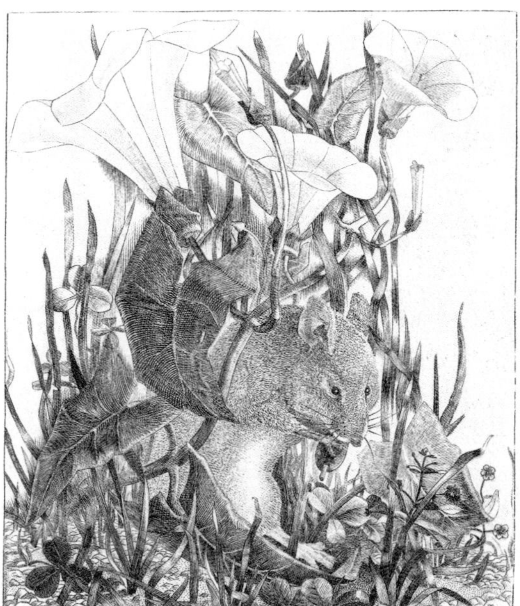

64 FIELD MOUSE or MOUSE 1948

LINE ENGRAVING 103 x 83 mm

EDITION 30 *1st state. Final state 1948*

EXHIBITED Royal Academy, 1948, No. 1142: CPE, 1949: Götene, 1975

ILLUSTRATED Catalogue, Ontario Royal Museum Exhibition, 1949

A field mouse feeds on a berry. A number of identifiable wild plants appear, a characteristic which developed much in future work. This was the artist's first completed engraving whilst a student at the RCA. A large leaf over the mouse in the 1st State is replaced in the final engraving by another flower.

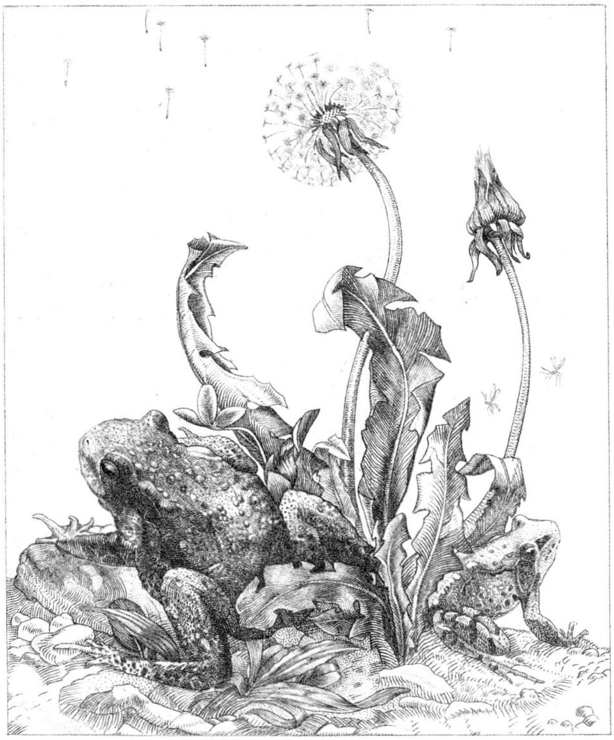

65 FROG AND TOAD
1948

Line engraving

127 x 102 mm

Edition 30

Exhibited RE, 1950, No. 207: Götene, 1975

The toad to the left and the frog to the right of a dandelion clock. Completed whilst a student at the RCA.

66 WREN 1948

Line engraving

90 x 88 mm

Edition 30

Exhibited Götene, 1975

A wren perched on a twig from a larch tree. Also buttercups, dandelions seed, rye grass and wood millet.

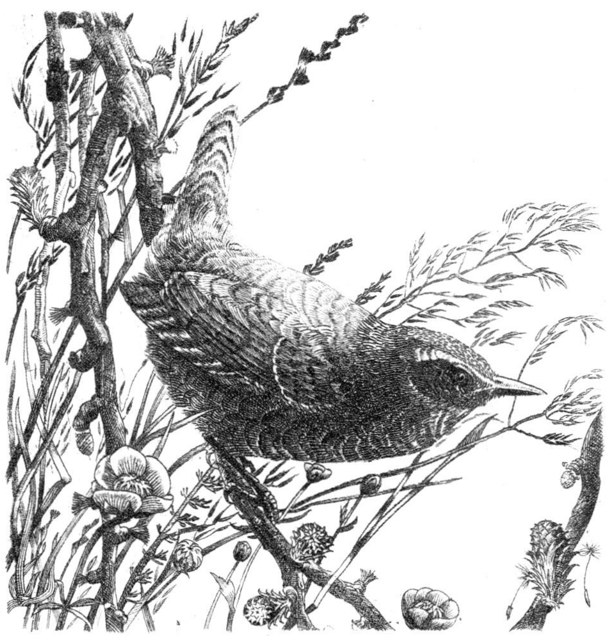

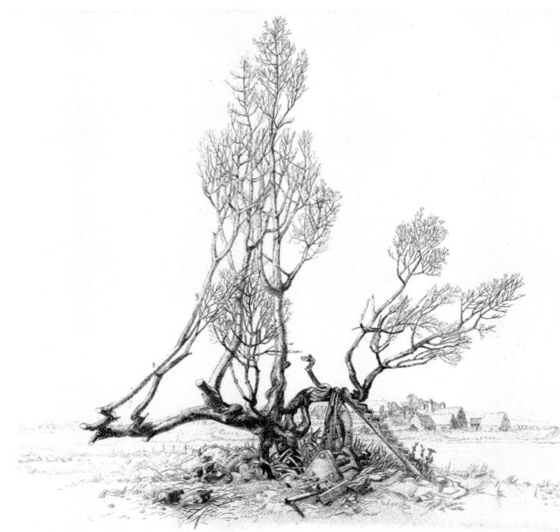

67 FARM CORNER (Dickens Farm) 1948

LINE ENGRAVING 175 x 180 mm

EDITION 30

EXHIBITED Royal Academy, 1948, No. 1132: RE, 1950, No. 87 and CPE, Hamilton, 1949: CPE Archive Exhibition, Hamilton, 1978: Götene, 1975

COLLECTIONS Archives Collection of the CPE, No. 30

ILLUSTRATED Reproduced in *Artviews* (Toronto, Canada), Vol. 4, No. 5, November/ December 1978, reviewing the CPE Exhibition in Hamilton.

Dickens Farm, Chorleywood can be seen in the distance behind an old tree. This was the artist's presentation print to the Society of Canadian Painter-Etchers and Engravers in 1949. The artist said of this print: 'Farm Corner, so far as I remember, was about my third completely engraved plate, where I started to design and engrave various isolated subjects, — i.e. young ash tree, various incidental odds and ends, and farm buildings, to make one subject. I have continued and enlarged on this practice of engraving old tools and machines from various farms and museums and now have a number of such plates.' In the collection of the author, there is a print of this plate annotated as having been printed by Robert Austin at the Royal College of Art.

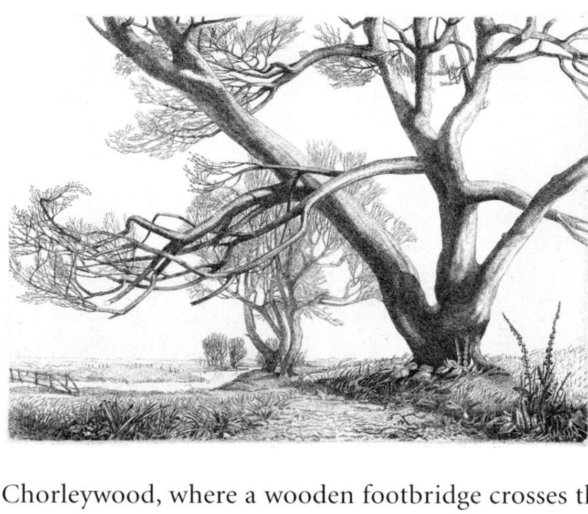

68 EARLY SPRING or TREES ON THE CHESS 1948

LINE ENGRAVING 143 x 187 mm

EDITION 50 *extended to 75*

EXHIBITED CPE, 1950, Toronto, No. 20: CPE Archives exhibition, Hamilton, 1978

COLLECTION Archives Collection of the CPE, No. 31

ILLUSTRATED *SK Araborgs Länstidning*, 20 May 1975

An ash tree near the River Chess, Chorleywood, where a wooden footbridge crosses the river and foxgloves bloom. Diploma plate for the artist's Associateship of the CPE 1950, and Honorary Members' Print 1950.

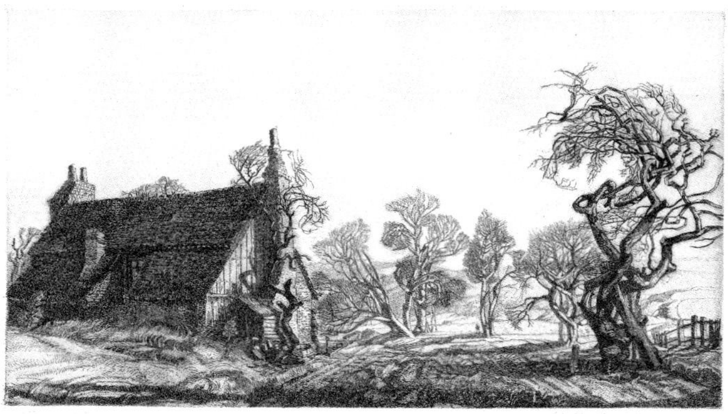

69 EVENING LIGHT — CHESS VALLEY 1948

LINE ENGRAVING
185 x 325 mm

EDITION 20

EXHIBITED CPE Toronto, 1950, No. 19

A farm worker's cottage overlooks the Chess Valley near Chorleywood where the trees cast long shadows over the fields. Engraved whilst a student at the Royal College of Art.

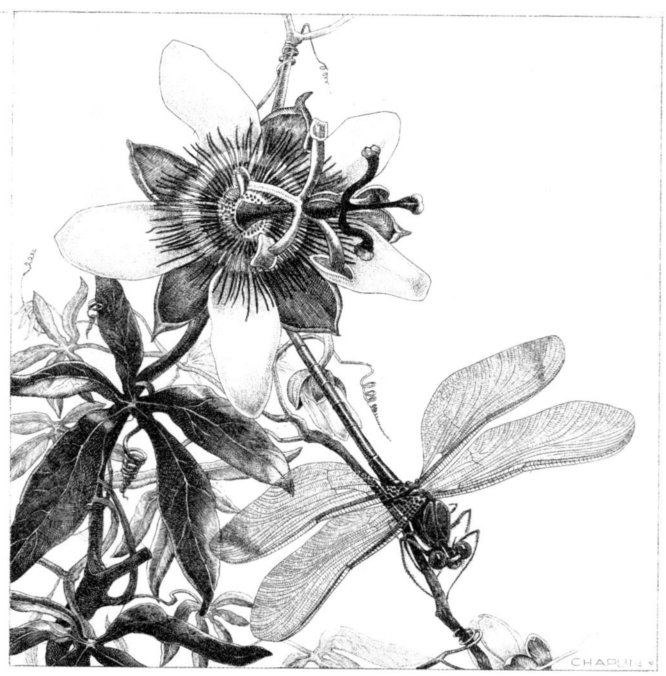

70 DRAGONFLY & PASSION FLOWER 1949

LINE ENGRAVING
125 x 120 mm

EDITION 30

ILLUSTRATED *Picture Post*, 28 May 1949, Vol. 43, No.9

EXHIBITED Götene 1979: RE, 1950 No.93

A dragonfly, wings extended, rests on the stem of a passion flower plant immediately below a passion flower fully open. The artist's name is engraved bottom right. The artist noted: 'Dragonflies of all shapes and sizes are often found in my garden. This one was sketched without any previous drawings direct onto copper plate, then engraved. This was also the method used for the Passion Flower, said to have religious significance. The white petals represent the Apostles, rays of the corona, the crown of thorns; 5 anthers, the wounds; 3 stigmas, the nails; the coiling tendrils, the whips; and the five lobed leaves, the cruel hands.'

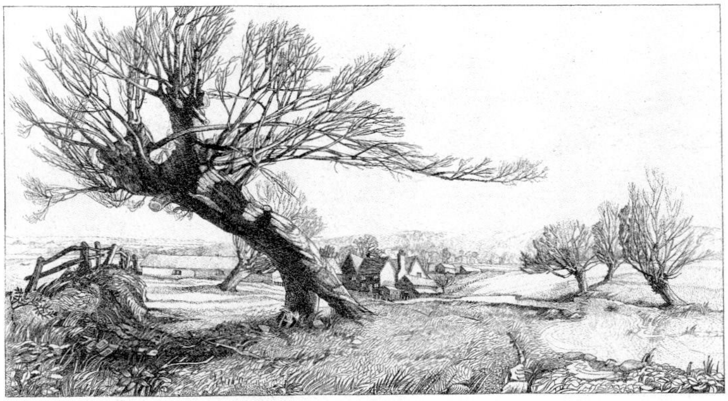

71 CHESS VALLEY or CHESS VALLEY FARM 1949

Line engraving
123 x 220 mm

Edition 30 *(some printed in 1951)*

Exhibited RE, 1950, No. 39: Götene, 1975

An old pollarded willow tree leans away from the river Chess near Chorleywood, with farm buildings in the background, and a broken fence to the left.

72 FROG 1949

Line engraving
123 x 100 mm

Edition 30

Exhibited Royal Academy, 1949, No. 1113: Götene, 1975: RE, 1965, No. 2

Reference *Daily Telegraph*, 2 May 1949, critique of RA Summer Exhibition.

A frog is poised to jump in front of moss-covered stones. The 1st state of the engraving shows the frog alone with no background; a trial proof contains suggestions for the background pencilled in by Robert Austin RA, which were followed — to some extent — in the final plate.

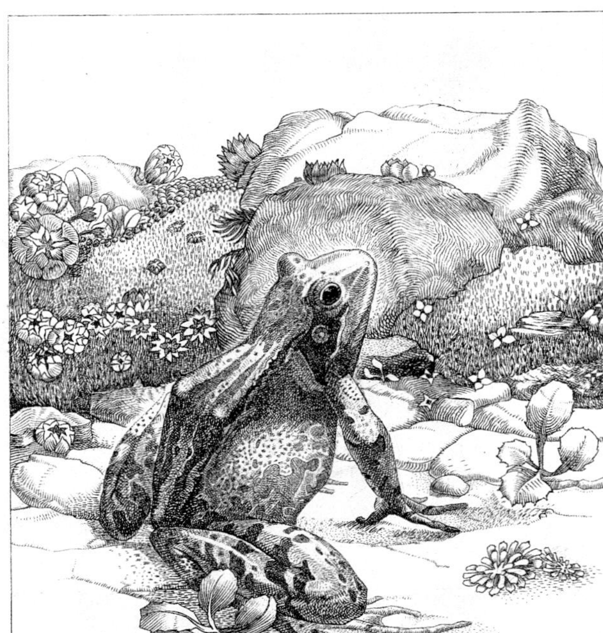

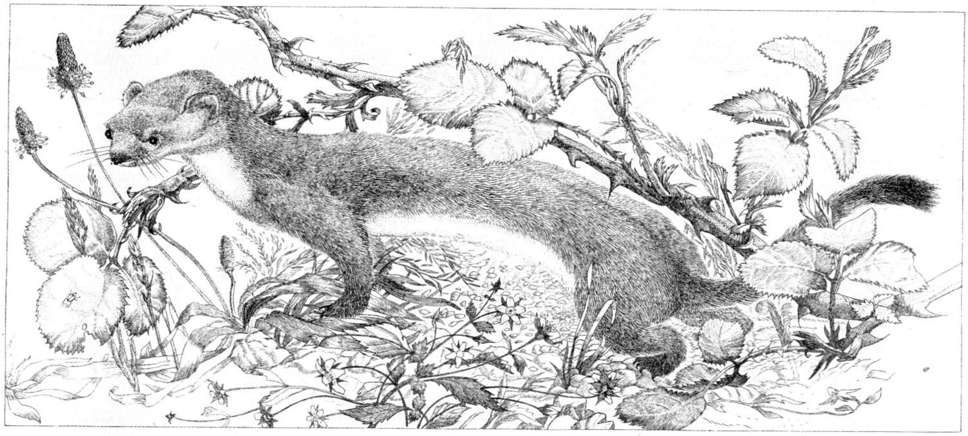

73 STOAT 1949

LINE ENGRAVING 92 x 200 mm

EDITION 30 *Some printed on antique paper*

EXHIBITED Royal Academy, 1950, No. 1162: RE, 1950, No. 209: CPE, Toronto, 1951, No. 26: Ashmolean Museum, Oxford, 1999, No. RE427: Götene, 1975

DIPLOMA Plate for the artist's Associateship of the RE, and presentation print for Print Collectors Club.

COLLECTION Ashmolean Museum, Oxford

ILLUSTRATED 'No Day Without a Line', Ashmolean Museum Exhibition, 1999, catalogue, p. 110.

Engraved from a drawing in pencil from a dead stoat sent to the artist by a friend. The plants are Hoary Plantain of Lamb's Tongue, in flower, Scarlet Pimpernel, and various grasses. The larger twig is the common Blackberry.

74 (Untitled) NUDE STUDY 1949

DRYPOINT
225 x 365 mm

NOT EDITIONED

Two nudes studied from models at Watford School of Art, needled direct onto copper.

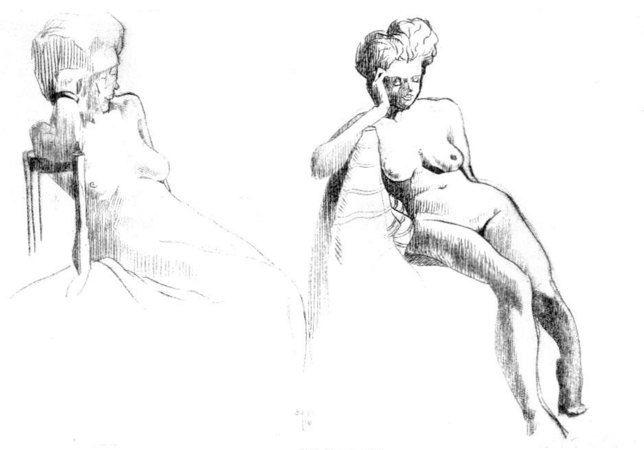

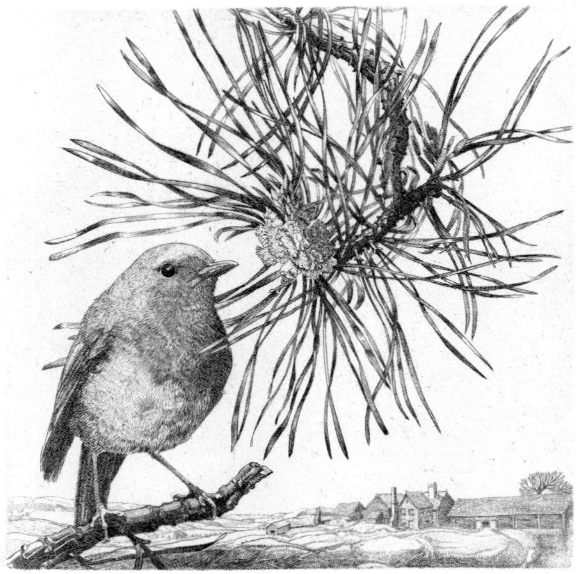

75 ROBIN 1950

LINE ENGRAVING 125 x 125 mm

EDITION 30

EXHIBITED Götene 1975

A robin perches under a twig of the twin leaves and cone flowers of the Scots pine. In the background appears the Black Horse pub on Chorleywood Common, where, as the artist records, 'during the second world war whilst serving with the Royal Observer Corps I met and drank with many American Air Force men from their nearby base at Bovingdon.'

76 BUTTERFLIES AND BUDDLEIA 1950

LINE ENGRAVING 120 x 122 mm

EDITION 30

EXHIBITED RE, 1965, No. 6: Götene, 1975

Two butterflies settle on a buddleia flower. Commenced whilst student at RCA. The name of the artist is engraved on the plate.

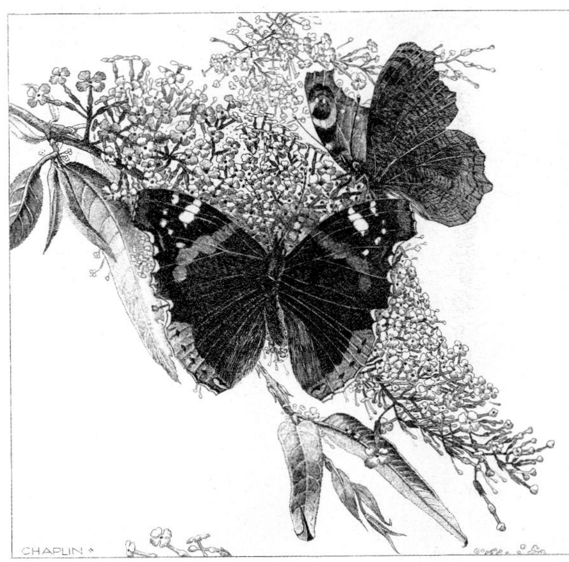

77 MOLE 1950

Line engraving
112 x 178 mm

Edition 30 *1st state* (1950): Final (1951) illustrated*

Exhibited
RE, 1951, No. 43

The mole has a beetle in his sights.

* The 1st state lacks the beetle and a little of the foreground detail.

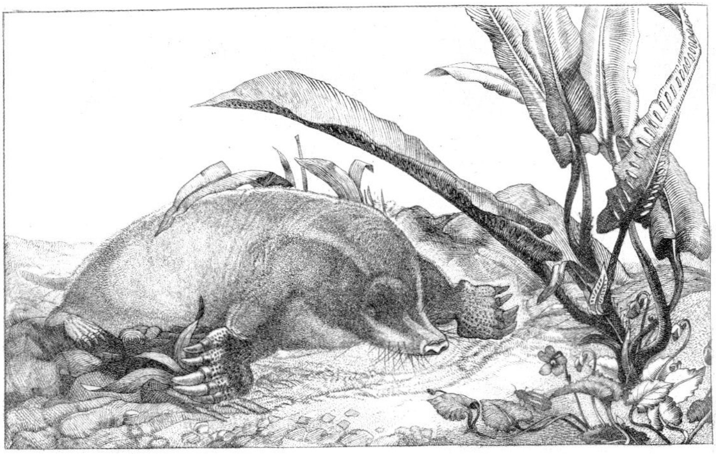

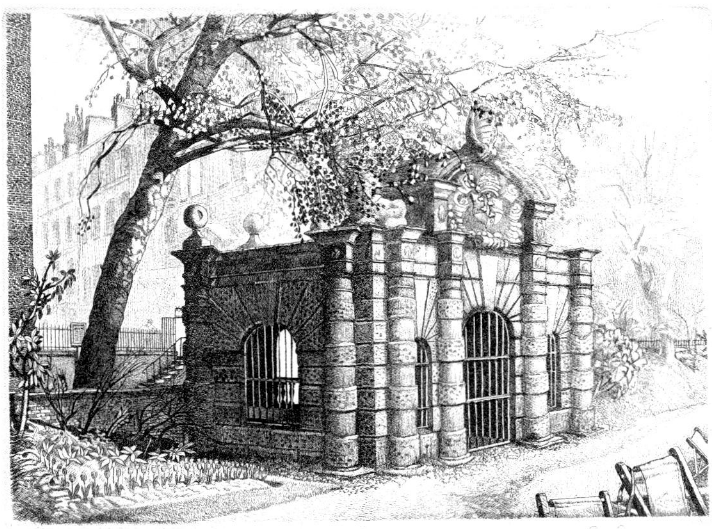

78 THE WATERGATE 1950

LINE ENGRAVING
192 x 258 mm

NOT EDITIONED
Plate commissioned for Sun Engraving Company. Some printed in 1951

EXHIBITED RE, 1951, No. 208: CPE, Toronto, 1951, No. 24

The Watergate, sited in Thames Embankment Gardens, has since been removed elsewhere. This was one of very few commissions. Chaplin was less comfortable with architectural drawing than with representations of living and natural things.

79 SQUIRREL 1950

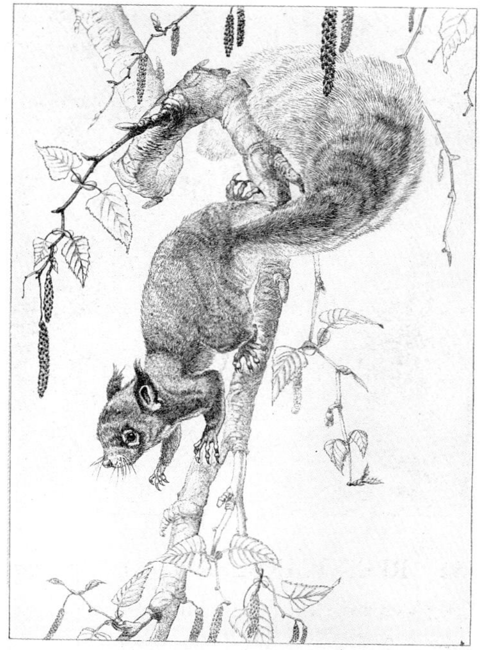

LINE ENGRAVING 190 x 133 mm

EDITION 30

EXHIBITED RE, 1951, No. 29: Götene, 1975

ILLUSTRATED *Everybody's Weekly*, 20 October 1951, p. 17

The artist noted: 'The squirrel on this plate is an old friend, often seen in our garden. It is a grey squirrel scampering down a branch of silver birch, also from the garden.'

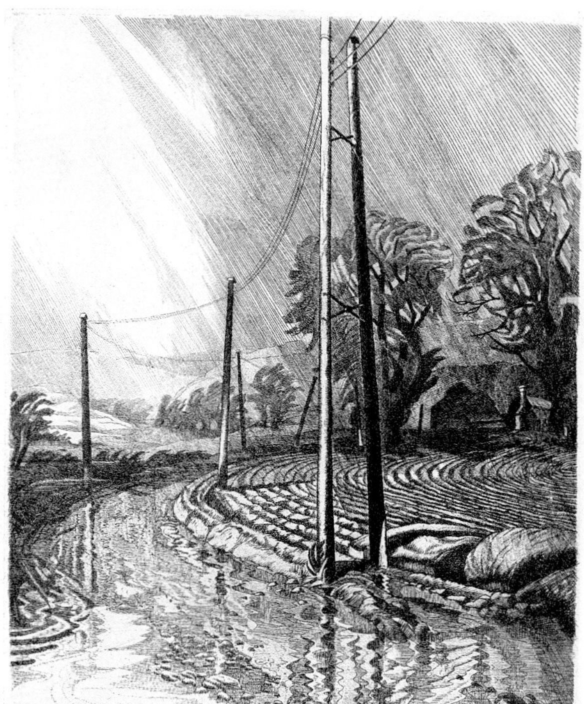

80 RAIN or SUNNY SHOWERS 1951

LINE ENGRAVING 246 x 193 mm

NOT EDITIONED *Some printed with alternative title in 1954*

Stark poles along a muddy lane in Sussex, as the rain pours down, and the sunshine emerges from the left.

The artist recorded that the sketch for this was made by two artist friends whilst sitting in a car with the rain pouring down all day: 'Don't leave out the poles,' they said, 'it will help to ruin it!'.

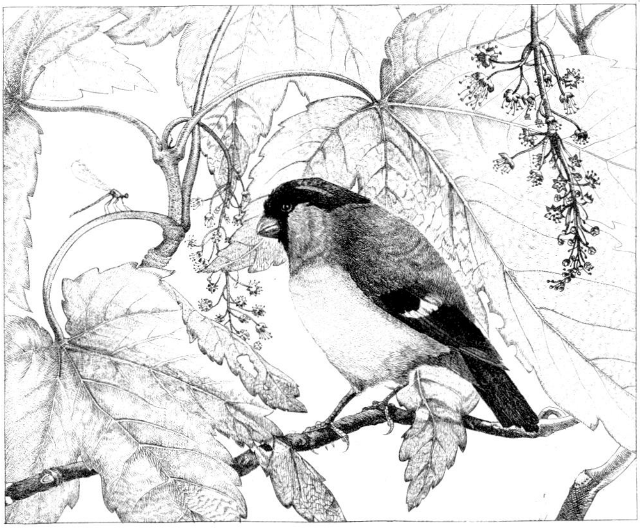

81 BULLFINCH 1951

LINE ENGRAVING
170 x 200 mm

EDITION 30

EXHIBITED Royal Academy, 1951, No. 1010: RE, 1951 No. 59: Götene 1975: City of Liverpool Art Gallery, 1951 No. 17: CPE, Toronto, 1951 No. 25

A bullfinch perched on a sycamore leaf stares at a damsel dragonfly.

82 REED WARBLER 1951

LINE ENGRAVING 223 x 150 mm

EDITION 30 *1st state:* Final printed mainly in 1952 (illustrated)*

EXHIBITED RE, 1952, No. 58

A reed warbler perched on a weeping willow twig stares hungrily at a caterpillar. The artist's initials are engraved on the footbridge, which is over the river Colne, at Rickmansworth.

* In the 1st state the twig hangs in the air and there is no background; the background, added in the final plate, includes a footbridge over a river with a punt moored by the bank and a cottage behind.

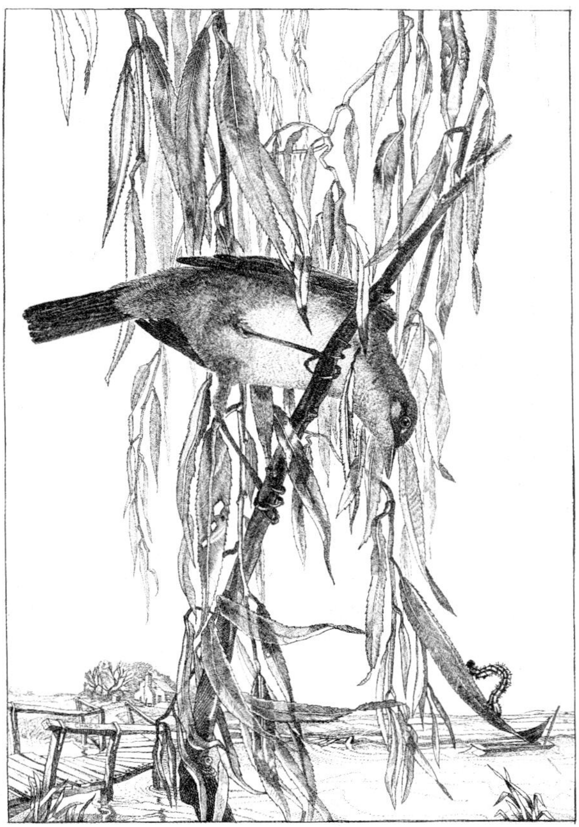

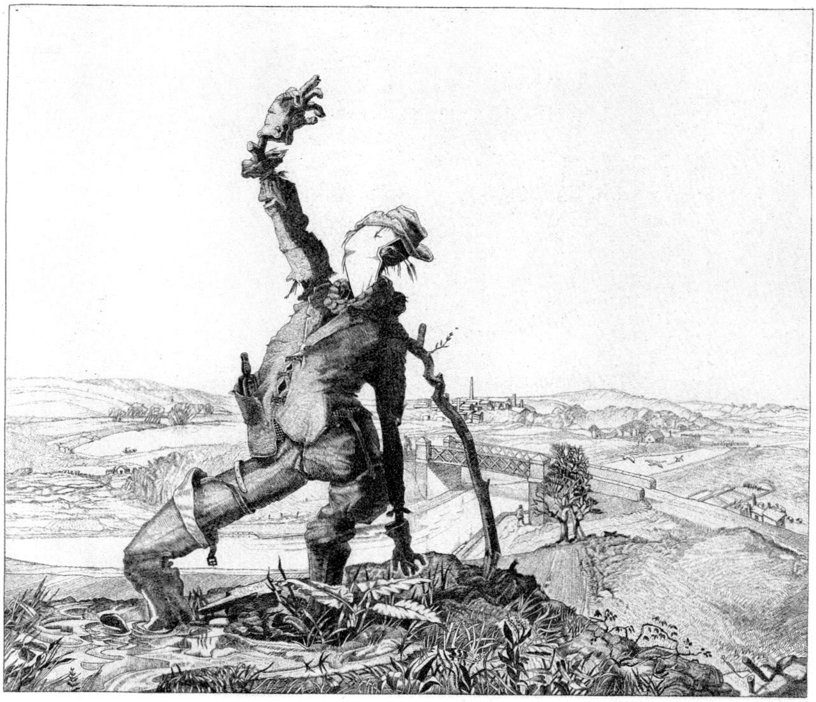

83 SCARECROW 1951

LINE ENGRAVING 220 x 252 mm EDITION 30

EXHIBITED RE, 1952, No. 189

ILLUSTRATED Cover of Catalogue for Exhibition of Artists works by Hilary Chapman Fine Prints, 20th Century Gallery, London, April 2003.

REFERENCE This plate is the subject of a lengthy (unpublished) analysis by the artist's nephew, John Francis Chaplin in 2003.

A scarecrow protects newly planted watercress in the beds at Cassiobury Park, Watford. In the background is Rousebarn Lane, a bridge over the Grand Union Canal, and a representation of the factory of Sun Printers Ltd, Watford, where the artist worked for nearly fifty years. Identifiable figures are James Fry, a pastel artist friend, passing under the bridge, and Mr Sansom, a watercress grower, by his beds: the lady with a feather in her hat was an acquaintance whom he met walking in his lunch hour most days. The name of a young lady is also engraved on the plate, a source of some mystery. The plate is engraved 'CHAC 1951'.

The mystery was partly solved some years later in 2003 when, following her death, the lady's daughter sold the prints forming the collection of the artist's work that he had given her over many years. (See catalogue Hilary Chapman Fine Prints, 20th Century Gallery, London, April 2003). The image is discussed further in the text, page 45.

84 MYSTERY OF SPAIN 1952

Mezzotint
210 x 270 mm

Not editioned Two inks

Exhibited RE, 1953, No. 269

Shadowy figures with donkeys in the moonlight near Segovia. Completed following the artist's visit to Spain in 1952, and the first of five prints with Spanish subjects.

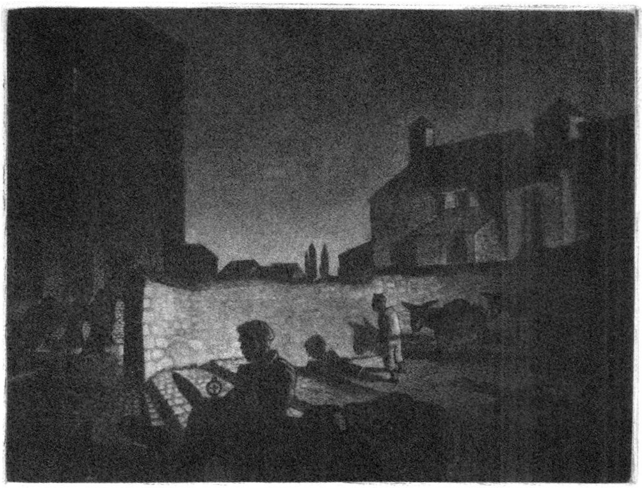

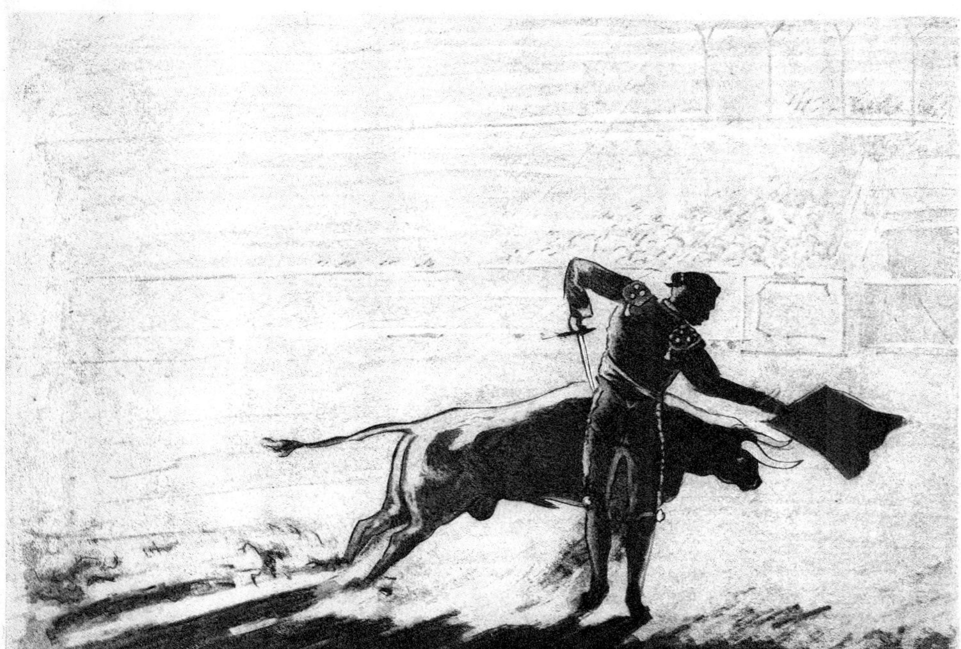

85 BULLFIGHT 1952

Soft ground etching and drypoint 210 x 300 mm

Not editioned *Printed in red brown ink*

Made following the artist's visit to Spain, from sketches in Malaga. This plate was rejected for exhibition by the RE on the grounds that the bullfighter was left-handed.

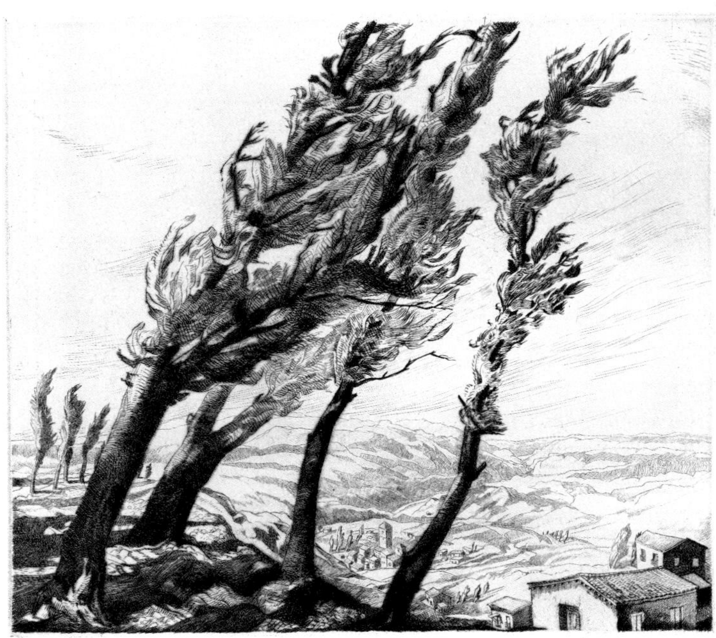

86 SPAIN 1952

DRYPOINT
247 x 275 mm

NOT EDITIONED

Tall trees overlook a small town in a hilly valley, Guidix, Spain.

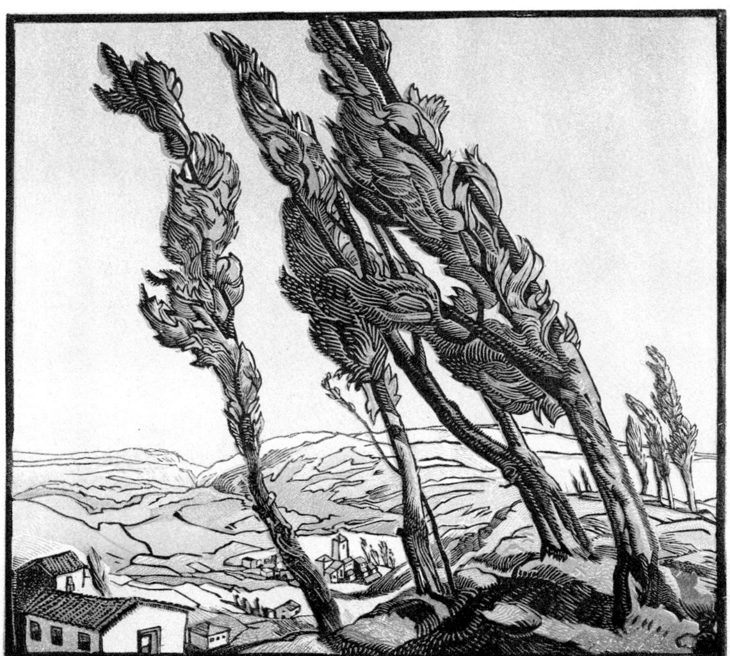

87 SPAIN 1952

LINOCUT,
5 COLOURS
265 x 285 mm

NOT EDITIONED

Very few prints exist. (An illustration of this linocut can be found on page 44.)

A linocut of the same subject as the drypoint (No. 86), in reverse.

88 UNDERHILL FARM (with cats) 1952

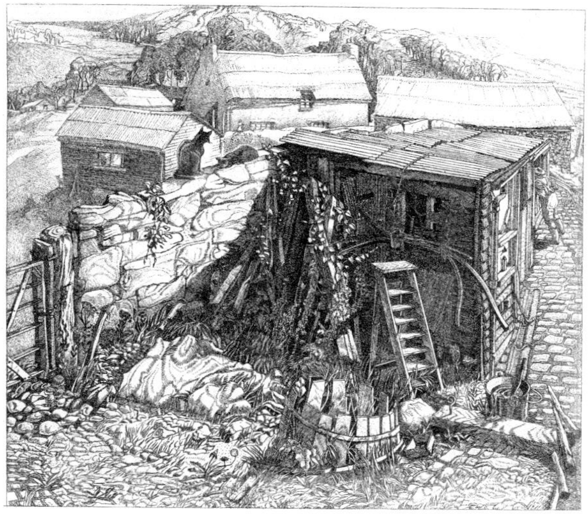

LINE ENGRAVING 225 x 250 mm

EDITION 30

EXHIBITED Royal Academy, 1952, No. 1231: RE, 1952, No. 16: Götene, 1975

The two plates of 'Underhill Farm' (Lyme Regis) are distinguished by the presence of two cats sitting on a wall in this one, and of Mr Bowditch, the farmer, in the other. The farmhouse was used on location for scenes in the film *The French Lieutenant's Woman*. This plate shows the early development of Chaplin's fascination with rural clutter and decrepit agricultural buildings.

89 SUMMER, UNDERHILL FARM (with Mr Bowditch) or UNDERHILL FARM 1952

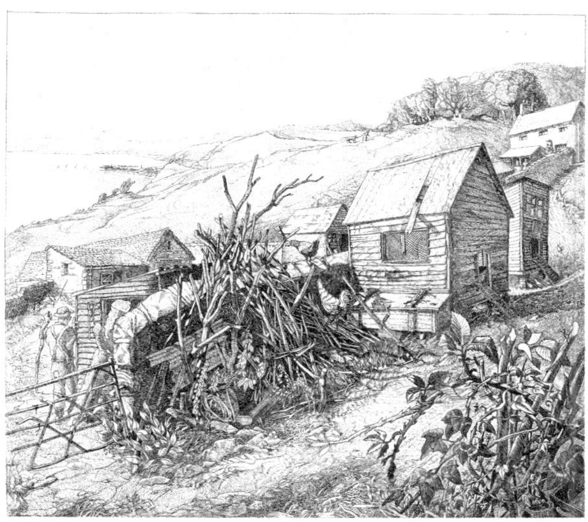

LINE ENGRAVING 225 x 250 mm

Edition 30

EXHIBITED Royal Academy, 1953, No. 1016: RE, 1953, No. 274: CPE, 1952: CPE Archives Exhibition, Hamilton, 1976

AWARD George A. Reid Silver Memorial Award of CPE, 1952

The two plates titled 'Underhill Farm' (Lyme Regis) are distinguished by the presence of Mr Bowditch, the farmer, in one, and two cats in the other. The plate is in mirror image as the Cobb at Lyme Regis can be seen along the shore — Underhill Farm is in fact to the west of the Cobb! The farmhouse was used for scenes shot in the film *The French Lieutenant's Woman*. 'CHAC 1952' is engraved on a stone in the foreground; the deleted initials 'CHAC' can also just be made out on a pot on which a robin stands in the right-hand corner.

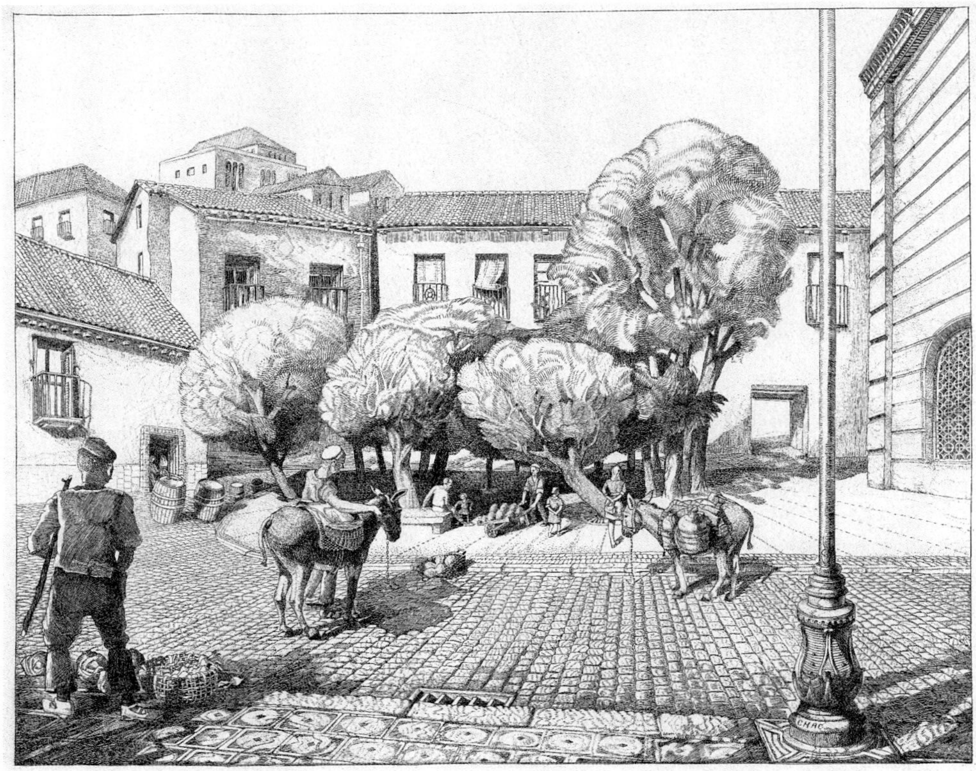

90 SEGOVIA, SPAIN 1953

LINE ENGRAVING 230 x 283 mm EDITION 30

EXHIBITED RE, 1953, No. 230

One of a small number of works completed following the artist's tour of Spain in 1952. A small cobbled square in Segovia with a figure and a lamppost in the foreground; and donkeys and trees in the background, all apparently in bright sunshine.

The artist records: 'We stopped for half-an-hour or so in this little square — the figures and donkeys were introduced from other sketches. I stood in a shop doorway sheltering from the pouring rain and made the sketch of the square. One donkey is loaded with sand, the other with water jars, and the little figure in the foreground is selling turnips and cabbages, and the one with the barrow is selling melons.

The tall post in the foreground is of cast iron and was made in Birmingham, England. The building on the right with a beautiful wrought iron grill over the window, was a bank. The trees were pollarded acacia trees.

The road was made of granite sets — set only in sand — and the pavement was paved with beautiful tiles.'

This image was reproduced from the original print from the collection of Jonathan Cave.

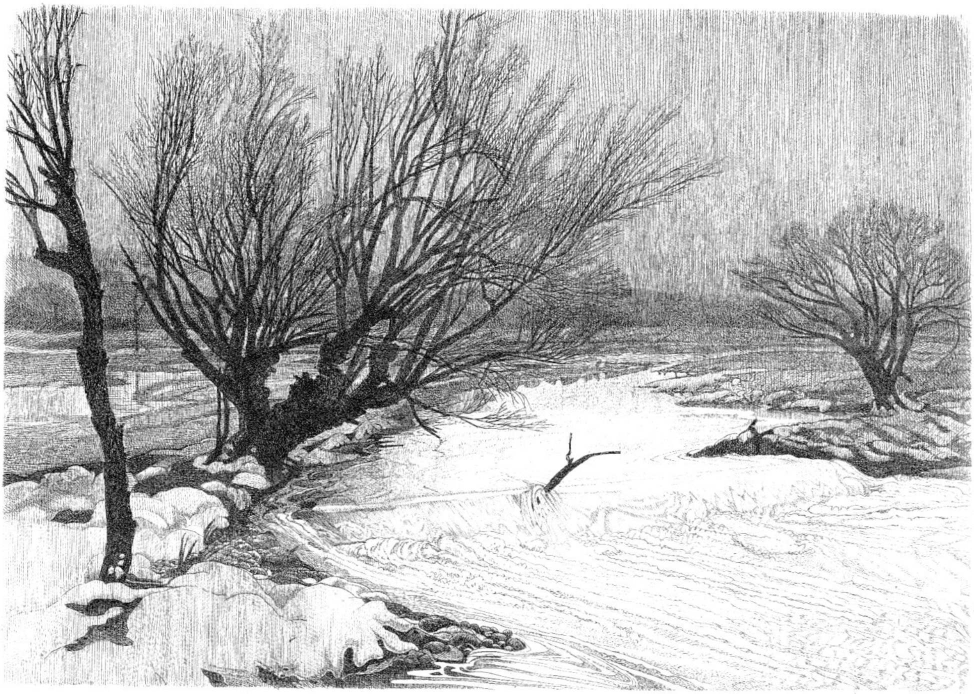

91 MELTING SNOW AND FLOODWATER 1953

ETCHING AND ENGRAVING 190 x 263 mm

EDITION 30 *Printed in blue-black and black ink*

EXHIBITED Royal Academy, 1953, No. 1073: RE, 1954, No. 115: Götene, 1979

REFERENCE *The Collector*, July 1953, Vol. 1, No.1, p. 18 — re the 1953 Summer Exhibition: 'The best of the engravings, in the writer's opinion, is No. 1073, by Charles Chaplin, "Melting Snow and flood Water". This is a notably good rendering of his subject in line. The colour of the ink is noteworthy. He should go far in his chosen mediums, if he can keep up such a standard.'

West Herts & Watford Observer, 1 September 1953: 'CHA Chaplin's somber "Melting Snow and Floodwater" captures to perfection the dull cold and clamminess of a wintry landscape.'

Depiction of winter snow and floodwater intrigued the artist, and this repeated the subject matter of his first exhibit at the Summer Exhibition of 1939, 'Melting Snow' (31). Here the River Colne at Rickmansworth is in flood, whilst the willow trees on the banks stand out against a dark threatening day.

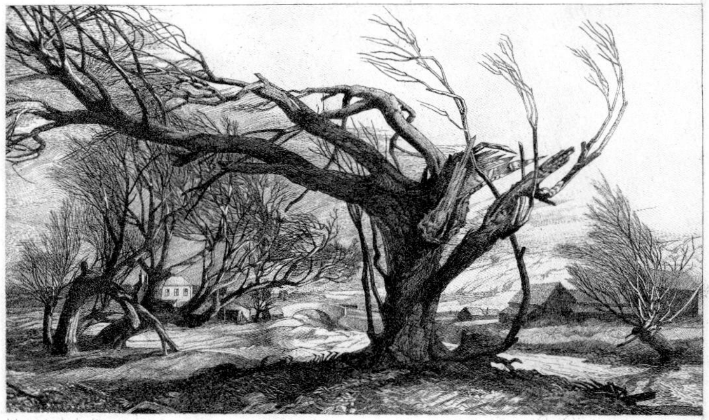

92 OLD WILLOWS or WILLOWS or BROKEN WILLOW or WIND AND WILLOWS OR WIND IN THE WILLOWS 1954

LINE ENGRAVING
186 x 308 mm

EDITION 30 *Some printed in brown ink*

EXHIBITED Royal Academy, 1964, No. 981: RE, 1954, No. 301: CPE, Toronto, Vancouver, Regina, Prince Albert, Brandon: Götene, 1975

A broken willow tree dominates a view of Stockers Bridge Rickmansworth, and the River Colne. The artist not infrequently gave his works alternative titles, but with this plate he seems to have been quite unable to decide, each separate printing seemingly given a fresh title!

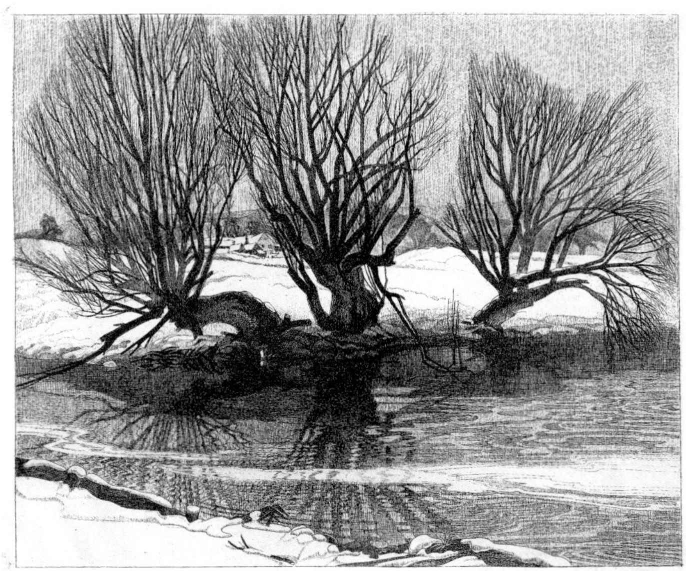

93 WINTER'S REFLECTIONS 1954

LINE ENGRAVING
230 x 277 mm

EDITION 30

EXHIBITED Royal Academy, 1954, No. 1108: RE, 1954, No. 337

The artist returns to his theme of winter snow and flooded waters, with three willow trees on the bank of the River Colne at Rickmansworth, their branches reflecting in the water.

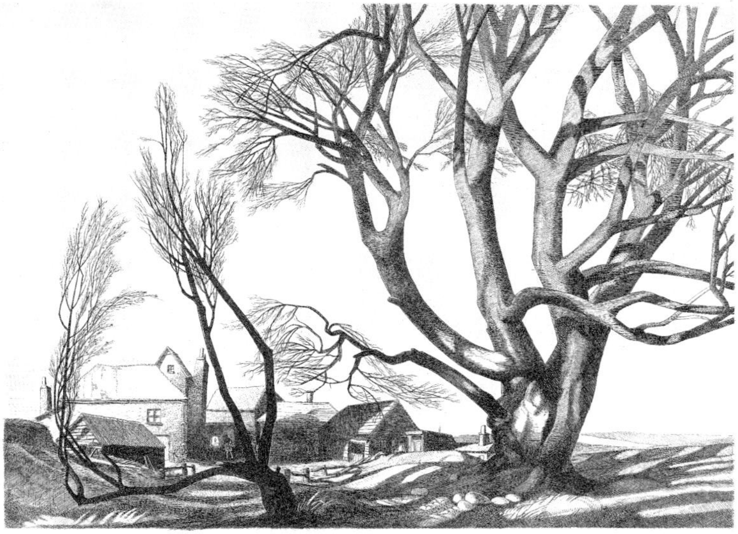

94 EVENING PATTERNS

1955

Line engraving

234 x 317 mm

Edition 30

Exhibited RE, 1955, No. 13: RE, 1956, No. 12: CPE, Toronto, Ontario, London, Willistead, Ingersoll, Waterloo, 1956–57

Evening light throws patterns of shadows of large trees by a farm cottage and buildings, Stockers Lake Farm, Rickmansworth.

95 TREE PATTERNS

1955

Line engraving

220 x 250 mm

Edition 30

Exhibited Royal Academy, 1955, No. 1030: RE, 1955, No. 141

The sun shining directly behind a group of trees in winter throws patterns of shadow over the foreground. Stockers Farm is in the background.

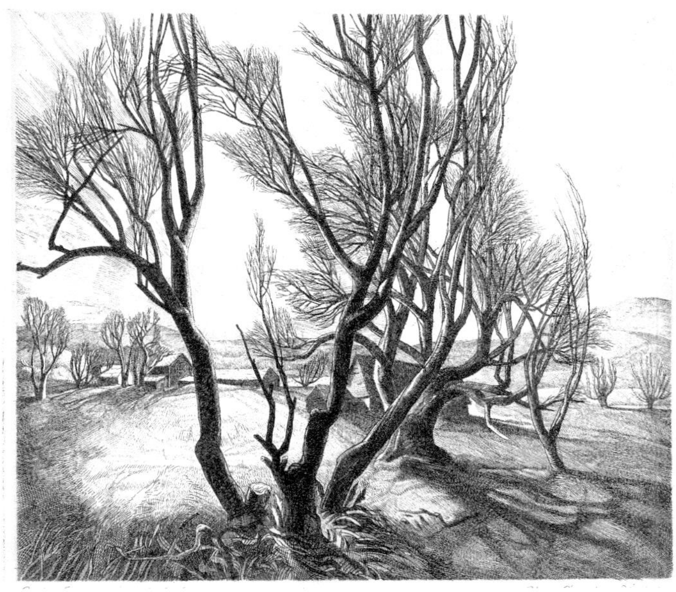

96 WINTER SNOW 1957

LINE ENGRAVING
167 x 280 mm

EDITION 30
extended to 50

EXHIBITED
Götene, 1975: RE, 1957/8, No. 24

Trees in deep snow in front of barns and farm buildings near Thame, Oxfordshire.

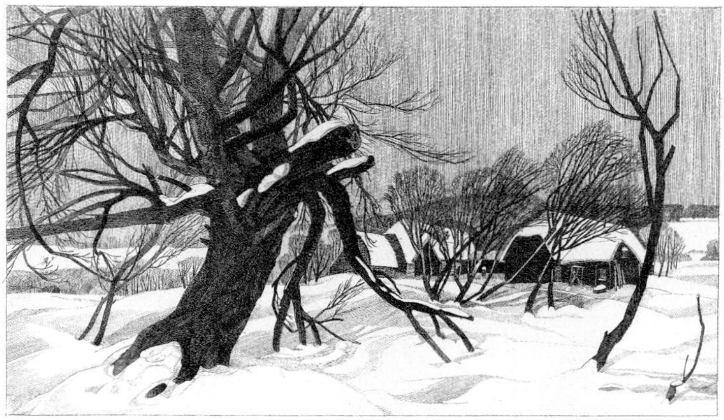

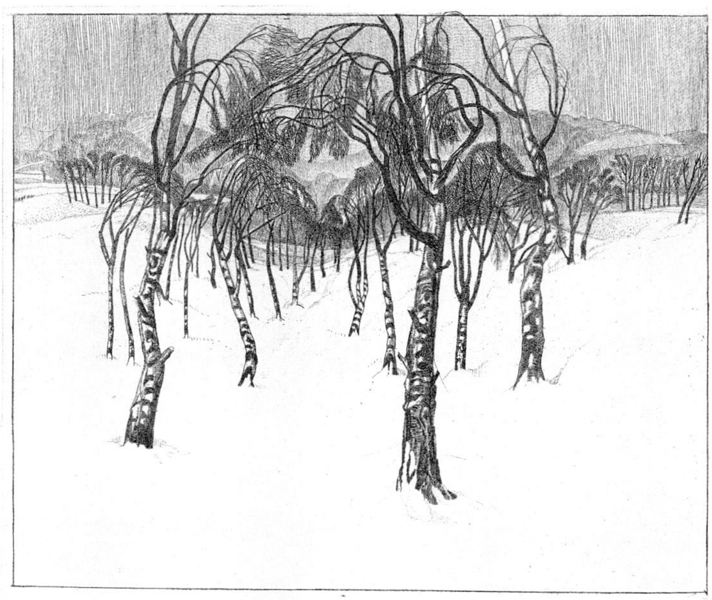

97 SILVER BIRCHES IN WINTER 1958

LINE ENGRAVING, ON ALLOY BI-METAL PLATE 185 x 218 mm

EDITION 30 Most prints are dated 1959

EXHIBITED Royal Academy, 1959, No. 1260: RE, 1959, No. 97

A copse of silver birches in snow in Whippendell Woods, Watford. Engraved on alloy bi-metal plate which was used experimentally to replace copper for half tone plate work by the Sun Engraving Company. These plates were hard and gritty to engrave but very clean to remove ink from the surface.

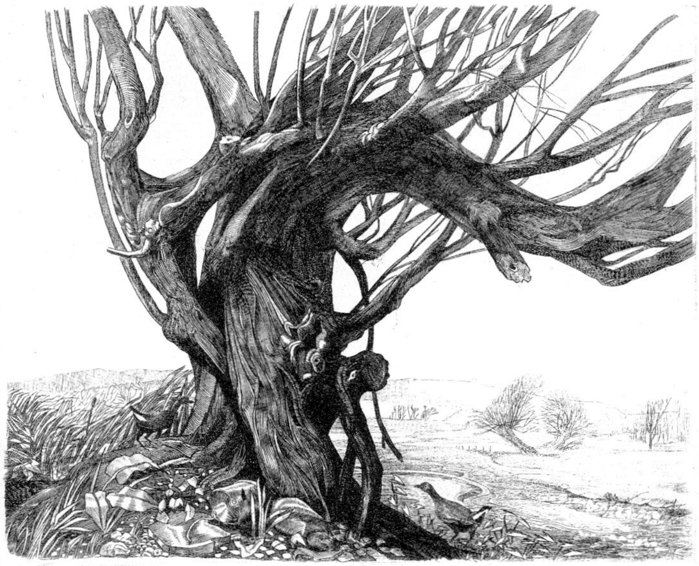

98 OLD WILLOW AND MOORHENS 1959

LINE ENGRAVING
172 x 205 mm

EDITION 30

EXHIBITED Royal Academy, 1959, No. 1253: RE, 1959, No. 93

A pair of moorhens explore around the roots of an old willow tree by the river.

99 IN THE NEW FOREST (with pheasant) 1960

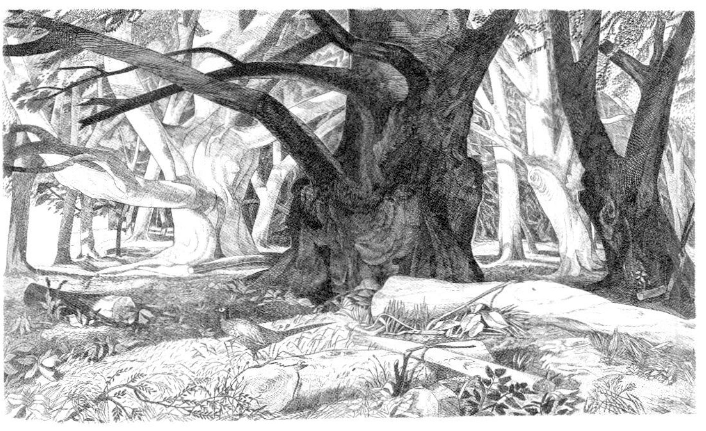

LINE ENGRAVING
147 x 243 mm

EDITION 30

EXHIBITED Royal Academy 1960, No. 1239: RE, 1960, No. 37

ILLUSTRATED *Tree News*, Autumn/Winter 2003, pp. 38, 39, Felix Publishing

The titles of the six New Forest subjects, of which this is the first, are distinguished by an identifying parenthesis — in this case a cock pheasant struts in the foreground. 'This is a study of light and shade of very old beech trees at Burley, in the New Forest. I have added a cock pheasant and a few twigs, plants and flowers.'

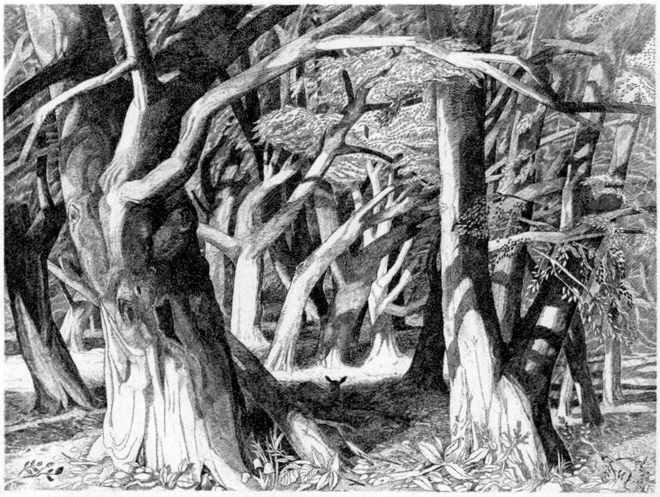

100 SUNLIGHT AND SHADOW, NEW FOREST (with deer) or LIGHT AND SHADE — NEW FOREST 1960

LINE ENGRAVING
183 x 240 mm

EDITION 30

EXHIBITED Royal Academy, 1961, No. 1164: RE, 1961, No. 149

In this study of bright sunshine filtering through the dense beech trees of the New Forest, a deer rests quietly in the shade.

101 SIESTA 1960

LINE ENGRAVING
138 x 235 mm

EDITION 30
Red/brown ink

EXHIBITED RE, 1960, No. 339

At midday in the Spanish countryside, three workers rest from their labours under the shade of the overhanging branches of a tree.

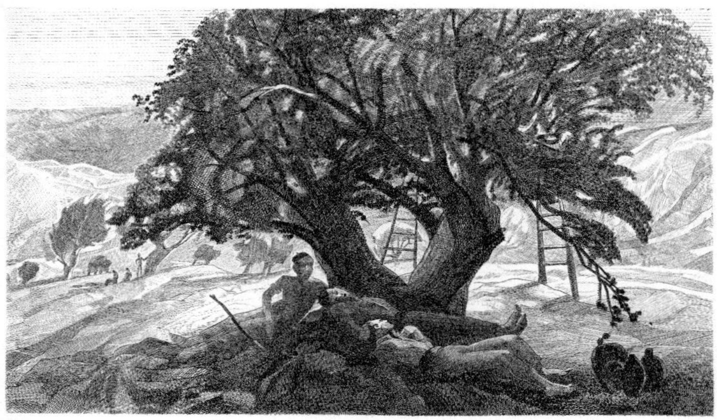

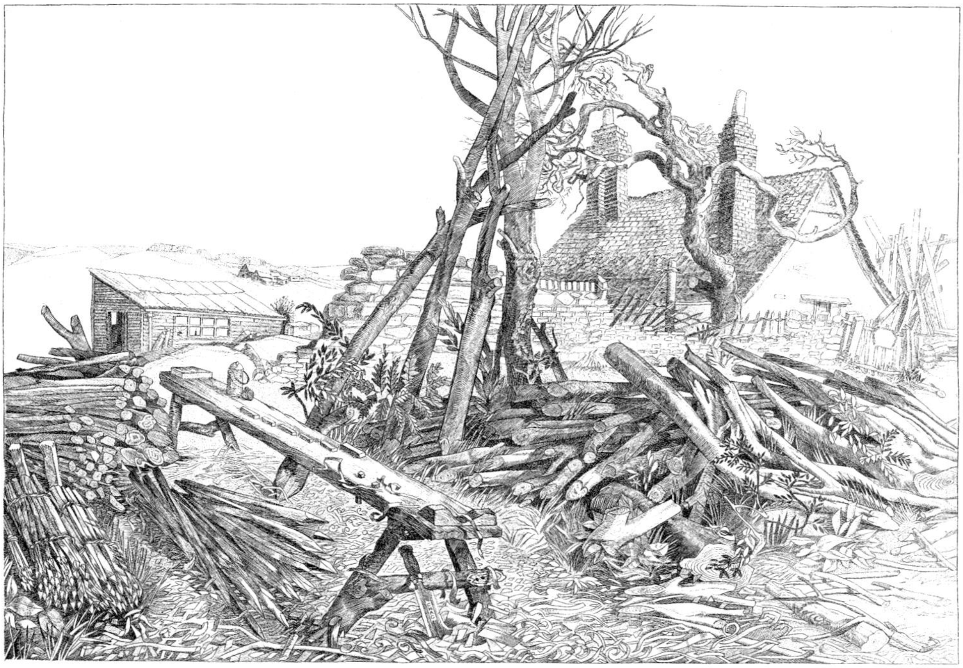

102 ANCIENT CRAFTS 1962

LINE ENGRAVING 172 x 242 mm

EDITION 30

EXHIBITED Royal Academy, 1962, No. 917: RE, 1962, No. 150: CPE, Toronto: Götene, 1975

The craft of split chestnut fencing is displayed in front of an old country cottage in Lickfold Sussex. The artist's initials are engraved on the billhook.

Chaplin noted: 'The making of split chestnut fencing and fencing stakes was a rural country craft carried on outside this cottage, and by a nearby wood where chestnut tree logs were available. The logs were sawn off in lengths, split down with an axe, or split with wedges, sharpened to a point and the bark mostly removed and then bundled. The rough bench with marking stops on was used for this purpose — the bundles were tied up with the twisted skin bark and later were wired up, as seen in the old chestnut fence on the broken brick wall in front of the cottage. This cottage, by the way, served teas which were mostly of home made jams and scones.

Very little was rearranged on this plate. It is a faithful rendering of the spot in all ways — the ground was deeply covered with wood shavings, and on the bench stood a blue enamel beaker with lid for tea, a cup, and a billhook used for cutting. Swallows were flying in and out of their nests on the cottage.'

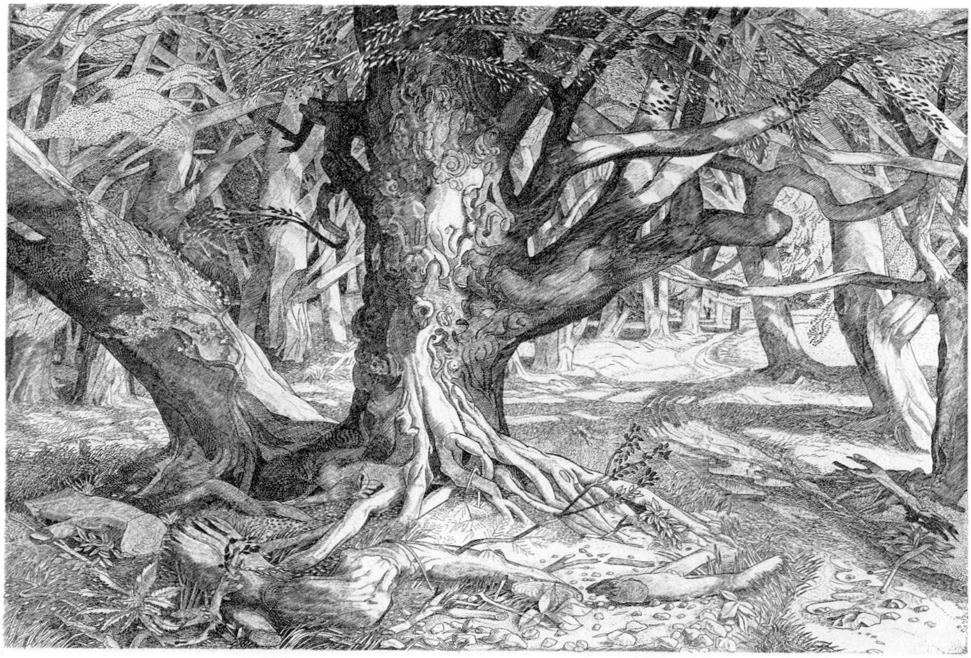

103 FOREST GLADE (with Teddy Bear) or NEW FOREST GLADE or IN THE NEW FOREST GLADE or GLADE IN THE NEW FOREST 1962

LINE ENGRAVING 172 x 247 mm

EDITION 30 *1st state (December 1962):* Final 1963*

EXHIBITED Royal Academy, 1963, No. 1101: RE, 1963, No. 56

DIPLOMA Plate for artist's Fellowship of Royal Society of Painters-Etchers and Engravers

PRESENTATION PRINT Engravers Print Collectors Club, 1962

COLLECTION Ashmolean Museum, Oxford

In the New Forest, a gnarled old tree partly obscures a sunny glade beyond. This, the third of the New Forest engravings, is identified by a teddy bear lying on the grass in the glade. Chaplin wrote: 'The teddy bear belonged to my small granddaughter, Elizabeth Louise, who left it in the exact spot shown in the engraving. The trees are bad examples, overgrown and no use for timber cutting but a great source of enjoyment to engrave.'

For more about the teddy bear see the biographical section, page 81.

* The 1st state is almost indistinguishable from the final plate.

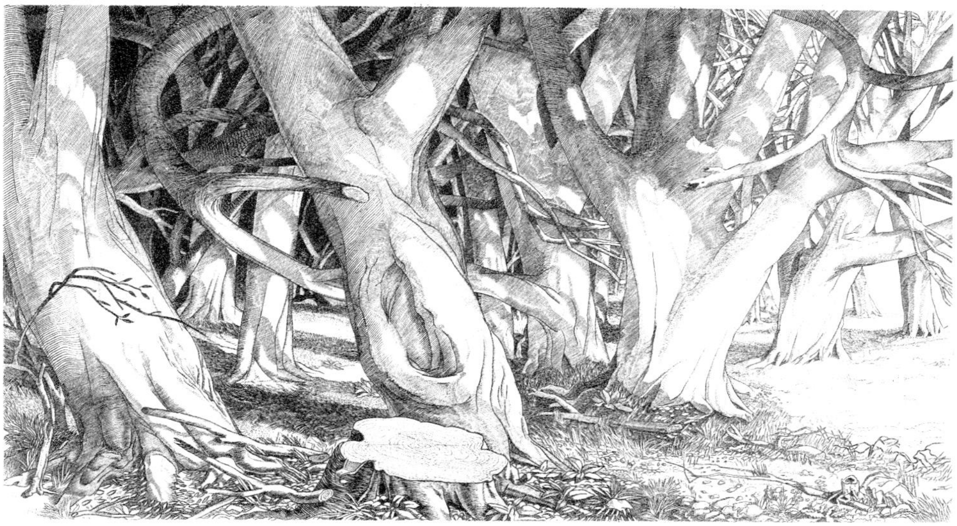

104 EDGE OF FOREST (with tree stump) 1964

LINE ENGRAVING 150 x 268 mm EDITION 30

EXHIBITED Royal Academy, 1965, No. 1343: RE, 1964, No. 57: Götene, 1975

A scene of dense trees on the edge of the New Forest, distinguished by a prominent sawn-off tree stump in the foreground.

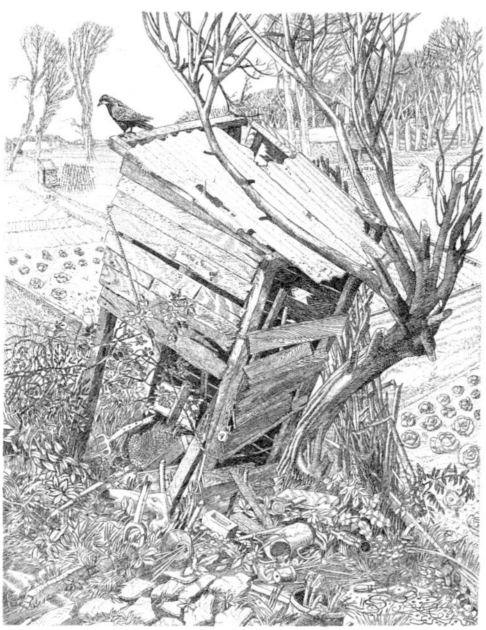

105 ALLOTMENT HUT 1966

LINE ENGRAVING 233 x 178 mm

EDITION 30 *Some printed on antique paper*

EXHIBITED Royal Academy, 1966, No. 1039: RE, 1966, No. 35: CPE: Götene, 1975

ILLUSTRATED *Knitware & Stocking*, May 1966, Vol. 20, No. 5

At the edge of some neat allotments stands a tumbledown hut out of which pours the debris of broken tools and abandoned artifacts. A crow surveys the scene from the roof of the hut. The name of a friend 'Ernie Collins' is engraved on the label of a bottle. How this plate came to be reproduced in such an esoteric magazine is not known!

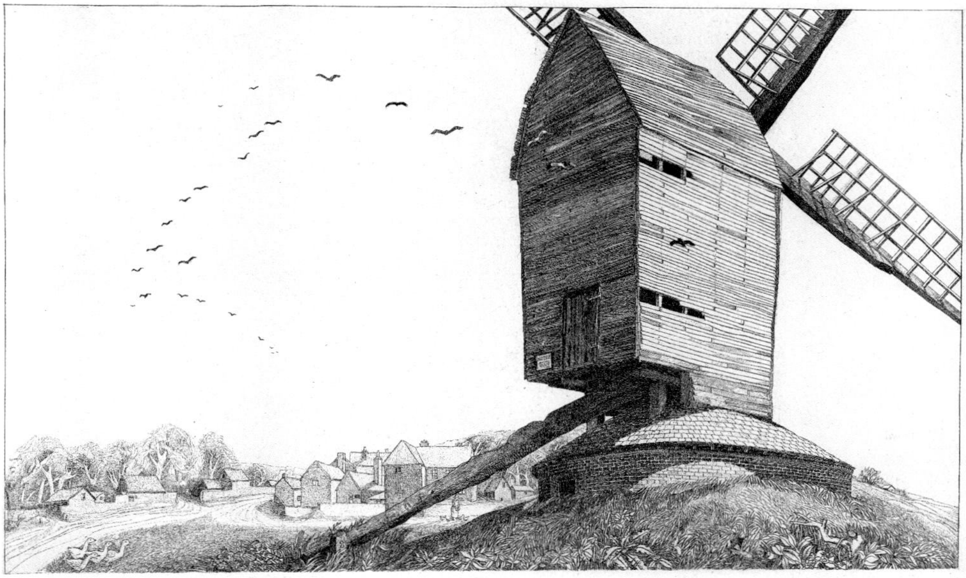

106 WINDMILL, BRILL 1966

LINE ENGRAVING 190 (l/h) / 194 (r/h) x 315 mm (Note irregularity of image)

EDITION 30 *Black and brown inks*

EXHIBITED Royal Academy, 1966, No. 1035: RE, 1967, No. 112: CPE, Hamilton, London, Toronto Canada, 1967/68: Götene 1975

'There are few remaining windmills left in this country in such a good condition as the one at Brill in Oxfordshire. It stands facing wide open country, with the village of Brill close by as shown in my engraving. The village is still very rural and unspoilt. Brill stands 603 ft above sea level, dates from 1689 and looks across countryside of Buckinghamshire and Oxfordshire. One of the oldest post-mills in England with its machinery intact. The grassy mounds surrounding the windmill were thrown up when the ground was quarried for the clay from which the bricks of Brill were made.

I have made many black and white sketches and many pastel sketches of this windmill. My granddaughter's name, "Sara, 1965", is engraved on the beam supporting the mill as she was with me and it was her birthday when we visited Brill.

The birds, crows, were added to help the design of the plate.'

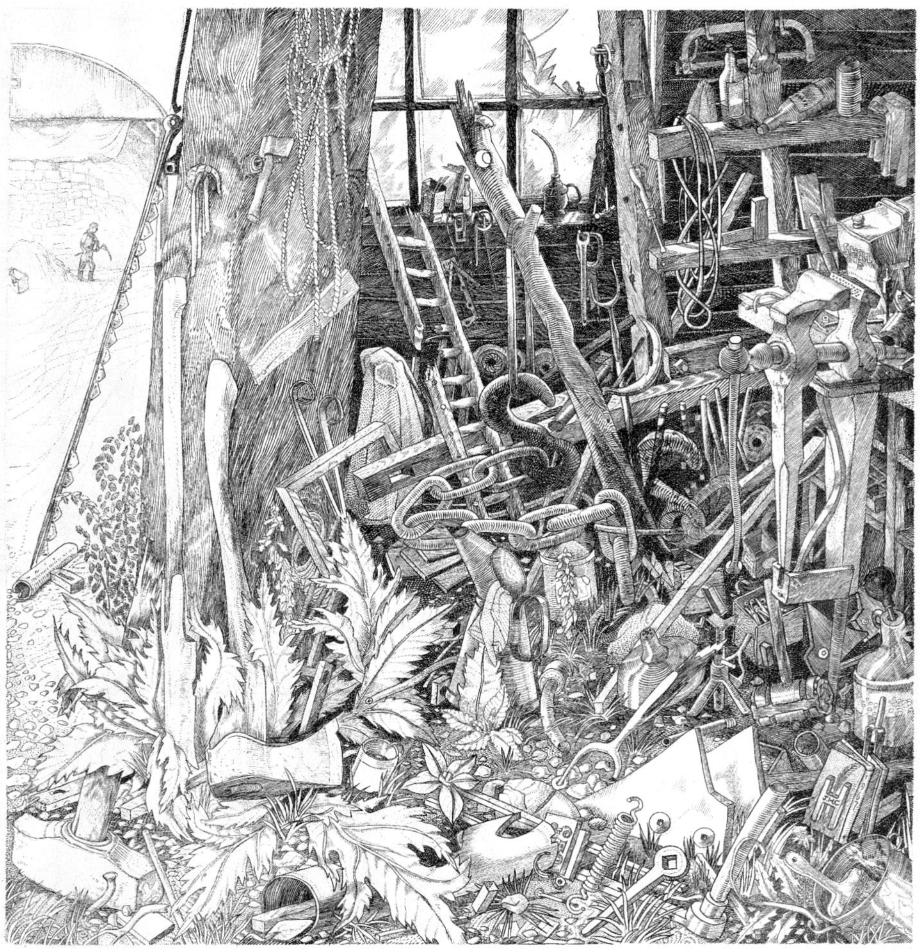

107 FARM CORNER (Knightscote Farm) 1967

LINE ENGRAVING 220 x 205 mm

EDITION 30 *(A few non-editioned prints of this plate were also made by Corrie Graddon on Japanese Paper; the illustration is from one of these.)*

EXHIBITED Royal Academy, 1967, No. 1149: RE, 1968, No. 60: CPE, 1969: Götene, 1975

A glimpse inside the corner of a farm building at Knightscote Farm, Harefield, with the chaos of abandoned farming artifacts. The artist's brother, Edward, was tenant of the farm at this time.

Chaplin noted: 'This plate has now become, along with others of this nature, of great interest to collectors, and is a recording of many old tools and crafts.' The plate includes a reference to a promotion in the career of his son, Jon, as well as the first of the little naked ladies (see page 77).

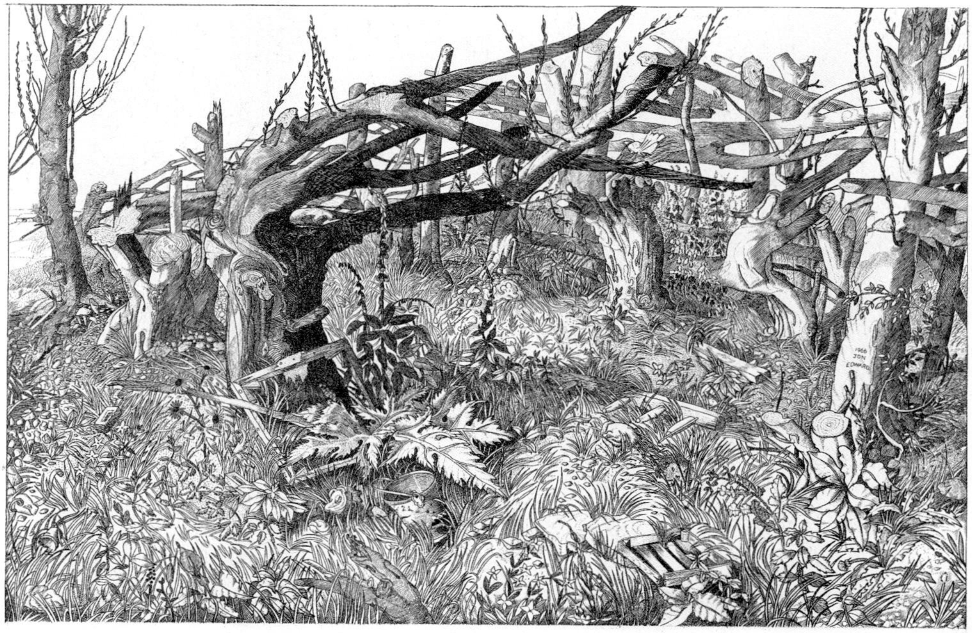

108 HEDGEROW STUDY 1967

LINE ENGRAVING 176 x 272 mm

EDITION 30

EXHIBITED Royal Academy, 1967, No. 1146: RE, 1967, No. 55: CPE, Hamilton, London, Toronto, Canada, 1967/68: Götene, 1975

A detailed study of a hedgerow in Green Lane, Chorleywood in early spring with foxgloves and a hedgehog. The plate also contains the name of the artist's wife 'E. M. Chaplin' and a reference to the birth of his grandson '1966 Jon Edward'.

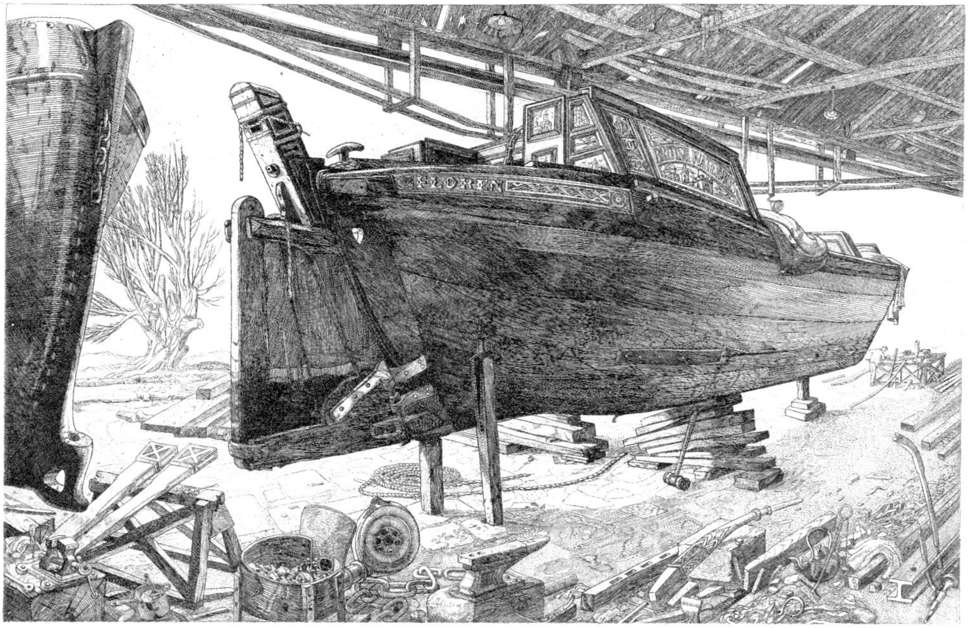

109 UNDER REPAIR 1968

LINE ENGRAVING 204 x 305 mm

EDITION 30

EXHIBITED RE 1968, No. 223: Götene 1975

A narrow boat 'Floren', rests on the drydock of a boat yard on the Grand Union Canal at Rickmansworth. The artist wrote: 'Drawings were made for this plate at Walker's Boat Yard. My son, Jon, was working there, filling in time before going to Oxford, chipping inch-thick rust off old iron barges, later helping to paint the traditional decorations on the wooden narrow boats which were made and repaired on the canal-side yard. He was proud of his painting and wanted me to see — that's when the sketches were made (1954). Many sketches went into the making of the plate.* Many years later I engraved the plate from the drawings, and went along to the boatyard to check one or two things. The yard and all the slipways and wonderful workshop had completely gone, and all the old craftsmen with them.'

The site is now a Tesco's superstore. In the right hand corner the artist engraved two of the small tools he used on the plate. A small nude also appears. No less than eight signed trial proofs exist of this plate in every stage of its development.

* See example of sketch on page 40.

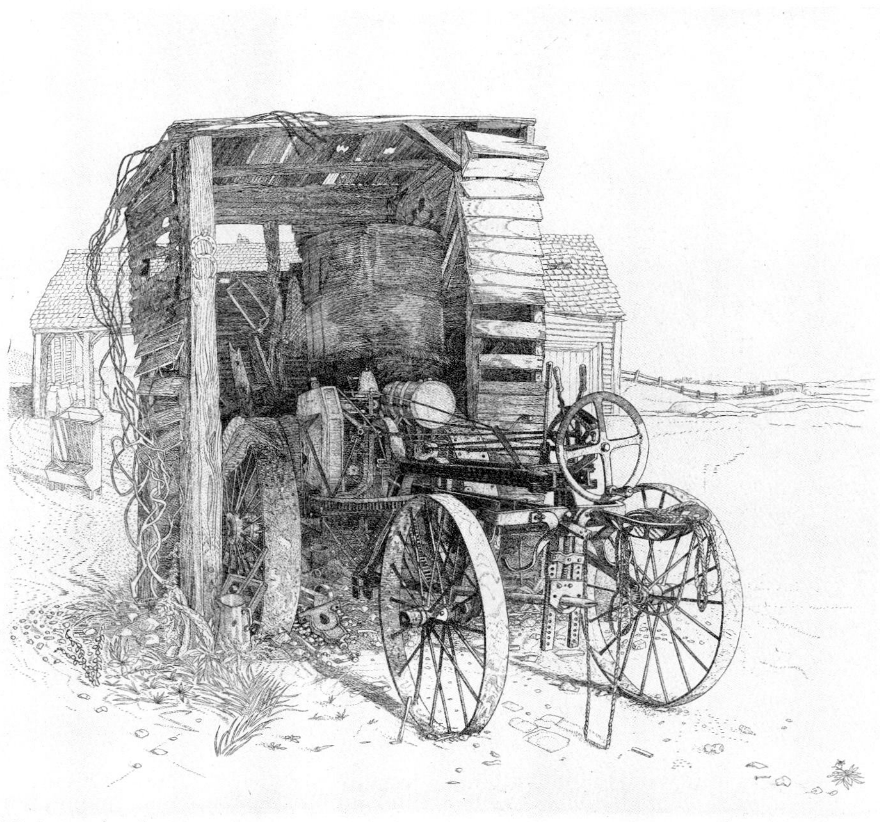

110 GOING FOR A SONG 1969

LINE ENGRAVING 245 x 263 mm EDITION 30 *Some artists proofs printed in 1977*

EXHIBITED Royal Academy, 1969, No. 941: RE, 1969, No. 59: CPE, Toronto, Canada, 1970: Götene, 1975

Chaplin wrote: 'This tractor is one of two believed to be in this country. It was made by Moline Plow Co, USA, Universal Tractors, Moline, Illinois, USA (Name Plate on Tractor).

Made about 1913/15 in USA, it is a twin cylinder 16 HP tractor. It won a bronze medal in Nebraska in 1921, the original price being £540. It was in use until 1946 and is still now in good running condition in 1977 and attends many old tractor rallies. The tractor is located at Knightscote Farm, Harefield, Middlesex. I helped to renovate this tractor and engraved my small grandson's name, Jon Edward, on the plate as he took great delight in sitting on the seat and turning the steering wheel when he was 3 years old.

The background and shed, which is a farm oil shed, are from a farm near Great Missenden, Bucks. The plate is a mirrored image, as I preferred the left to right effect although other experts did not. The title "Going for a Song" was suggested by the name of a programme on antiques on BBC1 television.'

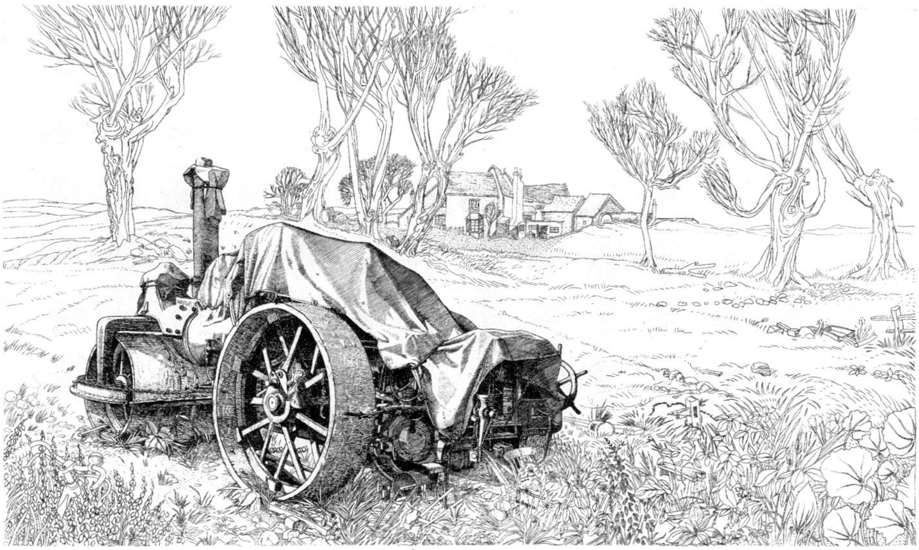

111 PUT OUT TO GRASS 1970

LINE ENGRAVING 183 x 302 mm EDITION 30 *1st state trial**

EXHIBITED RE, 1970, No. 54: Götene, 1975

ILLUSTRATED Götene Konstförening Exhibition Catalogue, 1975 and Nya Läns, Tidningen, 20 May 1975

The artist wrote: 'This old steam roller was a very long standing resident on Knightscote Farm Museum, Harefield, Middlesex and various attempts were made from time to time to recover it from its very dilapidated condition. It was made about 1913 by Aveling and Porter, of Rochester, Kent. Finally it was hauled into a field and left for further repair. A tarpaulin was dragged over it, an old-fashioned blacksmith's vice clamped to it for further action, then "Put out to Grass" looked like a war horse. I understand it has been renovated into mint condition and made a great showpiece and a very valuable antique. It was also a feature in the film *The Revenge of Smokey Joe.*

For a background, I added Coleshill Pond Farm, Bucks, and introduced various small items chiefly for fun and to fill up the design, including part of an old bicycle in some nettles, the names of two very good friends who live in Sweden and who collect my work, an old chair, a saucepan, sledge hammer (broken), bottles and jars, carpenter's saw bench, gate post, spanners, bolts, many grasses, leaves and flowers, including moon daisy, lords and ladies fingers and a little nude lady sitting in an old tin (just for fun). This plate was engraved the year I retired, hence the title "Put out to Grass".'

The plate is also engraved "CHAC, 1970" and the names of Kerstin and Lief Lundström, the artist's Swedish friends, also appear.

* The 1st state contained detail of the steam roller, some of the foreground, and an outline of the background. The finished machine with completed foreground and background appeared in the final state.

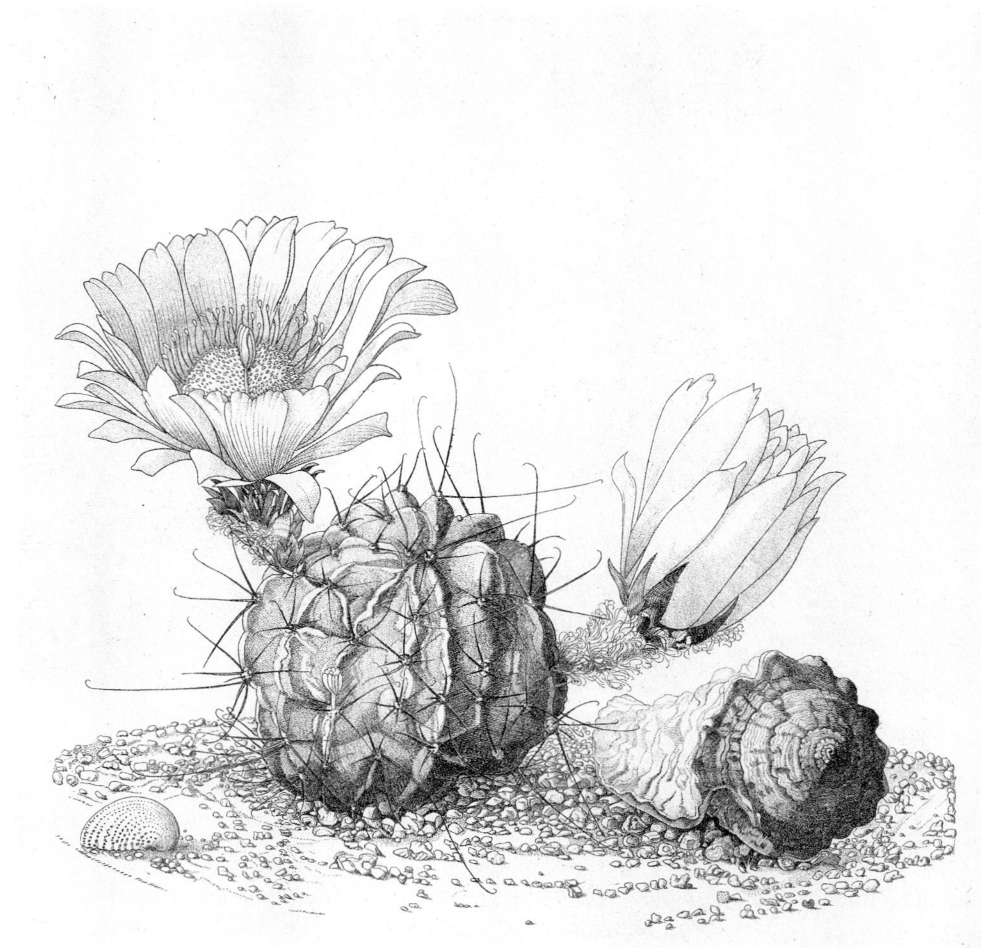

112 CACTUS AND SHELLS 1971

LINE ENGRAVING 198 x 198 mm

EDITION 30

EXHIBITED Royal Academy, 1971, No. 225: RE, 1971, No. 45: CPE, Montreal, 1971: Götene, 1975

The artist noted: 'The cactus in a 4 inch pot was given to me by a friend; the flower was a very pale yellow. This plate was accepted and hung at the Royal Academy; they preferred to hang this plate instead of "Tree Patterns, New Forest", which was a disappointment to me.' A small nude lady sits on a pebble.

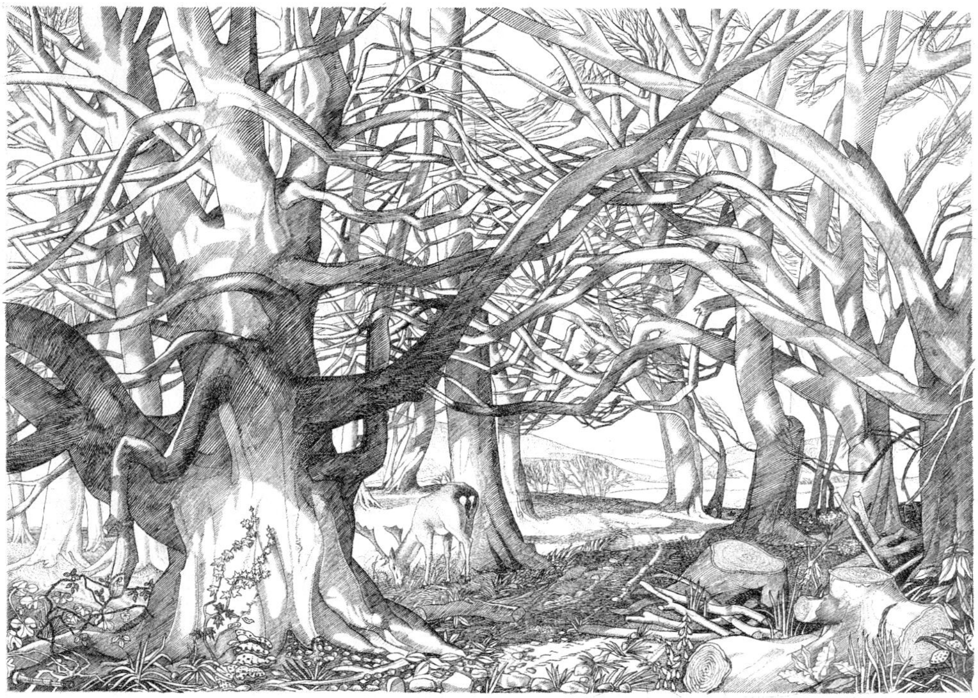

113 TREE PATTERNS, NEW FOREST (with large stag) 1971

LINE ENGRAVING* 174 x 237 mm

EDITION 30

EXHIBITED RE, 1971, No. 37: CPE, Toronto: Götene' 1975

The fifth in the series of studies of the New Forest, this one identified by the presence of a stag. The artist wrote of this engraving: 'This plate was a complete departure from my usual method of working. No drawings or preliminary studies were made at all for this most complicated plate. I made a few scratches on a copper plate with a steel point, of the general design and pattern, standing on the spot holding the clean copper plate in one hand — taking in all about 15 minutes. The main scratch lines remain on the plate and can be seen on the finished proof. Many weeks later I proceeded to engrave direct on to this plate, without further reference of any kind, the complicated pattern of beech trees and branches, interwoven and broken off. All sorts of wild plants and flowers and toadstools are worked into the design. In the left hand corner a graver used to engrave the plate can be seen, and on a sawn-off branch a small nude is engraved (just for fun).'

* Signed and dated 1st, 2nd, 3rd and 4th trial proofs also exist.

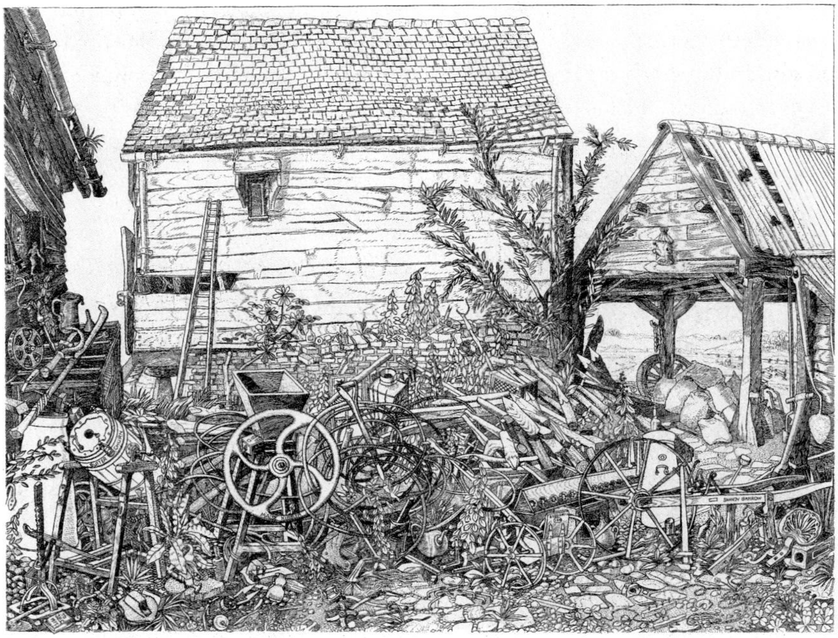

114 SHANDY BARROW, MAIZE KIBBLER AND BUTTER CHURN 1974

LINE ENGRAVING 190 x 244 mm EDITION 30

EXHIBITED Royal Academy, 1974, No. 988: RE, 1974, No. 51: Götene, 1975

ILLUSTRATED *The Royal Academy Illustrated*, 1974, p. 32

COLLECTION City of Sheffield, Graves and Mapin Art Gallery

A jumbled collection of old machinery and tools lies abandoned between some barns at Knightscote Farm, Harefield. The plate was dedicated to the artist's grandson — 'To JEC 1973' is engraved on a book in the bottom left hand corner. Two nudes appear in this plate, one named 'Eve'! Also a caricatured self portrait of the artist! The three items of the title are engraved on the respective machines portrayed in the plate.

The artist recorded an inventory for the plate as follows: 'Oxalis Corniclata (yellow sorrel), moon daisy, chestnut tree, ash tree, nettles, plantain, dock, blackberry, convolvulus, dandelion, weeds and grasses, shandy barrow, seed drill, maize kibbler, butter churn, 2 milk churns, wagon jack (hand forged), seat tractor, old flat iron, hedge slasher knife for trimming cow's hoof, 2 horseshoes, number of old spanners, jug, funnel, small book, hand-forged adjustable spanner, meat hook, old gear wheel, split-handled screw driver, bottle, old rabbit hutch, iron mallet, old handlebars with bell, coiled spring, pipe with tap on end, wine bottle, small oil can, ballcock, broken chopper, 2 wrought iron gutter brackets, coils of rubber hose, 2 broken pitchforks, 7 wire straining hooks, old kettle, old Wellingtons, straining bracket for holding walls together, old pair steel tongs, fruit picking ladder, sharpened wood stakes, sheep shears, bean dibblers, old paint tin with brush in, cider flagon, tomtits' nesting box, old rabbit hutch, banded oak barrel, old iron teapot, broken hammer, rake, seed sacks, old wagon wheel, bucket handle (broken), 'H' section iron girder, butcher's meat chopper, old window frame, very small box with lid, old round sieve, padlock, duck on pond, large iron shod dibber, rick tester, turfing iron, sack trolley, old brick wall, granary, bits of old pipes and tubes, old brush, broken fork handle, handsaw, bracket, sickle, house-brick.'

The artist clearly had much fun with this plate.

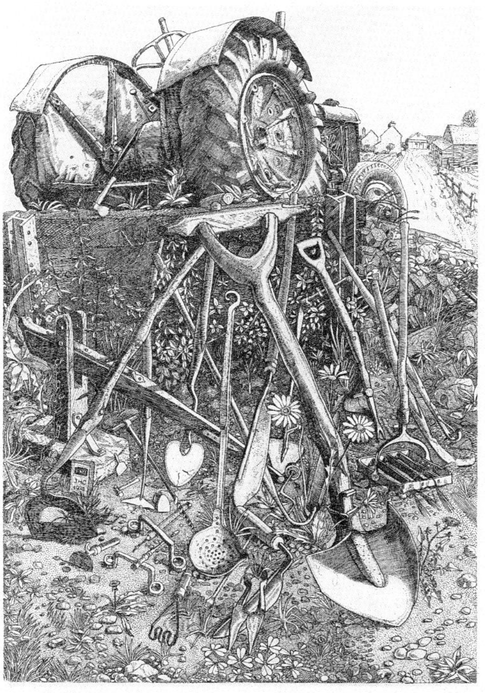

115 BREAST PLOUGH AND BARLEY HUMMELLER 1975

LINE ENGRAVING 268 x 183 mm

EDITION 50

EXHIBITED RE 1975, No. 56: Götene, 1975

ILLUSTRATED Götene Konstförening Exhibition Catalogue, 1975

A number of old tools are displayed beneath a veteran tractor, at Knightscote Farm, Harefield. In the background is Langley Farm. A reference to a promotion in the career of the artist's son, Jon, appears in the engraving.

The artist noted: 'This breast plough is 100 years old and has been well used. The ironwork is blacksmith forged and the main handle has been fashioned out of a Y forked branch of an ash tree. It is driven by force with one's breast, and is commonly used in preparing the turf in burn beating. The barley hummeller is an instrument for separating the awns (spiky bits) of the barley plant from the seed. The print includes bull hook, hedge slasher, dock grubber, turfing iron, silage cutter, small hoe, ditching tool, old ladle, sheep shears, sheep branding iron, flat iron, silage knife, large hoe, small hand hoe — (this I have discovered now is for scraping pigs' bristles and the hook for pulling out the toes), coach wheel spanners, old screw driver, chopper, old fire tongs, braced screwdriver, hammer, drainage tool, old wooden jack, old Fordston tractor (about 1936, 4 cylinder, 25 horsepower) for future renovation, just arrived from Ireland on loading ramp.

Various flowers, plants and grasses found on the farm during the year, include moon daisies (much enlarged as are most of the other flowers) dandelions, nettles, dock, convolvulus, ivy, plantain, sow thistle, yellow sorrel, and there is a small acknowledgement to my son, Jon, on being made secretary of EMI.'

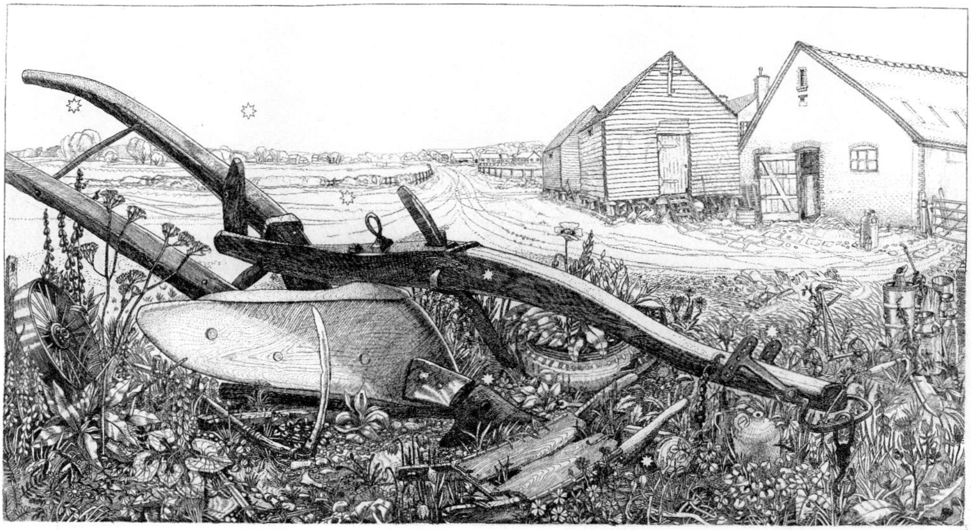

116 THE PLOUGH 1975

LINE ENGRAVING 175 x 310 mm EDITION 50

EXHIBITED RE, 1975, No. 71: Götene, 1975

COLLECTION Brunel University, 1975

An antique plough rests in a corner by two old granaries and a calf-rearing building at Knightscote Farm, with Harefield village in the distance. The farmer's name, Frank Townsend, is engraved on the plate. Chaplin's notes record: 'This wooden and iron plough is over 100 years old and was found hanging in a barn in Buckinghamshire, the wooden Mould Board full of woodworm, the rest fairly free from it. The iron share (also known as Sock) and the principal cutting part of the plough is well worn, The beam is the main member of the structure, running from back to front, to which all other parts are attached, and is of one piece of timber and beautifully shaped and curved. Mould Boards were made of wood until 1760 when cast iron was used: wooden Mould Boards were still in common use until 1830. This plough was designed and made to plough one particular field called "The Great Tit".

Besides the plough, there are various small tools, objects and wild flowers, including pig dressing cradle, very old scythe, drainage tool, a small 2-wheel pig trolley for transporting a plough such as this, a small pig trough, plough spanner, iron drum, stoneware jar, mild churns, old tyre, silage knife, oil drams, oil pump and accessories, old wheel, Banbury billhook. Wild flowers include plantain, lords and ladies finger, dandelion, corn poppy, foxglove, stinging nettle, wild snakeshead, winter heliotrope, cow parsley, harebells, red campion, blackberry, teasel, greater stitchwort, moon daisy, ivy, dock. All can be found at the farm during the seasons.'

Stylised stars representing the eponymous constellation range across the image.

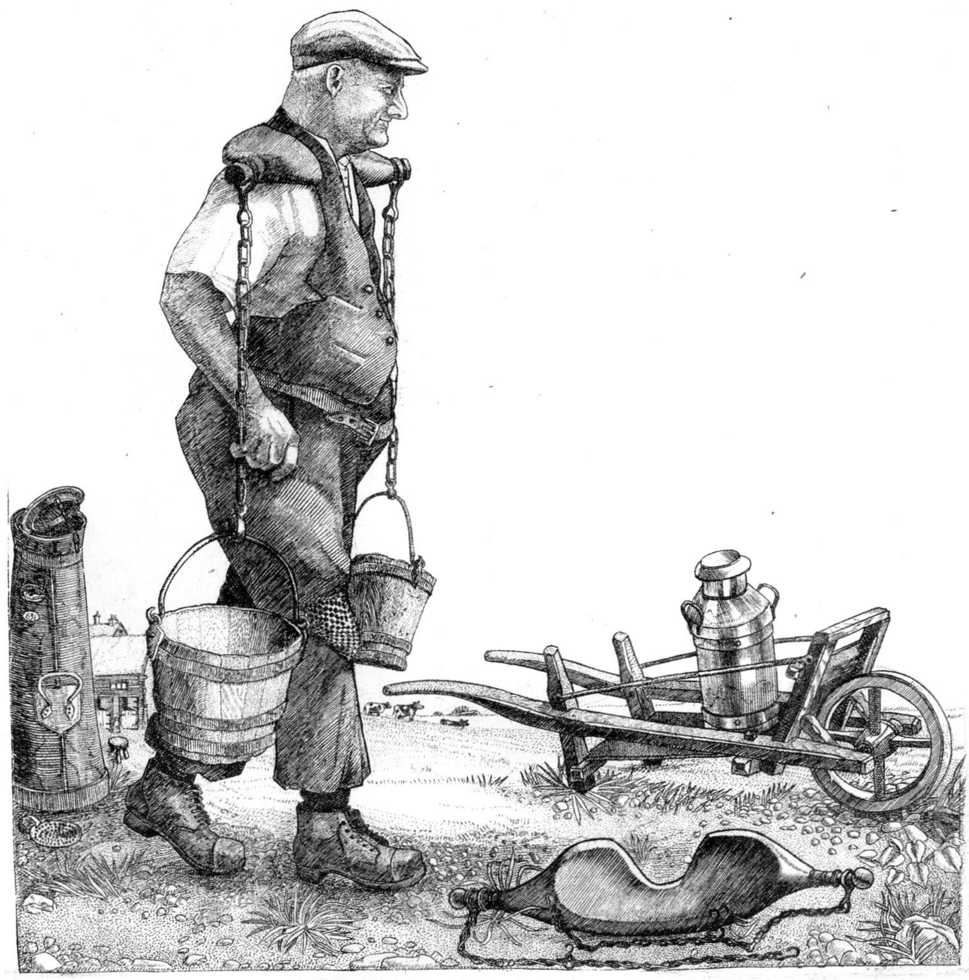

117 DICK TAYLOR AND YOKE OR YOKE, MILK BARROW AND DICK TAYLOR 1976

LINE ENGRAVING 155 x 143 mm EDITION 50

EXHIBITED RE, 1976, No. 61

The artist noted: 'Mr Dick Taylor farmed at Brooks Farm, Bicester, Oxfordshire. It is a faithful portrait of Dick after he had finished hand milking his cows and carrying the milk in wooden buckets with the aid of a milk yoke. The yoke on the ground and milk churn, and milk churn or sack barrow are from the farm collection at Knightscote Farm.'

Another nude appears in this plate.

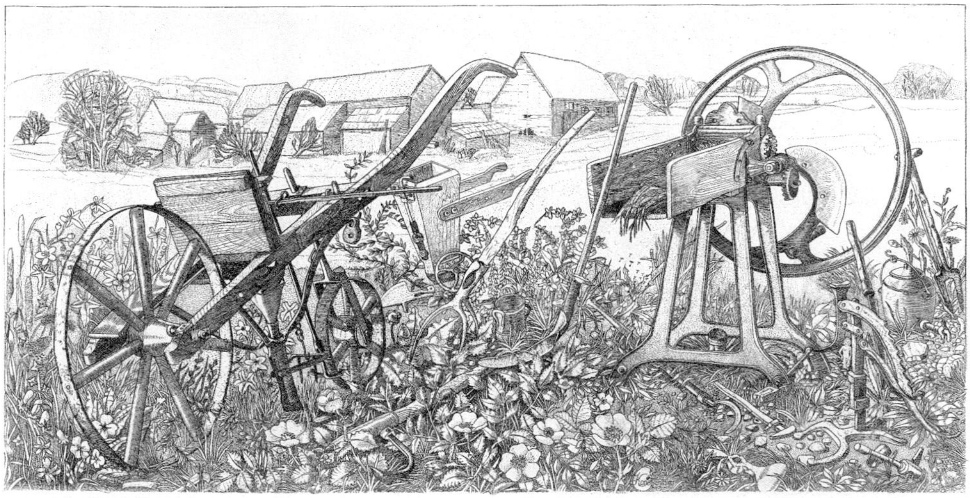

118 SURREY DRILL, DOGROSE AND CHAFF CUTTER 1976

LINE ENGRAVING 166 x 317 mm

EDITION 50

EXHIBITED RE, 1976, No. 68 and 1981, No. 269: Götene Konstförening, Sweden, 1979

A surrey drill and a chaff cutter lie in a field with a ground cover of dog roses; Stockers Farm, Rickmansworth, is in the background. The double cut chaff cutter was made by H. G. Singlehurst and the seed drill by J. Gibbs, Bedfont. The plate contains an acknowledgement — 'Götene Konstförening 1975' — of an exhibition of much of the artist's work in Sweden. A little nude also appears.

Chaplin noted: 'Besides the dog roses, I have added the following flowers and plants: Wood speedwell, bluebells, primrose, acorns, rye grasses, ox-eyed daisy, white bryong, plantain, little willow and elm trees in background. Amongst these plants I have introduced the following tools: swede lifter and top chopper, dog roller, bean drill, head of ditching tool, mill bill, 3-pronged striffle, log roller, bean drill, head of ditching tool, cheese press made of brass and steel, long handled ditching knife, long handled hedge slasher, drop ditching fork, cauldron, hand forged spanner, hand forged jack.'

See also the text for further commentary on this plate, page 86.

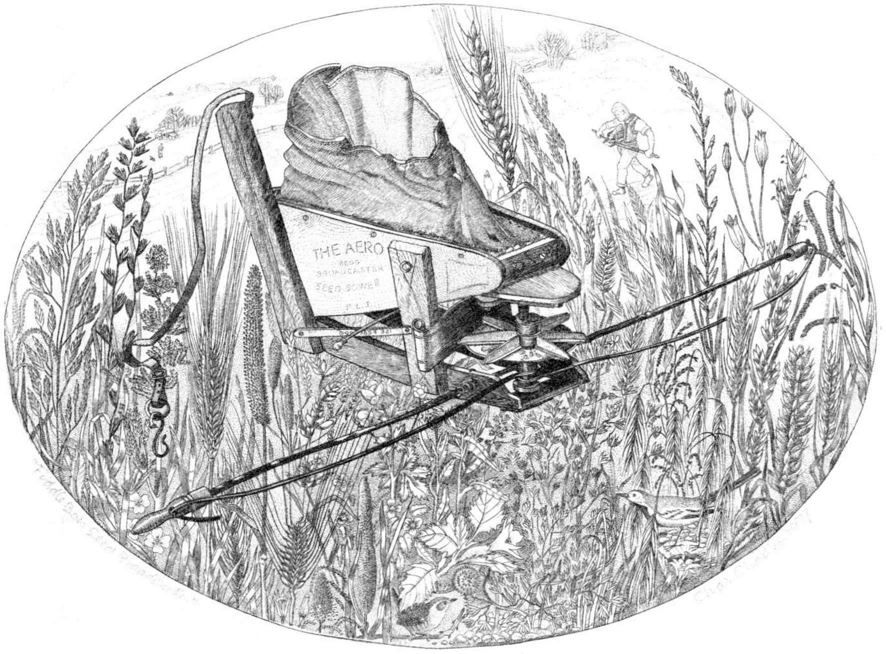

119 FIDDLE BOW SEED BROADCASTER 1977

LINE ENGRAVING Oval image 183 x 240 mm (rectangular plate) EDITION 50

EXHIBITED RE 1977, No. 170

'The Aero Regd. Broadcaster Seed Sower PLJ' rests on the ground, surrounded by the seeds of various grasses collected on Knightscote Farm, Harefield, while a small figure in the background shows the 'fiddle bow' in use. A wren and a wagtail enjoy the fallen seeds. This was the only oval image engraved by the artist.

The artist noted the large number of plants represented in the engraving as follows: 'Wheat emmer or two-grained splet, splet battledore, fan or peacock, winter bere barley (all old seeds not now in use), rye grass, globe flower, goats beard, thornapple, wheat, interrupted broome, broome, cockfoot, meadow barley, rye, speedwell flower, wheat seeds, wood fake broome, rush leaved fescue, barron broome, broad leaved willow herb, meadow grass, sands cats tail, cats tail timothy grass, tall fescue, wild radish flower, creeping twitch couch, plantain, and rampion sandstwitch.

One for the pigeon;
One for the crow;
One to wither;
And one to grow.

That's the fate of careless sowing of seed, according to the proverb. The seed broadcaster helps to dispel the proverb.'

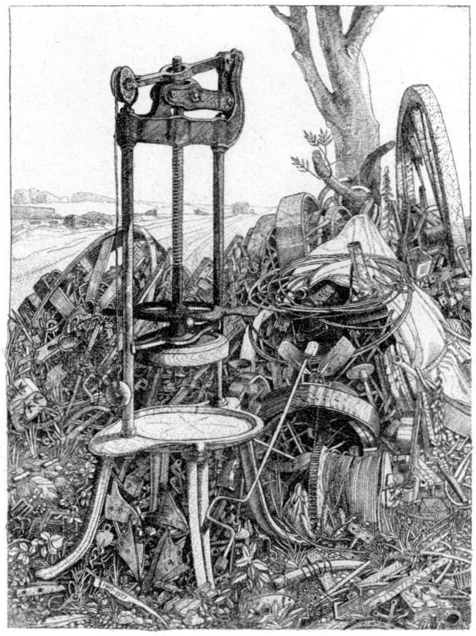

120 CHEESE PRESS 1977

LINE ENGRAVING 233 x 170 mm

EDITION 50

EXHIBITED Royal Academy, 1977, No. 1374: RE, 1977, No. 38: Götene, 1979

ILLUSTRATED *Journal of RE*, No. 7, 1985, p. 19 ('CHA Chaplin RE discusses his engravings.')

REFERENCE *Yorkshire Post*, 4 June 1977 — Harrogate Exhibition of RE

An old cheese press stands abandoned in a field amidst a pile of junk metal. The plate records the seventy years of the artist's life, '1907–1977'.

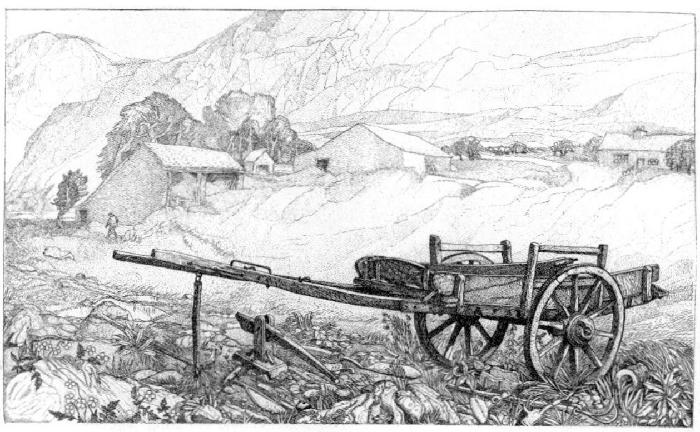

121 WELSHCART 1978

LINE ENGRAVING 165 x 265 mm

EDITION 50

EXHIBITED RE, 1978, No. 50: Turner House Gallery, Penarth, 1978

COLLECTION Purchased by the National Library of Wales

The cart, the first in a series of six carts, was drawn at the Old Kiln, Museum, Tildford, Surrey; the shafts are 8 feet long and the body 10 feet by 4 feet. The artist notes: 'The background is freely adapted from a sketch I made in pastel of a farm near Talyllyn, Towyn, Merioneth, Wales. I have introduced into it an old wooden wagon jack, skid pan, long handled ditching tool, long handled hedge slasher, coulter scraper, wooden iron banded mustard seed barrel, adze head, small hand-carved wooden grain ladle, hay or silage knife, and a strange double hooked, long handled muck knocker, used to spread cow pats on the Midland fattening pastures.

Some of the weeds and flowers added are dock, moon daisy, plantain, nettles, ivy, various grasses and Welsh poppy, which is yellow in colour and only grows near damp and shady rocks in Wales and S W England. I have made various pastel studies of this area of Wales and have endeavoured to make this subject closely associated with the background, as well as to blend as a whole into a picture and design, instead of an isolated engraving of a cart.'

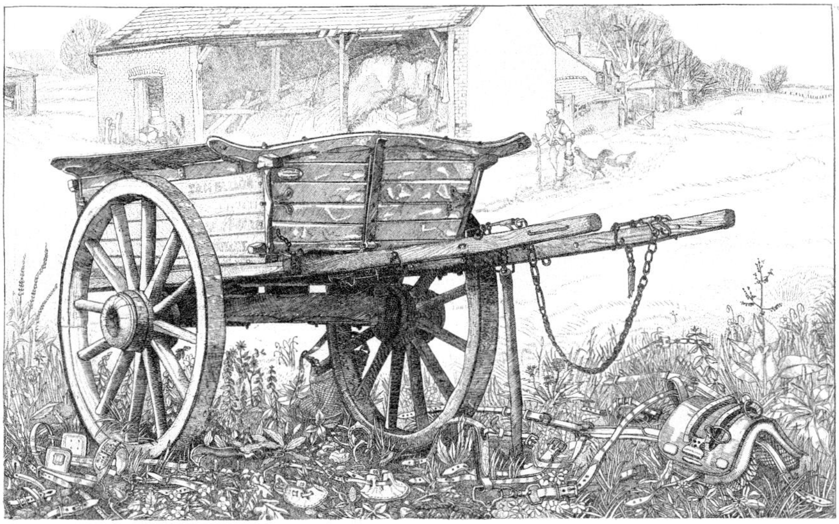

122 SCOTCH CART 1978

LINE ENGRAVING 165 x 260 mm.

EDITION 50 *Signed and dated 1st, 2nd and 3rd trial proofs also exist**

EXHIBITED Royal Academy, 1978, No. 810: RE, 1978, No. 54, and 1981, No. 258: Götene, 1979

COLLECTION Durham County Council, Bowes Museum

Drawn at the Greater London Council Museum at Knightscote Farm, Harefield. The background is a freely adapted mirrowed image of Tring Farm, Tring. Chaplin wrote: 'These carts were originally made in Scotland, then in East Anglia — and are variously called Tumbrils, Tip-up Carts, Scotch Carts, Dung Carts. This cart was made (see oval iron plate on front) by E & H Ronerts, Ltd Deanshanger, Stony Stratford. The last owner's name was J R H Ellson of Higham Perres, Northants — this is barely distinguishable on the side of cart. The workmanship in wood and iron is of the highest craftsmanship. The balance of the tip up and down can be easily accomplished by one man standing between the shafts, holding the shaft with one hand, and the other pulling a small lever. The cart can easily be pulled by one man in the shaft. The overall balance is perfect.

The working horse saddle and bridle bear a brass plate on the bridle with the maker's name on a hinged brass plate "Hutson Maker Uxbridge". All the harness straps and buckles in brass are made of the finest craftsmanship. There are a pair of horses' overshoes worn to prevent damage to grass lawns when worn by the horses. Also included is an old horse's nosebag, hoof paring knife, various horseshoes, and skid pan for a wagon. Some of the plants and flowers include hawkweed, dandelion, lords and ladies fingers, speedwell, stinging nettles, plantains, crimson clover, daisy, dock, poppies and foxglove.'

* In the 1st and 2nd trial proofs the cart is complete but the background is incomplete. The little nude appears again.

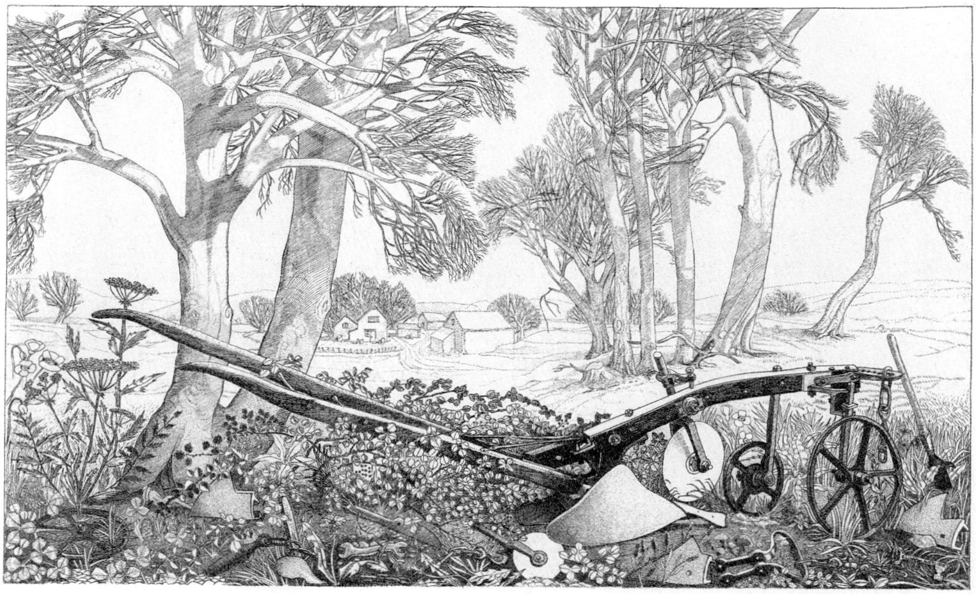

123 BRAMBLES AND PLOUGH 1978

LINE ENGRAVING 165 x 265 mm EDITION 50

EXHIBITED RE, 1979, No. 42: Götene, 1979

COLLECTION Durham County Council, Bowes Museum

This antique plough was drawn at the Greater London Council Museum at Knightscote Farm, Harefield. The background trees are from pencil studies made at Batchworth Lake, Rickmansworth with some buildings at Langley Farm, Harefield. The coming of age (eighteenth birthday) of the artist's eldest granddaughter, Elizabeth Louise, is celebrated on a key in the right hand corner. The little nude lady, now almost a trademark of the artist, lurks in the undergrowth.

The artist's detailed notes give some further information: 'This two-wheel plough (both wheels adjustable) is constructed with wood, cast iron, also hand forged part and steel parts, the overall length being 9 ft 10 ins, and was made *circa* 1850. The plough consists of beam (wood encased with iron), handle or stilts (wood), handle stay or brace, quadrant head, draught chain, breast or mould board (steel), breast stay, mould board rest, share, land wheel, land wheel standard, furrow wheel, furrow wheel standard, coulter, coulter clip, and disc coulter. Two types of plough shares are shown — a drag weight and chain - rake and chain — plough spanner, disc coulter and skim coulter, and in the left-hand corner some odd plough wheels. A coulter cleaner leans on the front of the plough.

The bramble or blackberry bush around the plough is the main plant. Others include hearts tongue fern, dandelion, crimson clover (not a weed), poppy, beech trees, timothy grass, wood mushroom, white clover (not a weed), and hemlock.'

124 SNOW DROPS AND MOWING MACHINE

1979/1983

LINE ENGRAVING

173 x 233 mm

EDITION 75 *1st state 1979, 2nd state 1983 (final):* 2nd state illustrated*

EXHIBITED RE, 1979, No. 47 and 1983, No. 104

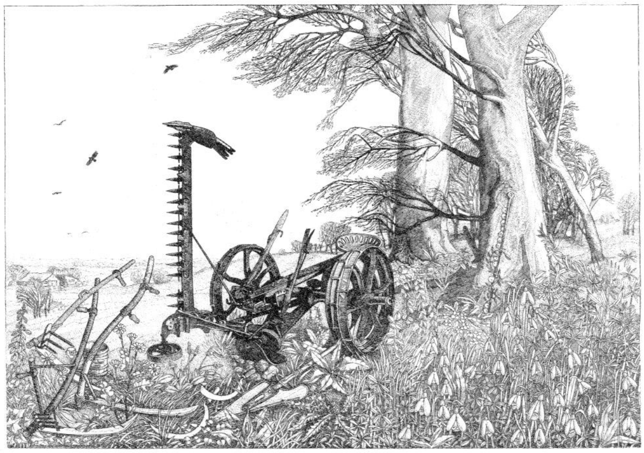

An old rusting, derelict and broken horse-drawn mowing machine by Barnlett, Thirsk, Scotland lies abandoned in a clump of snowdrops. Drawn at the Greater London Council Museum at Knightscote Farm, Harefield, it is an imperfect example. Also appearing is the Art cup, awarded to the artist's granddaughter, Sara Ann, at the Arts Educational School, Tring in 1978, and a source of much pride to him.

Chaplin had clearly studied this machine closely. 'The things that interest me are the cutter bar raised into the sky (lowered to the ground when mowing), the unique pair of wheels and the odd shaped ironwork. There are two large travelling wheels and an independent gear frame from which the cutter bar and finger beam hangs in such a manner as to allow it to follow freely over all the irregularities of the ground. In this engraving, the cutter bar is raised to allow for transporting. The track board is missing from the end of the cutter bar, but one is engraved directly under the machine. Also the cutting blades which move between the fingers are shown leaning against the tree. It is a horse-drawn machine. The shaft and whippletrees are missing, and there are a number of broken parts, and various bits missing. It is all rusted up, and will require a great deal of renovation.

The reason for the snowdrops is that many years ago there were some farm workers' cottages on this museum site, and, each year since, snowdrops appear as well as other garden flowers. However, this year will be the last for the snowdrops as the site for the museum building was so turned over by the bulldozer, that I do not think they will survive.

Also included in the engraving are an old reaping scythe, bagging hook, cradle scythe, sickle, common scythe, track board, a wooden mustard seed barrel, cutter blades, snowdrops, cleavers or goosegrass, stinging nettles, teazle, stemless thistle, foxglove, cuckoopint, hoary plant, moon daisy, primrose, dock, ivy, rough hawksbeard, feverfew or batchelor buttons, which is reputed to cure migraine.'

* In the second state, printed in brown ink and exhibited at the RE in 1983, Chaplin engraved a flock of crows circling on the left of the image, and more foliage to the left of the tree trunks; also, the background to the mowing machine was filled in to a greater extent.

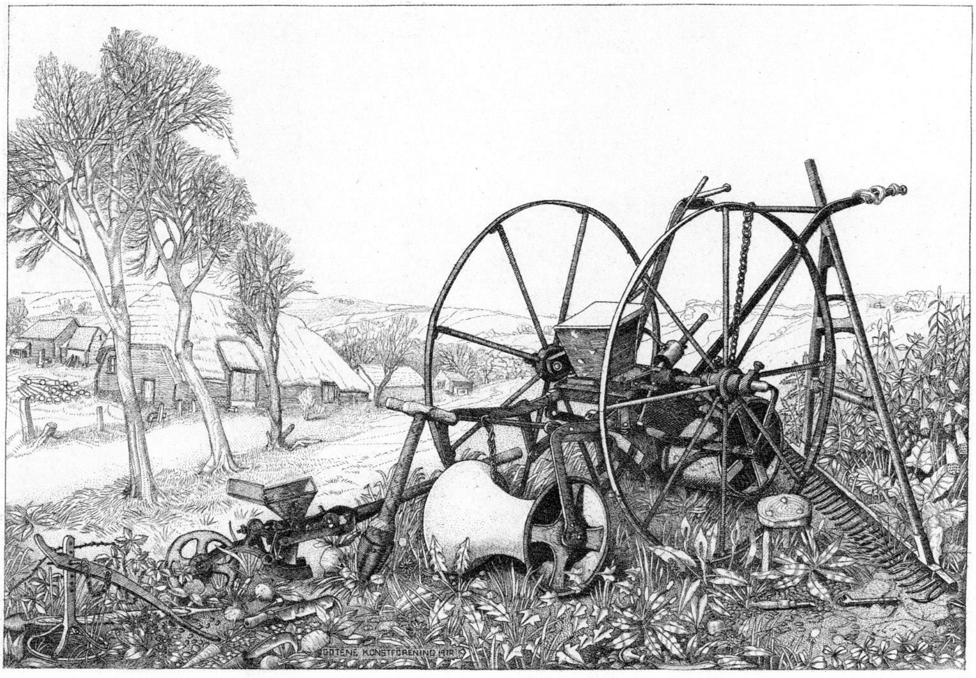

125 TURNIP SEED DRILL 1979

LINE ENGRAVING 162 x 222 mm

COMMISSIONED Götene Konstförening, Sweden. One edition of 60, plus 20 artist's proofs

EXHIBITED RE 1981, No. 273: Götene, 1979

COLLECTION Durham County Council, Bowes Museum

The seed drill was drawn at the Greater London Council's museum at Knightscote Farm, Harefield. The background shows a reed-thatched barn in Sussex, and a fine little nude also appears.

Chaplin notes: 'Turnip seed and other small seeds were scattered by hand or sown by hand in shallow drills made with the hand hoe, until this machine was invented and made by J Elcott & Sons of North Petherton, Somerset, England about 1900. The unusual and interesting feature of this Turnip Drill is the concave front roller. The small seed drill also shown is called a "Seed Dodger" — an aptly named hand pushed drill used to fill in the gaps where seed has failed to germinate. Also shown is a large dibber, an old three-legged milking stool, large hay-rake called a hobby rake, a mole-catcher's staff, one very small horseshow nail, hand forged wagon jack, pea and bean cutter, turnip cutter, spanner and two engraving tools as used to engrave this plate. Some of the plants are thistle, stinging nettles, foxglove, blackberries, lords and ladies fingers, plantain, swedes, mangolds, turnips, parsnips, daisy, dandelion, ivy, edible toadstools and various grasses.' For further reference to this plate, see page 78.

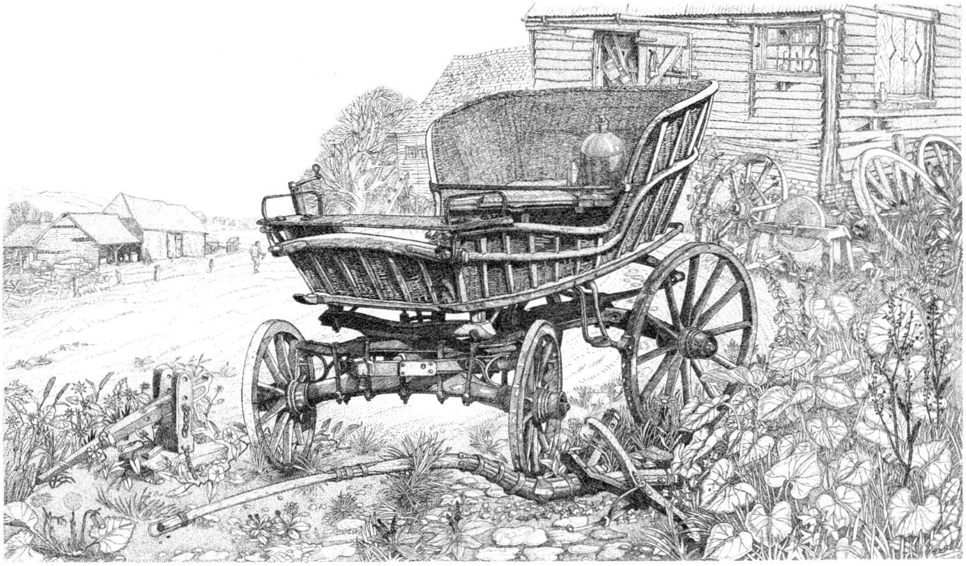

126 LIGHT CARRIAGE 1979

LINE ENGRAVING 170 x 275 mm

EDITION 50

EXHIBITED Royal Academy, 1982, No. 868: RE, 1981, No. 235

The four-wheel carriage, originating in Towcester, Northamptonshire, rests outside farm buildings with a whetstone grinding wheel. The farm is in Pitstone, near Tring, with Sussex barns in the background. The little nude appears again.

The artist's notes reveal: 'This unique light 4-wheel carriage has many features that are original in structure; i.e. the single pole shaft, with whipple-trees on one side only, is a peculiar bent shape and reinforced with iron sheeting, as are many other parts of the body work, all being carefully shaped. There is considerable cane work which is unfortunately damaged, although the rest of the carriage is in a remarkable state of preservation. There is a turndown brake on the rear wheels which are leaf sprung across the bodywork. All the woodwork is of light structure and beautifully shaped and chamfered, especially the front pair of wheels. There is a large amount of hand wrought ironwork on the whole of the body. There are three old stone jars in the carriage seat. Included also is an old wooden jack. The wild flowers and plants are lambstail, plantain, catstail, timothy grass, coltsfoot, field bindweed, stinging nettles, moon daisy, lesser celandine, and old seeds of purple loosestrife.'

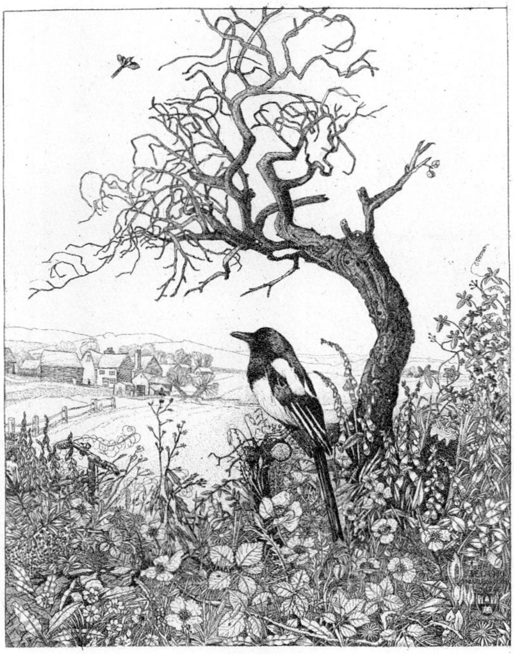

127 TWO'S COMPANY 1980

LINE ENGRAVING 208 x 162 mm

EDITION 50
2nd state — with magpie in sky

EXHIBITED RE, 1991, No. 267

In the foreground a magpie perches against a dead tree outlined against the sky, whilst its mate soars in the sky above. The background is a farm in the Chess valley. In the right hand corner appears the coat of arms of Marlborough College, in order to celebrate his grandson, Jon Edward, gaining admission there in 1980.

The title of the work derives from the gift of a print of the 2nd state to the parents of the artist's daughter-in-law Betty, William and Maggie Cave, on the occasion of their golden wedding anniversary. In the 2nd state the artist engraved an additional magpie in the sky to accompany the one perched on the tree — 'Two's Company'. The little nude is well concealed in the dense undergrowth of the 2nd state.

The artist added: 'I was demonstrating to a friend how I would draw an old apple tree on Knightscote Farm, Harefield, without being too realistic. The tree was dead and contorted — however, I put a little apple on it. Then, like all my plates, it began to develop on at least six pieces of tracing paper — no complete drawing but many little sketches. Magpies are mostly seen about in pairs and quite often in my own garden. The plants included are all from little thumbnail sketches I have made including: lambs tongue plantain, common poppy, bryony, foxglove, last year's seed heads, odd leaves, stinging nettle, lords and ladies, primrose, blackberry, dog rose, many grasses and an old bicycle.

I have since discovered that the little dead apple tree was a plum tree.'

128 CHRIST CHURCH, CHORLEYWOOD 1981

LINE ENGRAVING 172 x 236 mm

NOT EDITIONED *1st state, 2nd state:* (1st state illustrated)*

A view, or views, of the church on the common at Chorleywood, Hertfordshire, representing an example of perhaps the most extreme form of artist's license. The image is reproduced from two quite separate angles, the churchyard, lych gate and body of the church from one position, and the tower from another, enabling the right buttress and

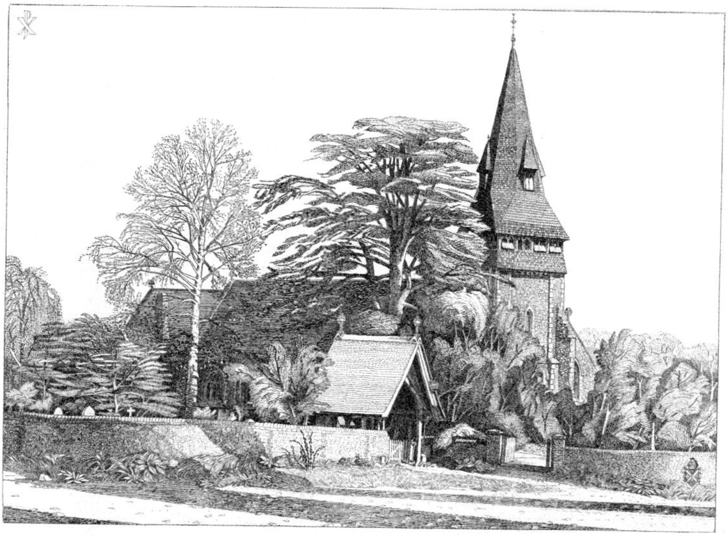

cross to be visible; the resulting image might not have been recognized by the architect in 1875, although it is instantly recognizable to all those who know the church.

Charles Chaplin wrote of this engraving: 'I do not know the history or the architectural details of this little church delightfully situated on Chorleywood Common, but I do know a little about trees, and this picturesque church has two wonderful specimens, a cedar and a silver birch. I could therefore only make a careful statement of what I could see, and this I have endeavored to do — a portrait of the church and trees.

The symbol in the top left-hand corner is called the CHI-RHO monogram. The Greek word for Christ is Χριστος, pronounced "Christos". A combination of the first two letters chi(X) and rho(ρ) was adopted by the early Christians as a symbol of Christianity and was often found in primitive and Christian art from the 4th century on sarcophagi and eucharistic vessels, (so I am informed). The greek word is translated into English as 'Christ' or 'Messiah', a title rather than a name which literally means 'anointed' or 'chosen one'. Jesus is called 'Christ' because he was chosen by God and anointed with the Holy Spirit to bring salvation to all people.

The crest in the bottom right-hand corner indicates that Christ Church is in the Diocese of St Albans. My son was married in the Church on 1st August, 1959 and this is recorded in the plate in the bottom right-hand corner— "Jon and Betty August 1959".' *(2nd state)

The huge 150-year-old cedar tree was blown down by the great storm of January 1990, a few days before Jon Edward, Charles Chaplin's grandson, was married there on 3 February, 1990 to Nicola Tippetts. His granddaughters Elizabeth Louise and Sara Ann had also been married there on 4 August, 1984 and 3 August, 1986 respectively. Charles Chaplin's funeral service was held in this church on 5 May, 1987, and that of his wife Elsie May, on 9 August, 1999.

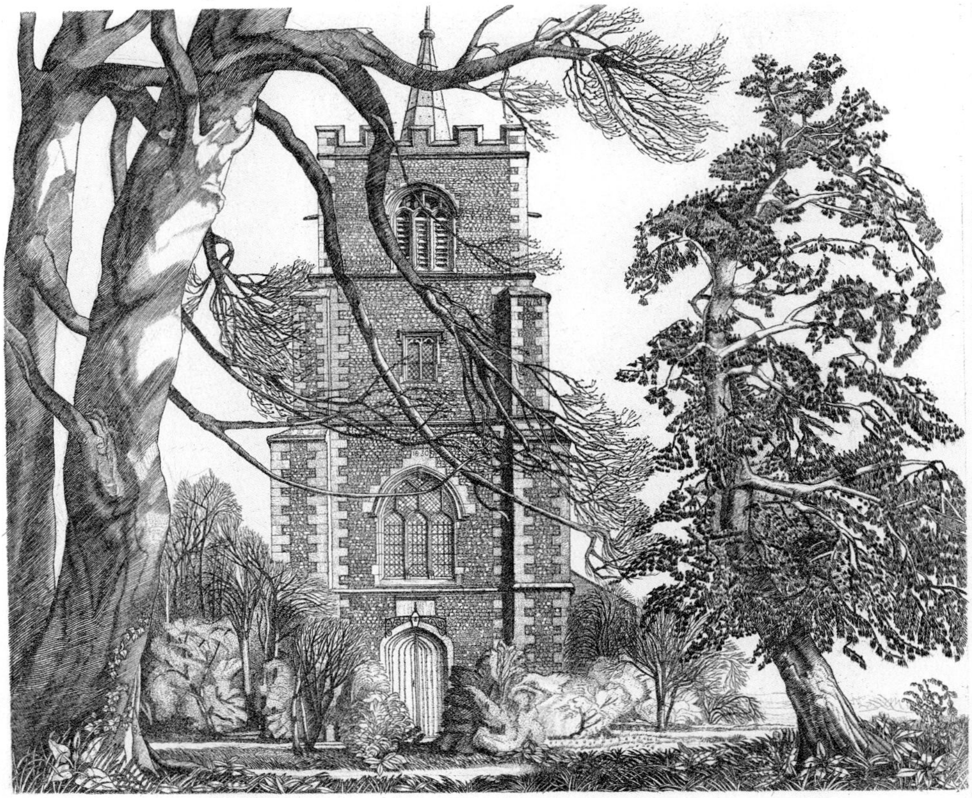

129 ST MARY'S CHURCH, RICKMANSWORTH 1981

LINE ENGRAVING 204 X 240 mm

EDITION 75

EXHIBITED RE 1982, No. 67

A view facing the tower of St Mary's. A number of signed and dated trial proofs of this plate exist, showing the trees and foreground gradually emerging round the tower. Unusually, many of the final proofs were not signed.

Chaplin wrote of this engraving: 'I have made five visits to make sketches of this Church, in freezing cold — once it snowed whilst sketching. A kestrel was sitting on the peak of the top window when I was sketching. West door and tower dated 1630 and window 1933. "Our Lady of the Island" — this was once the popular name for St Mary's Church, the island being formed by the rivers Chess and Gade and the town streams. The age of the Church is uncertain but the oldest parts of the tower are 14th century. The Church has been extensively rebuilt at different dates, notably after it had been damaged by fire by dissenters.'

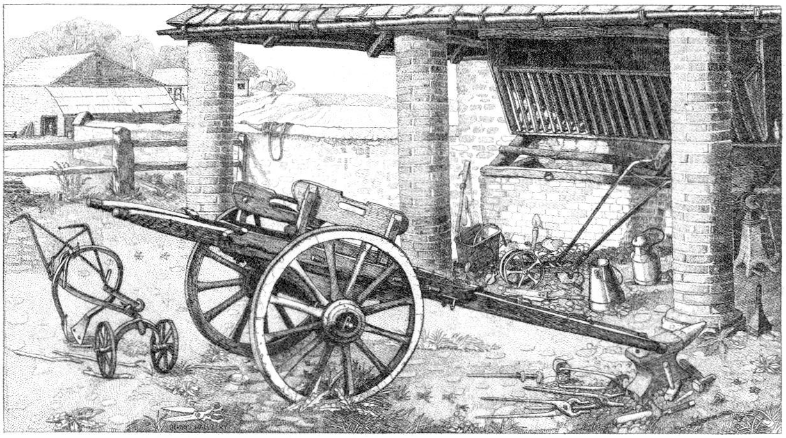

130 JINTY CART 1982

LINE ENGRAVING 128 x 225 mm

EDITION 75 *Brown ink. Printed Millbourn hand made paper*

EXHIBITED RE, 1982, No. 58

A small cart is parked in front of a lean-to shed with round brick pillars. The rural background contains many pieces of machinery and tools.

The artist wrote: 'The extremely rare and unique cart I believe is of Irish origin, although I have been unable to trace the makers, or where it came from, apart from the fact that it was in the possession of a farmer at Glyme Farm, Chipping Norton, Oxford. The farmer is the cousin of my friend, Dennis Hallbery*, who tells me the River Glyme rises from the farm, and the cart has now been sold to another collector. I think it is a cart chiefly for carrying people and goods, as it is not a heavy looking affair — a single plank seat was supported by the two sides.

The exceedingly unusual rounded brick pillars supporting the lean-to shed with a hay rack are on a farm I visited with Dennis, and the whole background is from the same farm. Pillars of this kind are most unusual and are the personal efforts of the farmer.

The very rare horse-drawn 'beet' lifting plough is now in the Greater London Council's Museum, Harefield, where I and my friend Dennis spend much time renovating and repairing antique farm implements, carts and wagons, tools, etc.

Also included in the plate are a blacksmith's anvil, shoeing hammer, swage, tongs, pincer, rasp file, 3 horseshoe nails (if you can find them), a hand forged adjustable spanner, wagon skid pan, cream separator, small hand cream separator, large oil funnel, small seed drill, sheep drenching bottle, coulter cleaner, a wood hoist block, trowel, small tank, bill hook, small sickle, a 100 year old pair of American tailors' shears which belong to Dennis, who is a Master Tailor, and who helps me with the studies for my plates in many and various ways.'

* Name engraved on plate.

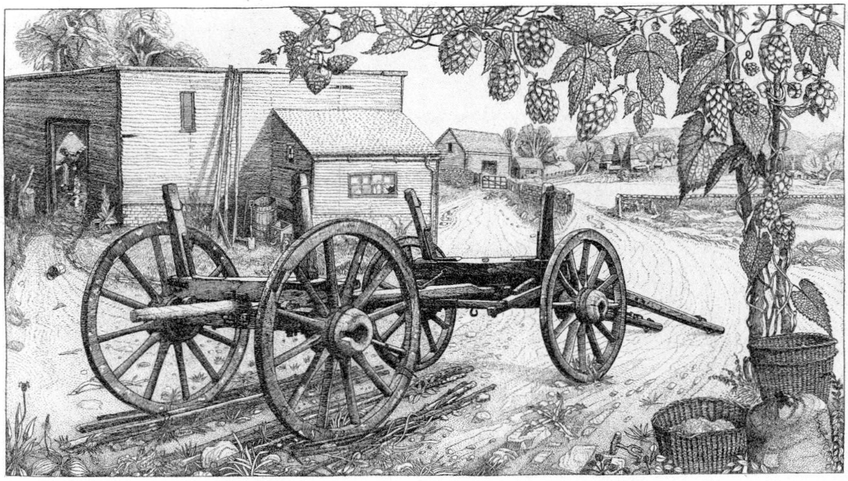

131 HOP POLE TUG 1982

LINE ENGRAVING 158 x 280 mm EDITION 80 *Brown ink on Millbourn paper*

EXHIBITED RE, 1983, No. 14

ILLUSTRATED *RE Journal*, No. 7, 1985 p. 20 ('CHA Chaplin RE discusses his engravings')

A special cart for carrying hop poles is positioned in front of farm buildings, with oast houses from Crookham Hill, Kent appearing in the background. To the top left is a garland of hops. This is the fifth in a series of images of carts — the others being Welsh Cart, Scotch Cart, Light Carriage and Jinty Cart. Another cart, Banham Waggon was never completed. The plate, as so often, contains a small naked lady.

A family connection was recorded by the artist: 'This interesting wagon from the Kent-Sussex borders is owned by my nephew, John Chaplin*, of Lewes, Sussex, who is a collector of farming antiques. It is in a very good condition and is called a "Bavin" or hop pole tug, for use in the hop gardens. Bavin is the Kentish word for a bundle of brushwood, and the main task of the tug was to carry long hop poles, which were mainly of larch, chestnut, or ash, 12–14ft long, the hops being ready for picking during mid-September. The chief feature of this tug, which is a smaller version of the much heavier timber tug used for hauling heavy timber, is that there is no body as such, and there are no rear tail boards or floor or sides. The body consists of a very heavy single pole fixed to the front wheel assembly, but the rear wheel can be moved forwards or backwards along the pole. There are four upright stifers (standards) mortised into the front and rear bolsters.

My nephew sent me along a box of hops so I engraved a garland of hops across the picture. The hop sacks called 'pockets' are very long and contain about 112 lbs of hops. The wicker hop baskets are shown. Also engraved is a sack grab, hairy plantain, nettles, docks, dandelion, and narrow leaved plantain.'

* Name engraved in plate.

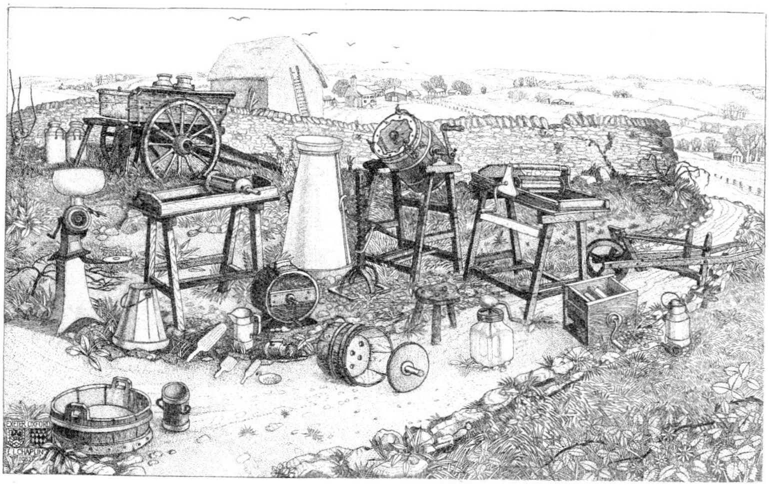

132 MILK, BUTTER, CHEESE 1982

LINE ENGRAVING 149 x 233 mm EDITION 80 *Brown ink*

EXHIBITED RE 1983, No. 104

COLLECTION Durham County Council, Bowes Museum

A collection of old tools and objects associated with the dairy industry is assembled on a farm lane in front of a Cotswold stone wall, with a Cotswold farm in the background. The arms of Exeter University and Magdalen College, Oxford, in the left hand corner acknowledge the achievement of the artist's granddaughter, Elizabeth Louise, in gaining her degree at Exeter, and her post-graduate place at Oxford in 1982.

The artist notes: 'Some years ago I came across an old dung cart being used by a farmer in the Cotswolds as a milk pick-up platform for his milk churns. His farm being across the fields, this old "Scotch Cart" served as a convenient loading and unloading platform for the milk lorries going down the lane. I also saw old wartime Anderson air raid shelters being used for the same purpose at other farms — these were not so picturesque.

All the other objects I have repaired and renovated at some time or other, now belong to the Greater London Council and are collected together at Knightscote Farm, Harefield. I have made small sketches of them all in the past. Besides the old dung cart, the other objects relate is some way to milk, butter, or cheese and include up and over butter churn, 1 gallon glass butter churn (I found 5 woodworm grubs in the little wooden paddles), wooden square box 4 paddle butter churn, wooden round box 2 paddle butter churn, 3 leg milking stool, 3 wooden butter pats, 1 small butter mould, 1 butter worker paddle turned by hand, (removes excess water from butter), 1 butter worker paddle turned by hand roller, (removes excess water from butter), large wooden cheese mould, large milk churn, milk churn barrow, milk churns of various sizes and shapes, various milk measures, small cream skimmer, old upright cream separator, metal cheese mould, wooden cheese mould, and an iron wagon jack.'

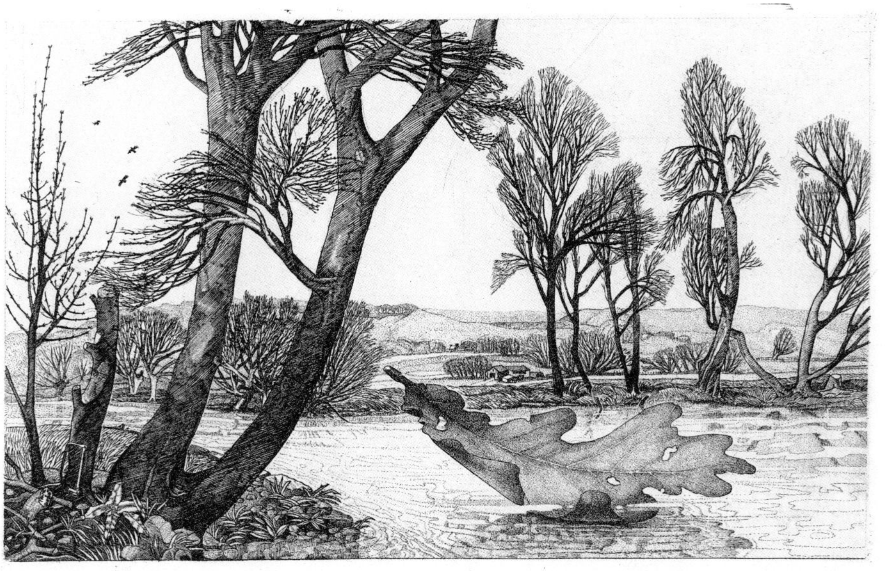

133 FLOATING OAK LEAF 1983

LINE ENGRAVING 138 x 213 mm

EDITION 75 *Printed 1984. Some signed 3rd trial proofs dated 1983 lack some detail in the river surface and the flying crows to the left; also some trial proofs of the final engraving.*

EXHIBITED RE 1984, No. 174

An oak leaf floats down the River Colne at Rickmansworth; the lakes and a farm can be seen in the background. A surrealist feature is that the scale of the oak leaf is many times that of its setting. The names of friends, Frank and Barbara, are engraved on the plate. This is the last plate by the artist of his beloved area, the lakes at Rickmansworth, which had inspired so much of his work in the previous fifty years since acquiring his house and studio there. He was seriously ill at this time, having to give up his studio and move to a flat which, fortunately, overlooked and was close to the lakes. He was therefore able, for a couple more years, to work in the area.

Another friend, Paul Wigmore, wrote a verse, inspired by this image:

ALTERNATIVE ECOLOGY

Downstream a secret runnel flows
Through microcosmic rural land
Where man is brash and bellicose
Because he cannot understand

Upstream there is a giant oak
Whose leaves are broader than a span
Where dreadful yellowhammers croak
And feed on unrepentant man

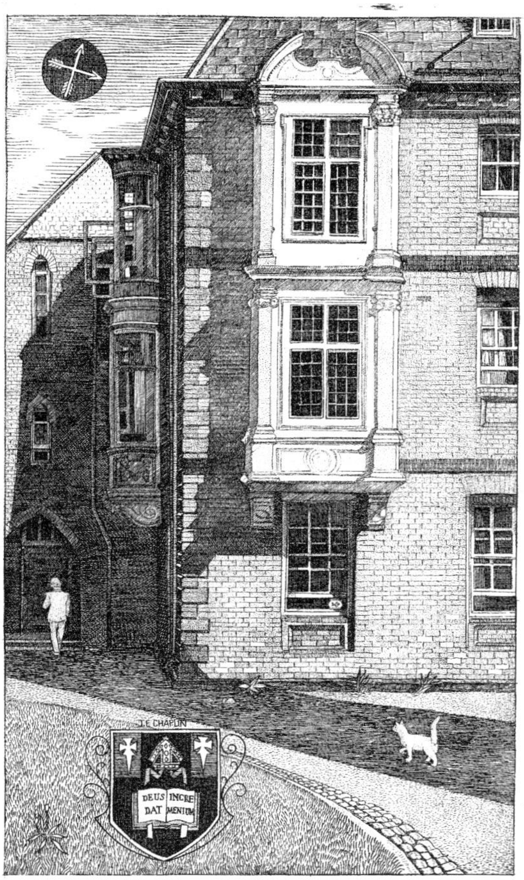

134 ORIEL WINDOWN, THE COLLEGE MARLBOROUGH 1984

LINE ENGRAVING 182 x 105 mm

EDITION 30 *originally, extended to 75*

EXHIBITED RE 1985, No. 75

An oriel window in B2 House at Marlborough College, Wiltshire. A student enters the building on the left, whilst a cat walks up the path, and a goldfish bowl props the sash window open. The arms of the College appear in the foreground, and the House badge appears at top left. The plate was dedicated by the artist to his grandson, Jon Edward, who attended the College 1980–86, and at one time occupied the room known as the 'goldfish bowl'.

A letter from the artist to his grandson about this plate is reproduced in the text, page 82. The artist also gave his grandson a portfolio with the original rough ideas for the plate, the detailed pencil sketches and architectural notes, and five trial proofs at progressive stages of the engraving.

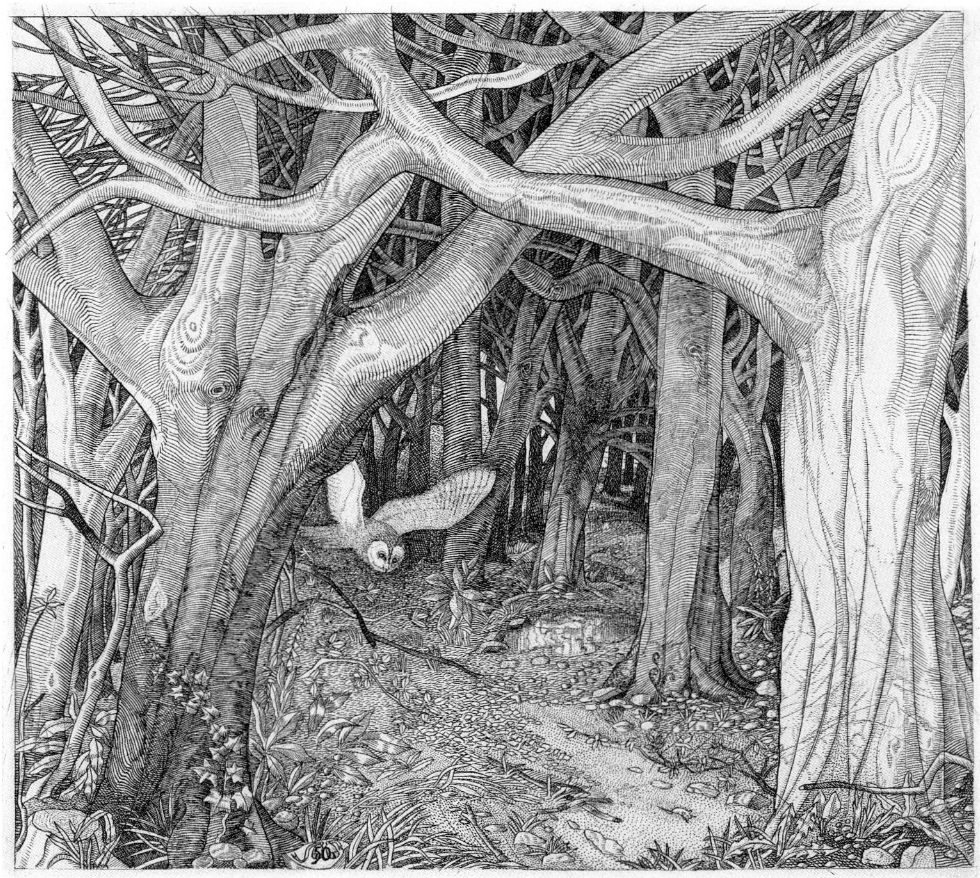

135 NEW FOREST GHOST 1984

Line Engraving 157 x 167 mm

Edition 75 *Black and brown inks. Signed and dated 4th trial proofs virtually identical*

Exhibited Royal Academy, 1984, No. 1591: RE 1984, No. 65

Illustrated *RE Journal*, No. 7, 1985, p. 19 (CHA Chaplin RE discusses his engravings)

Reference (i) 'New Forest Ghost'. Poem by Paul Wigmore (see page 63): (ii) *RE Journal* No. 7, 1985, p. 30 (described as 'mystical')

A dark corner of the New Forest, from which an owl swoops on a mouse. A tiny garland engraved at the foot of the plate commemorates the artist's fiftieth wedding anniversary. This was the artist's last exhibit at the Summer Exhibitions, and indeed the last engraving to be completed by him. The artist's notes on this subject appear in the text, page 62.

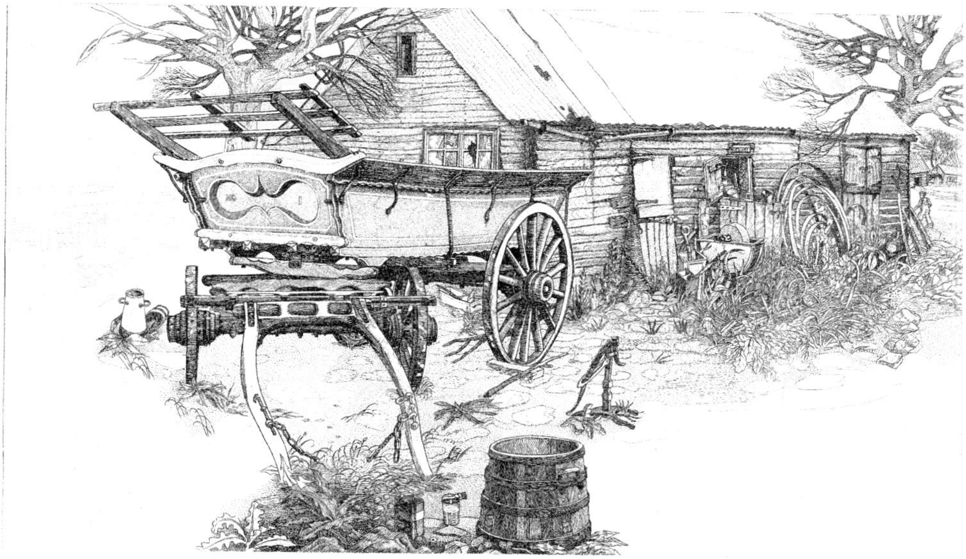

136 THE BANHAM WAGGON 1985

LINE ENGRAVING 152 x 257 mm

Not completed. 3rd trial proofs exist, signed and dated 1985. Signed and dated 1st and 2nd trial proofs also exist.*

A large wagon stands in front of a rural stable block, surrounded by various rural artifacts. The plate was abandoned when the artist had to give up his studio upon moving house. Chaplin was seventy-nine, and was suffering from cancer, which was to claim his life less than two years later. The plate may have been potentially his best ever, and represents an outstanding achievement in the circumstances.

* The left background, and the left and right foregrounds are incomplete.

Index of Titles of Prints and Alternative Titles

INDEX

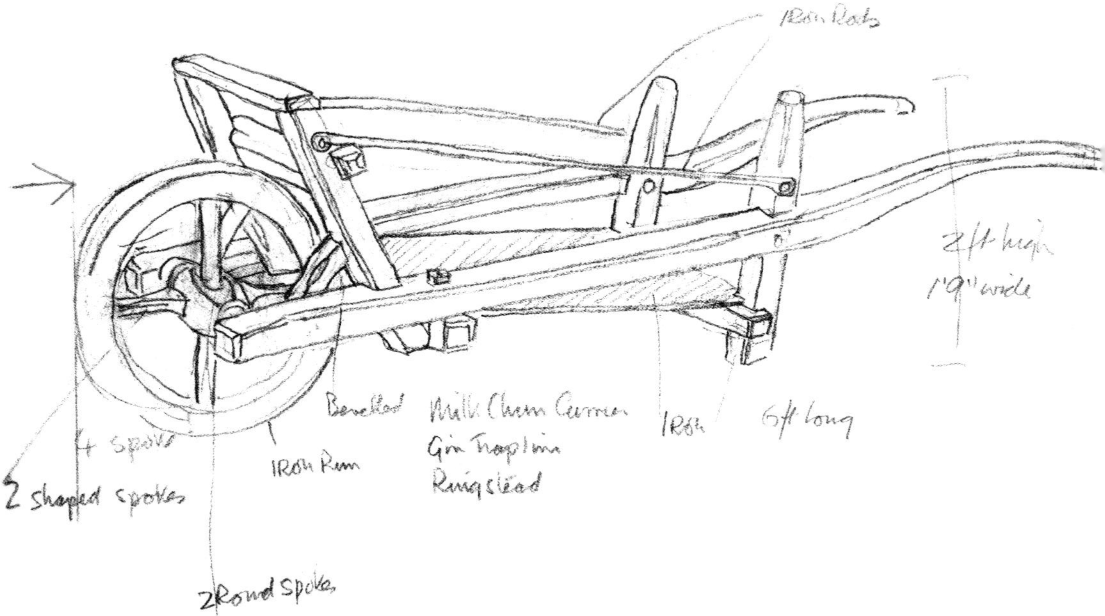
2ft high
1'9" wide
6ft Long
4 spokes
IRON Rim
2 shaped spokes